Short Takes

Short Takes

MODEL ESSAYS FOR COMPOSITION

Ninth Edition

Elizabeth Penfield

University of New Orleans

PEARSON
Longman

New York   San Francisco   Boston
London   Toronto   Sydney   Tokyo   Singapore   Madrid
Mexico City   Munich   Paris   Cape Town   Hong Kong   Montreal

Executive Editor: Lynn M. Huddon
Senior Marketing Manager: Sandra McGuire
Senior Supplements Editor: Donna Campion
Production Manager: Ellen MacElree
Project Coordination, Text Design, and Electronic Page Makeup: Nesbitt Graphics, Inc.
Cover Design Manager: Wendy Ann Fredericks
Cover Designer: Base Art Co., Ltd.
Cover Photos: *Clockwise from top left:* Sang An/Botanica/Jupiter
    Images; Dominic Burke/Alamy Images; Tom Walker/ImageState/Jupiter
    Images; and Paul Ridsdale/Alamy Images
Manufacturing Buyer: Roy Pickering
Printer and Binder: R. R. Donnelley & Sons, Inc.
Cover Printer: Phoenix Color Corp.

Library of Congress Cataloging-in-Publication data on file with the Library of Congress.

Please visit us at http://www.ablongman.com

ISBN: 0-321-48815-6

1 2 3 4 5 6 7 8 9 10—DOH—09 08 07 06

CONTENTS

3 On Using Definition 77

4 On Using Example 108

5 | On Using Division and Classification   **142**

6   On Using Comparison and Contrast   172

8 On Using Cause and Effect   232

9 On Using Argument   265

10 For Further Reading: Multiple Modes, Varied Opinions   308

THEMATIC GUIDE

Scenes and Places

The Individual

Relationships

Society

PREFACE

This book combines the old and the new. When the first edition was only an idea, I was teaching freshman English in a structured program that emphasized rhetorical modes and final product. My dilemma then was one that many teachers still face: how to incorporate the modes with the whole tangle of the writing process. But once I focused on the aims of discourse, the modes fell into place as means, not ends, and as patterns of organization used in combination, not just singly. There remained the problem of the textbooks, many of which contained essays of imposing length and complexity that intimidated and overwhelmed many a student. Often, any short essay was so because it was an excerpt. *Short Takes* was the result of my frustrations. This ninth edition still reflects the rhetorical framework of the first one, but it is flexible. You can even ignore it and use the thematic table of contents. But if you find the modes useful, you'll see them here.

This edition remains a collection of short, readable, interesting essays written by professionals and students, and the commentary continues to focus on reading and writing as interrelated activities. Much, however, is new:

- Revised chapter introductions that highlight the most important points and are therefore more accessible for students
- Fresh topics and eighteen new essays that engage students by analyzing subjects as varied as what makes a perfect ice cream sundae and the place of morality in the college curriculum
- Emphasis on subordinate modes so that students can more clearly understand how various modes are used singly and together
- Five sets of paired essays that present differing arguments on timely subjects so students can construct their own arguments in response
- Revised chapter on argument that pairs essays and includes a cartoon and comic strip so students can analyze differing views and different ways of presenting them
- Some writing assignments include the use of the Internet, a ready resource for most students

At the same time, features that teachers particularly liked are still here. The text

- Opens with "Freeze Frame: Reading and Writing," a brief section that introduces students to the principles of critical reading and writing.
- Provides chapter introductions directed to students that emphasize the writing process (as well as the kinds of choices and decisions all writers face).
- Presents short, engaging, accessible essays and helpful introductions to each rhetorical pattern.
- Contains complete essays, not excerpts.
- Describes each author, context for the essay, and its notable stylistic features.
- Includes questions on organization, ideas, technique, and style after each essay, engaging students to think critically about the readings.
- For each selection, suggests a number of topics for writing journal entries and essays.
- Concludes each chapter with more writing suggestions for each rhetorical mode and for essays that ask students to compare two or more of the selections.
- Additional writing prompts at the end of each chapter that call for an evaluation of two or more essays.
- Includes a variety of authors, styles, and subjects.
- Emphasizes how the rhetorical modes interact with invention and the entire writing process.
- Provides an alternate thematic table of contents.
- Comes with an Instructor's Manual that includes key words and phrases for each essay, suggestions for group work, and additional writing suggestions keyed to the thematic table of contents.

Each chapter builds on the previous one and leads to the one that follows, culminating in argument, but argument with a difference. The chapter on argument is a basic introduction, an extension of the kind of emphasis on thesis and evidence that exists throughout the text. Within each chapter, the essays are presented in order of difficulty. All the supplementary information—the chapter introductions, background information, notes on style, questions on the essays, and suggestions for writing—balance process and product, working on the premise that the two, like reading and writing, are so closely interrelated that one cannot be considered without the other.

As always, I welcome responses from students and teachers to this new edition, along with suggestions for the future. You can e-mail me direct <epenfiel@uno.edu> or in care of Longman's English Editor at Pearson Longman, 1185 Sixth Avenue, 25th Floor, New York, NY 10036.

The Essays

This edition contains 52 essays, 18 of which are new. Because most of the papers assigned in composition courses fall in the 400- to 1000-word range, most of the essays are short—about 1000 words at most—and as such easily lend themselves to scrutiny and emulation. A few are longer and rely on the kind of research that students may be asked to carry out. And a few illustrate the problem–solution organization often found in argumentative pieces. Two essays also serve as a basic introduction to the Modern Language Association's system of documentation. All of the essays are complete pieces, not excerpts, illustrating the arms of discourse and rhetorical modes.

To write is to choose among alternatives, to select the most appropriate organization, persona, diction, and techniques for a given audience and purpose. Each of the essays included in this edition was chosen because it exemplifies the author's choices, and the apparatus emphasizes those choices and alternatives. The essays, therefore, serve as illustrative models of organization and stylistic techniques available to the writer. The essays were also chosen because their authors represent different genders, ages, and cultures; as a result, the subjects of the essays are accessible and their perspectives are lively, qualities that also allow them to serve as sources of invention, as jumping-off places for students to develop their own ideas in their own styles.

Rhetorical Modes and the Aims of Discourse

Anyone who has used a reader with essays arranged by mode has probably run into two problems: first, few essays are pure examples of a single mode; second, most collections of essays treat argument—an aim of writing—as though it were the equivalent of description, comparison/contrast, and so on. *Short Takes* addresses these inconsistencies by emphasizing the difference between mode—how an essay is organized—and purpose—how an essay is intended to affect the reader—and by pointing out how writing frequently blends two or more modes.

Because essays usually employ more than one mode, the essays here are grouped according to the *primary* rhetorical pattern that guides their organization; the questions that follow each essay point out the subordinate modes. As for the aims of discourse, the essays represent the various purposes for writing. The writers' self-expressive, informative, and persuasive purposes are underscored in the discussion questions. In addition, the apparatus connects academic writing and the kind of writing found outside the classroom.

Apparatus for Reading and Writing

The apparatus makes full use of the essays. Chapters 1 to 9 begin with a brief introduction to the student that depicts the mode or purpose under discussion, showing how it can be used in formal essays and in practical, everyday writing tasks. The introductions point out specifically how the modes can be shaped by considerations of audience, purpose, particular strategies, thesis, and organization, ending with advice on finding a subject, exploring a topic, and drafting a paper. This division of the writing process approximates the classic one of invention, arrangement, and style but is not intended to imply that these are separate stages.

To emphasize both what a text says and how it says it, each essay in Chapters 1 to 9 is preceded by background information on the author and the text and a brief discussion of a stylistic strategy. Two sets of questions—"Organization and Ideas" and "Technique and Style"—follow the essay, along with ideas for journal entries and essays. Throughout, process and product, as well as reading and writing, are interrelated, emphasizing the recursive nature of the act of writing. Writers constantly invent, organize, and revise; the lines that distinguish those activities are narrow, if not blurred.

"Suggestions for Writing" follow each essay and contain options for both journal entries and essays, all related by theme, organization, or ideas to the work that has just been read. The assignments allow a good deal of flexibility: some lend themselves to general information or personal experience, some to research papers, many to group work (outlined in the Instructor's Manual), some to the classic technique of imitation. In addition, at the end of Chapters 1 to 9 you'll find prompts for using the mode or aim under discussion and for comparing and evaluating the essays.

Whether working alone or in groups, once students select their subjects, they will find flipping back to the introduction helpful. There, "Exploring the Topic" shapes questions so that no matter what type of paper they are writing, students can generate information. "Drafting the Paper" then helps organize the material and points out some of the pitfalls and advantages inherent in a particular mode or aim.

The Instructor's Manual

An Instructor's Manual (ISBN 0-205-53944-0) includes key words and phrases, responses to the questions, and teaching suggestions for both the questions and the longer writing assignments. The manual also contains an additional argumentative essay by a student and writing prompts for the text's Thematic Guide.

Acknowledgments

I have many people to thank for their help in bringing this book to publication: Lynn Huddon for her good advice and encouragement; Hope Rajala, Leslie Taggart, Karen Helfrich, and Liza Rudneva for their able assistance with past editions; James Postema, and Nancy Braun, for their help and that of their students; and Theodora Hill for her sound recommendations, patience, and help with the more mundane aspects of preparing a manuscript. Peg Markow's careful copyediting of this edition is much appreciated. The following reviewers all provided guidance and advice that improved the manuscript: Elizabeth Barrows, Isothermal Community College; Anna Deadrick, Northern Virginia Community College; Edward Glenn, Miami Dade College; Alexander Howe, University of D.C.; Linda Nugent, Delta College; Terry Lee Schifferns, Central Community College; Joyce Stoffers, Southwestern Oklahoma State University; and Jane Thompson, Mount Mary College.

ELIZABETH PENFIELD

Short Takes

Freeze Frame
Reading and Writing

This Book

In filmmaking, a "short take" is a brief scene filmed without interruption. Similarly, short essays move quickly toward their conclusions, with only the small breaks caused by paragraph indentations. Those are the kinds of essays you will find in this book, short essays that explain, argue, express the writer's feelings, or simply entertain. The essays carry out their purposes by drawing on various patterns of organization, patterns that can describe, tell a story, define a subject, provide examples, set up comparisons, or analyze a process or a cause and effect. These are the same patterns you will draw on when you write your own papers. The essays, then, can serve as models.

And just as the essays collected here are "short takes," this essay is a "freeze frame," as though you had stopped the film on one particular shot to get a better look at the details. That's just what this essay will do, stop and take a close-up look at what goes on when you read and when you write.

You, the Reader

A skilled reader interacts with the words on the page: reshaping, evaluating, selecting, analyzing. After all, you have your own world, one made up of everything you have experienced, from your first memory to your most recent thought—all of which you bring to what you read. An essay about why people love to walk on beaches, for example, will remind you of any beaches you know, and your associations will probably be pleasurable. As you begin to read the essay, you discover that the writer's associations are also pleasant ones, reinforcing yours. You

1

read on, constantly reassessing your ideas about the essay as you add more and more information to your first impression. Now and then, you may hit a sentence that at first doesn't make much sense, so you stop, perhaps to look up an unfamiliar word, perhaps to go back and review an earlier statement, then read on, again reevaluating your ideas about what the author is saying and what you think of it. The result is analytical, critical reading—not critical in the sense of judging harshly but critical in the sense of questioning, weighing evidence, evaluating, comparing your world to the one the writer has created on the page.

The idea of revising and tinkering is usually associated with writing, less so with reading. Yet just as you tinker and wrestle with your own writing, you should do the same with what you read. You should:

- scribble
- underline
- question
- challenge

Reading in this way, reading critically with pen or pencil in hand, will give you a fuller appreciation of what you read and a better understanding of the techniques the writer used to create the essay.

If you're not used to reading in this manner, it may seem foreign to you. After all, what's printed on the page should be easy enough to understand. But because words only stand for things and are not the things themselves, different readers find different meanings. If, for instance, your only memory of a beach was of nearly drowning in the Atlantic Ocean, then you would have to suspend that association when you read an essay that praises beach walking. And if your skin turns bright red at the mere mention of the sun, that adds one more obstacle to understanding why others enjoy the seashore. How then can a reader comprehend all that an author is saying? More specifically, how can a reader go about reading an essay critically?

Identifying the Purpose   It helps to know what different kinds of writing have in common. Whether business letter, lab report, journal entry, news story, poem, or essay, all focus on a subject, address a reader, and have a point. And, too, all have a purpose and a style; they are written for specific reasons and in a certain way. These shared elements are perhaps more familiar as questions used to spark ideas for writing, the familiar journalistic *who? what? where? when? how? why?* Yet these questions can be equally useful for reading, and thinking about them will give you a general overview of what you are reading:

- To whom is an essay addressed?
- What is the writer's main point?
- How is the piece organized?
- Why is it structured that way?
- Where and when does the action take place?

Many, many more inquiries can be spun off these seemingly simple questions, and they are useful tools for exploring an essay. Jotting down these questions and your answers to them in a notebook or journal can also sharpen your critical abilities and lead to a lively class discussion.

Looking for the Point   In much of the reading we do, we are looking for information. The election coverage reported in the newspaper, the syllabus for a course, and a set of directions all exemplify this kind of reading, but reading for information and reading for comprehension are as different as a vitamin pill and a five-course dinner. To understand not only what a writer is saying but also its implications and why that writer might have chosen to say it that way isn't easy.

The title of an essay is a good place to start, for most titles tip you off not only about the subject of the piece but also to the author's stand. You don't need to turn to the essay titled "Sweatin' for Nothin'" to figure out it may be about exercising and that the author doesn't see much point to fitness fads. Other titles, such as "Countdown," just imply a subject and raise your curiosity. What kind of countdown? Countdown to what? Some titles focus clearly on their subject, as in "Living with Cancer." Still others tip you off to the author's tone, the writer's attitude toward the subject: if an essay were called "Tube E or Not Tube E," the play on the familiar line from *Hamlet* suggests a humorous discussion of a chemistry lab course. Now and then, however, a title may announce a bald version of the thesis, such as an editorial headlined "Your Vote Counts." The editorial then would expand the idea so that a full version of the thesis becomes, "Your vote counts because a single ballot can change the outcome of an election—and it has."

Knowing or at least having a hint about the subject is the first step to discovering an essay's thesis, the assertion the author is making about the subject. The first paragraph or set of paragraphs that acts as an introduction will also help you form a tentative thesis. Sometimes the writer places the thesis in the first paragraph or introduction, but sometimes a bare-bones version of the thesis appears in the title. If you see it, you should mark it. If you don't spot a thesis, you should still write down a tentative version of your own so that you have a focus for what is to follow, an idea against which you can test other ideas.

This last option is a bit of a challenge. You must create the thesis by identifying key sentences and then mentally composing a statement that covers those ideas, a process that often takes more than one reading but is made easier if you underline the important sentences. Even then, you may well find that someone else who reads the essay comes up with a different thesis statement. And you both may be right.

What's happening here? If you think about how slippery words are and the different experiences that different readers bring to an essay, you can begin to see why there's more than one "correct" thesis. If you were to give the same essay to 10 critical readers, you would find that their versions of the thesis differ but overlap. Their readings would probably cluster around two or three central ideas. If an eleventh person read the essay and came up with a thesis that contradicted the 10 other readings, that version would probably be off base.

Sometimes writers unwittingly set traps, making it easy to mistake a fact for a thesis. If you keep in mind that a thesis is both a sentence and an assertion—a value judgment—those traps can be avoided. "The average American watches a lot of TV" states a fact most readers would shrug off with a "So what?" On the other hand, "Television rots the minds of its viewers" takes a stand that will probably raise hackles and a "Hey, wait a minute!"

Recognizing Patterns of Development

Once you've nailed down a thesis, go a step further to examine how that thesis is developed. Writers depend on various patterns of thought or modes of thinking that are almost innate.

- To tell a joke is to narrate.
- To convey what a party was like is to describe and to use examples.

- To decide which among many courses to take is to divide and classify.
- To figure out which car to buy is to compare and contrast (and if you think of your old car as a peach or a lemon, you are drawing an analogy).
- To give directions is to use process.
- To consider how to improve your tennis game is to weigh cause and effect.
- To explain how you feel is to define.

Narration, description, example, division and classification, comparison and contrast, analogy, process, cause and effect, and definition are the natural modes of thinking upon which writers rely.

These patterns of thought provide the structure of an essay. A piece on the ethics of using prisoners to test new medicines might open with a brief narrative that sets the scene, go on to define what kinds of medicines are involved, and then explain the effects of such experiments on the prisoners, the development of new drugs, and society's concept of ethics. As you read, you should note each type of mode the writer uses so you can more fully understand how the thesis is developed and how the essay is organized. Though you may find an essay uses many types of modes, it's likely that one predominates.

You, the Writer and Editor

Getting Started   Central to any kind of writing is the question "Why am I doing this?" The obvious answer for most students is "Because it's assigned." But face it—writing and editing are hard work, involving both time and effort, and while praise or a good grade can be a reward, neither may seem equal to the thought and struggle you put into writing an essay. By writing, however, you can learn about yourself and your subject, sharpen your mind, and increase your concentration. Even so, once you have written something you like, you may find that fear replaces enthusiasm, for the only thing scarier than putting words on paper is the idea that someone is going to read them. This kind of fear is something that most writers, whether students or professionals, experience. Yet you will find that having someone respond to your paper with "Hey, that was really good" or "I really liked that" more than makes up for the anxiety you experienced when you first sat down to write.

A blank sheet of paper or an empty computer screen can be a terrifying thing, so how should you begin? Off and on, you've been thinking about what to write, so in a sense you've already started your essay even though nothing is on paper. Or perhaps you've been able to talk about your topic with your classmates, generating ideas and finding a focus. Now you need to get those thoughts into print.

If you stare at a blank page and try to get that opening sentence just right, you're trying to edit too soon. Don't think of a finished piece or how your paper will begin or end; just start writing anything—notes, a title, a list of ideas, an outline, a paragraph—whatever comes to mind. At this stage, you're brainstorming, coming up with ideas and bouncing them off each other so that you can figure out what you are trying to say. Figuring out how you want your reader to respond, shaping your ideas, organizing and then polishing them, can come later. Now you just want to end up with ideas that can be loosely organized into a rough draft.

Thinking About Your Audience   If your class is run as a writer's workshop or uses peer groups, then at this point you have a draft of your essay, and your classmates can help you shape and refine it. Whether you're working on your own draft or one of your classmates', you'll need to keep in mind questions of purpose, audience, thesis, and organization.

What is the purpose of the essay? Should it inform, persuade, or entertain your reader, or perhaps all three? In writing, as in speech, the purpose determines the relationship among the subject, writer, and reader. Most of the writing you will be doing in college is intended to inform. For that reason, most of the essays included in this book are expository; their primary purpose is to explain a subject, to inform the reader. The focus is on the subject. In most of your other courses, you will find that your reading fits into this category, one occupied by stacks of textbooks. As for your writing, when you write a lab or book report, a précis, or an essay exam answer, you focus on your subject so that you explain it to your readers.

Though explaining may be your primary purpose, other aims enter in as well. In an essay exam question about a historical event, you are also trying to convince your reader that you know what you are writing about. Your reader, of course, is your teacher, someone who knows more about your subject than you do, so you aren't trying to explain the subject; instead you're trying to persuade your teacher that your interpretation of it is sound. Your focus is on the reader.

If you're writing a journal or diary entry or a personal letter, however, your focus is on yourself, the writer. You are writing to explore what you think and feel. That's also true if you're writing an opinion piece in the newspaper or a meditative essay. If, for example, your teacher asks you to keep a journal in which you respond to what you read, your responses may range from fury over an opinion you disagree with to mild musings on what you think about the author's subject. What is important is what you feel, and your writing expresses those feelings by communicating them clearly to your reader. You, not the subject, are center stage.

Discovering a Thesis   You will find that writing is a form of discovery, that writing about an idea helps clarify it. In your own experience, you have probably found that you usually don't have a clear grasp of your main point until you've written your way into it. You may start with an idea, a general focus, say, on professional wrestling, but that focus becomes clearer as you rethink your choice of a particular word or reread what is on the page to get a sense of what should come next. Gradually, your ideas become clearer and out of them an assertion emerges: professional wrestling may not be much of a sport, but it's splendid theater. And on you go, sometimes speeding, sometimes creeping, constantly revising.

Once your thesis is clear, then you must decide where to place it for the greatest effect. You may opt for placing it at the end of your introduction, but perhaps it would be best in your conclusion, or you may decide on a more subtle solution by weaving bits and pieces of the thesis into the essay as a whole. You may find it best to hold off a decision until you've worked some more on your essay's organization.

Organizing the Essay   Description, narration, cause and effect, and the like are modes that provide the structure of the essay, the means by which you support your major point, the thesis, and more often than not, you will draw on several patterns of development to support your major point. Rarely does an essay rely solely on one pattern of development. In the example above, the thesis—professional wrestling may not be much of a sport, but it's splendid theater—suggests a paper that might begin with a brief introduction that describes the cast of wrestlers and their costumes, then develops the thesis by defining what makes a sport a sport, comparing professional wrestling with that definition, and presenting examples as evidence that professional wrestling is theater. Most of the essay would concentrate on examples, which would be its primary mode of organization.

When you are writing, modes such as example, definition, and the like provide ways to think about your topic as well as ways to organize your essay. With practice they become as much second nature as shifting gears in a manual-transmission car. At first you might be a bit tentative about knowing when to shift from first to second, but with time you don't even think about it. Similarly, you might wonder if your point is clear without an example; in time, you will automatically supply one.

Knowing what you want to write and having a fair idea of how it should be organized still do not necessarily help you shape individual sentences so that they convey the desired tone, so that they *sound* right. That requires draft after draft. Even the idea of finishing is a shaky notion; many writers continue to revise right up to their deadlines. Hemingway rewrote the last page of *A Farewell to Arms* 39 times, and Katherine Anne Porter spent 20 years writing and rewriting *Ship of Fools*. Writing nonfiction doesn't make the process any easier. Wayne Booth, a distinguished essayist and scholar, speaks for most writers: "I revise many, many times, as many times as deadlines allow for. And I always feel that I would have profited from further revision." Poet, novelist, essayist, journalist, student, or professional, all continue in the tradition expressed in the eighteenth century by a fellow writer, Samuel Johnson, who said, "What is written without effort is in general read without pleasure." Pleasurable reading derives from a pleasing writing style, and though some writers strive for elegance as well as clarity, most readers will happily settle for clarity.

Far from following a recipe, you will find that writing an essay is like driving a car while at the same time trying to impress the passengers, talk on the cell phone, read a road map, recognize occasional familiar landmarks, follow scrawled and muttered directions, and watch for and listen to all the quirks of the car. You know vaguely where you are going and how you want to get there, but the rest is risk and adventure. With work and a number of dry runs, you can smooth out the trip so that the passengers fully appreciate the pleasure of the drive and the satisfaction of reaching the destination. That is the challenge the writer faces, a challenge that demands critical reading as well as effective writing.

Reading and Writing

Essays can be deceptive. What you see on the printed page resembles the writer's work about as much as a portrait resembles the real person. What you don't see when you look at printed pages are all the beginnings and stops, the crumpled paper, the false starts, the notes, the discarded ideas, the changed words. Instead, you have a finished piece—the result of the writer's choices. Don't be intimidated. The process most writers go through to produce their essays is very like your own. The writer Andre Dubus puts it another way: "There is something mystical [about writing] but it's not rare and nobody should treat it as though this is something special that writers do. Anybody born physically able in the brain can sit down and begin to write something, and discover that there are depths in her soul or his soul that are untapped."

As a writer and a reader, you tap into those depths, depths that help make meaning of the world we live in. The making of meaning is the heart of the essays contained in this book, together with its explanations, questions, and suggestions for writing. Stated concisely, this book reinforces a basic assumption: reading and writing are highly individual processes that are active, powerful, and interrelated ways to discover meaning.

To check out that statement, think of one day within the last week when something memorable happened to you. Isolate that incident so it's clear in your mind. Now think of all the other details of the day, from the time your eyes opened in the morning to the time they closed at night. That's a lot of detail, and most of it insignificant, meaningless bits and pieces of information you would probably discard if you were to write about that day. What you would be left with is that memorable thing that occurred and a few details directly related to it, some preceding it, a few following. In writing about that day, you would reshape events—evaluating, selecting, and recreating what happened so that what was most meaningful comes through clearly. As a result, someone reading your description would be able to experience at a distance what you experienced firsthand.

To write, then, is to create and structure a world; to read is to become part of someone else's. And just as reading makes a better writer, writing makes a better reader.

POINTERS FOR READING

1. **Settle in.** Gather up a good dictionary and whatever you like to write with, and then find a comfortable place to read.
2. **Think about the title.** What sort of expectations do you have about what will follow? Can you identify the subject? A thesis? Can you tell anything about the writer's tone?
3. **Look for a specific focus.** Where is the essay going? What appears to be its thesis? At what point does the introduction end and the body of the essay begin? What questions do you have about the essay so far? Is the essay directed at you? If not, who is the intended audience?
4. **Look for a predominant pattern of organization.** What are the most important ideas in the body of the essay? Note the patterns or modes the writer uses to develop those ideas.
5. **Identify the conclusion.** Where does the conclusion begin? How does it end the essay? What effect does it have on you?
6. **Evaluate the essay.** Did the essay answer the questions you had about it? How effective was the support for the main ideas? Did the writer's choice of words fit the audience? What effect did the essay have on you? Why?

POINTERS FOR WRITING AND EDITING

1. **Settle in.** Get hold of whatever you find comfortable to write with—computer, pen, pencil, legal pad, note paper, notebook—and settle into wherever you like to write. Start by jotting down words that represent a general idea of your subject. As words cross your mind, write them down so that at this point you have a vague focus.
2. **Focus.** Try writing right away and quickly. Get your ideas down on paper without worrying about organization or punctuation or whether what you write is right. If you run out of steam, pause and read over what you have written and then summarize it in one sentence. Then start up again writing as quickly as you can.

At some point you will have written your way into a tentative thesis that will help you focus as you revise what you have written. Now you have a draft and are ready to edit your own paper and, perhaps, those of your classmates.

3. **Reread.** Go over what's written, looking for sentences that state an opinion. Mark them in some way (a highlighter is useful). These sentences can become topic sentences that lead off paragraphs and therefore help organize the ideas.

4. **Organize what's there.** Go through the paper asking questions. What would make a good introduction? A good conclusion? What order best suits what's in between? What examples can you find? Where would they work best?

5. **Think about purpose.** As you reread, think about the kind of effect the paper should have on readers. Does it explain something to them? Argue a cause? Tell them about feelings? Entertain? Some combination of purposes?

6. **Think about the readers.** What do they know about the subject? The answer to this question may help cut out some information; and what they don't know can be a guide to what needs to be included. Do they have a bias for or against the thesis? The answer will reveal whether those biases need to be accounted for and suggest how to do that.

7. **Revise.** You've probably been revising all along, but at this point you can revise more thoroughly and deeply. You know your purpose, audience, and thesis—all of which will help you organize your paper more effectively.

8. **Proofread.** Now look for surface errors, checking for spelling and punctuation. If you're using a word-processing program, run your text through the spelling checker, but pay attention to anything offered as a substitute because it may be the wrong word. As for punctuation, if you have a grammar checker on your computer, try it. You may find it useful, but probably a handbook of grammar and usage will be much more helpful because the explanations are fuller and you'll find lots of examples. Just look up the key word in the handbook's index.

On Using Description

1

Description turns up in various guises in all types of prose, for it is the basic device a writer uses to convey sense impressions. For that reason, it is as essential to **objective**[1] writing as it is to **subjective** prose and, of course, to everything in between. A quick sketch of a family gathering that you might include in a letter to a friend draws on the same skills as a complex report on the effectiveness of a new product. Both rely on the ability to

- observe,
- select the most important details,
- create a coherent sequence for those details, and
- convey the result by appealing to the reader's senses.

To describe something, then, is to recreate it in such a way that it becomes alive again, so that the reader can see and understand it. Prose that depends heavily on description invites the reader to share the writer's initial sense of vividness and perception.

The role description plays in writing will vary. Personal narratives depend heavily on description to bring scenes and actions to life, to depict an outdoor wedding, for instance, or to convey what it feels like to have a toothache. Other types of informative essays use description in a less obvious role, perhaps to clarify a step in a process or make an example vivid. And persuasion often gets its punch from description, for it enables the reader to see the prisoner on death row or the crime that led to the death sentence. While no essay relies solely on description, each of the essays that follow uses description as its primary pattern of

---

[1]Words printed in boldface are defined under "Useful Terms" at the end of each introductory section.

organization. The essays' general subjects are familiar—a sandwich, a place, a person, a trip, a frog—but by selecting details, each author tailors description uniquely.

Audience and Purpose

Most writers start with a general sense of purpose and audience. Perhaps you want to explain an event or how something works or what you think about a particular place, person, or idea, in which case your purpose is expository and what you write is **exposition.** You focus on your subject so that you can explain it clearly to your reader. That's not as dull as it sounds. Odds are that if you wrote a description of your neighborhood in such a way that your readers felt as though they could see it, you'd have an interesting expository essay. Sure, it represents your opinion, how *you* see your neighborhood, but the focus is clearly on the subject; you are in the position of narrator, telling your readers about your subject, analyzing it, explaining it to them.

But imagine that as you begin to think about your neighborhood your thoughts turn to ways in which your life there could be improved. Perhaps the garbage could be picked up more frequently, the sidewalks could be repaired, or the property taxes lowered. All of a sudden you're off on an argumentative tear, one that can take a number of different forms—essay, letter to the editor, or letter to your city or state representative. But no matter who you write for, you're engaging in **persuasion** and your focus is on the reader, the person whose mind you want to change.

Writers who aim their work at a definite audience, say the readers of a particular magazine, have a head start by knowing the readership. One of the essays in this chapter comes from *Sierra,* the journal of the Sierra Club, an organization devoted to the preservation of American wildlife and nature. Writing for that audience, the author can assume a definite interest in animal life of almost any variety, so the only problem that remains is how to make the particular creature real and interesting.

If your audience is a more general one, say the readers of a newspaper or your classmates, the situation is quite different. The assumptions you can make must be more general. For a newspaper it's safe to assume, for instance, that most of the readers are educated and fall into a general age group ranging from young adult to middle-aged. Knowing that can help you estimate the distance between your subject and the audience. If your subject is old age, you will know that your readers are generally knowledgeable about the topic but that their experience is indirect. That means you must fill in the gap with descriptive details so that their experience becomes more direct, so that the readers can see and feel what it's like to be old. And if your audience is your classmates, a younger group, the gap between subject and audience is even wider so your description has to be even more full.

In addition to having a firm sense of what your audience does and does not know, it helps to know how your readers may feel about your subject and how you want them to feel. How you want them to feel is a matter of **tone,** your attitude toward the subject and the audience. Many readers, for example, are understandably squeamish about the subject of war, and that creates a problem for the writer, particularly one who wants to describe a scene realistically and at the same time elicit sympathy. One solution is to pretty it up, but that does a disservice to reality; however, too realistic a description can be so revolting that no one would read it. Nor would anyone want to read a dry, objective account. Rudyard Kipling, whom many of us know through his *Jungle Books,* faced this problem when he wrote *The Irish Guards in the Great War,* a history of a military unit in World War I. His description of the German positions before the British attack on the Somme can be summarized objectively by removing most of the details to create an intentionally flat, dull tone:

> The Germans had been strengthening their defenses for two years. It was a defense in depth, exploiting the smooth slopes ascending to their high ground. They fortified forests and villages and dug deep underground shelters in the chalky soil. They protected their positions with copious wire, often arranged to force attackers into the fire of machine guns. (Fussell 172).

Now compare that prose with how Kipling solves the problem of tone by finding a middle yet realistic ground:

> Here the enemy had sat for two years, looking down upon France and daily strengthening himself. His trebled and quadrupled lines of defense, worked for him by his prisoners, ran below and along the flanks and on the tops of ranges of five-hundred-foot downs. Some of these were studded with close woods, deadlier even than the fortified villages between them; some cut with narrowing valleys that drew machine-gun fire as chimneys draw draughts; some opening into broad, seemingly smooth slopes, whose every haunch and hollow covered sunk forts, carefully placed mine-fields,

machine-gun pits, gigantic quarries, enlarged in the chalk, connecting with systems of catacomb-like dug-outs and subterranean works at all depths, in which brigades could lie till the fitting moment. Belt upon belt of fifty-yard-deep wire protected these points, either directly or at such angles as should herd and hold up attacking infantry to the fire of veiled guns. Nothing in the entire system had been neglected or unforeseen, except knowledge of the nature of the men who, in due time, should wear their red way through every yard of it.[2]

Kipling's description is essentially an explanation, but note the argumentative twist he puts in his last sentence, his reference to the men of the Irish Guards and their valiant attack and huge losses, the blood of their "red way." There's no question about whose side Kipling is on. And there's no question about how he wants his readers to feel.

Details

No matter what the purpose or audience, descriptive essays are characterized by their use of detail. Note how many details are in the paragraph by Kipling, most of which are **concrete details.** The German defenses had not just been strengthened but "trebled and quadrupled." Nor is Kipling satisfied with **abstract words.** He tells us the quarries were "gigantic," an abstract word that has different meanings to different people, so he gives us a concrete sense of just how large those quarries are—they could hide whole brigades, groups of 1,500 to 3,300 soldiers. We get a visual idea of their size. Visual detail also helps us see the wire defenses. Because Kipling's book, from which the passage was taken, was published in 1923, shortly after the end of World War I, a time when tanks, missiles, and bombers as we know them were unheard of, the general particulars of trench warfare were still fresh in his readers' minds; they would know, for example, that the wire he refers to is barbed wire, but Kipling makes his audience (both then and now) see it by saying that it was "belt upon belt" of wire, "fifty-yard-deep" wire.

Visual details make us see what a writer is describing, but using other appeals to the senses also brings prose to life. Once you start thinking about it, you'll find images that draw in other senses. For auditory

---

[2]Quoted in Paul Fussell's *The Great War and Modern Memory.* New York: Oxford UP, 1977.

appeal, for instance, you might think of a time when you walked in snow so dry that a snowball turns to powder and you could hear the small squeal of your footsteps; and if your climate goes to the other extreme, you might remember a blistering night and the chirps, bleeps, squeaks, and rasps sung by a chorus of summer insects.

Comparison

Take any object and try to describe what it looks, feels, smells, sounds, and tastes like, and you'll quickly find yourself shifting over to comparisons. Comparisons enrich description in that they can:

- produce an arresting image
- explain the unfamiliar
- make a connection with the reader's own experience
- reinforce the major point in the essay

Comparing the unfamiliar to the familiar makes what is being described more real. Even the computer-illiterate among us get the idea embedded in the term *World Wide Web,* immediately imagining an electronic spider web that encompasses the globe. The image is a metaphor, and often comparisons take the form of **metaphor, simile,** or **allusion.**

Simile and *metaphor* both draw a comparison between dissimilar things; the terms differ in that a simile uses a comparative word such as *like* or *as.* As a result, metaphor is often the more arresting because it is a direct equation. If you were writing and got stuck to the point where nothing worked—the classic writer's block—you might describe your state as "sinking in the quicksand of words."

Unfortunately, the first comparisons that often come to mind can be overworked ones known as **clichés:** *green as grass, hot as hell, mad as a hornet, red as a rose,* and the like. While you can guard against them by being suspicious of any metaphor or simile that sounds familiar, clichés can sneak into your writing in less obvious ways. Watch out for descriptive words that come readily to mind—waves that pound or crash, clouds that are fluffy, bells that tinkle.

Analogy is another form of comparison. Think of it as a metaphor that is extended beyond a phrase into several sentences or a paragraph. You can understand how that can happen if you think of a metaphor for the way you write. Some may imagine a roller coaster; others might think of having to manage a busy switchboard; and for some it may be trying to build a house without having any blueprints or knowing what materials are needed. No matter which image, you can tell that it will take more than a sentence or two to develop the metaphor into an analogy.

Diction

The words a writer chooses determine whether the description is more objective or subjective, whether its tone is factual or impressionistic. Although total objectivity is impossible, description that leans toward the objective is called for when the writer wants to focus on the subject as opposed to emotional effect, on what something is rather than how it felt. Read the paragraph below by J. Merrill-Foster in which she describes an 85-year-old woman.

> She is frightened and distressed by letters from retired military men. They write that unless she sends $35 by return mail, the Russians will land in Oregon and take over America. The arrival of the daily mail looms large in her day. Once, every few weeks, it contains a personal letter. The rest is appeals and ads. She reads every item.

That passage comes from the first part of "Frightened by Loss," an essay by F. Merrill-Foster, which ends with this paragraph:

> I watch the woman—my mother—walking carefully down the frozen, snow-filled driveway to the mail box. She is a photograph in black and white, which only loving memory tints with stippled life and color.

The first description reports the unnamed woman's feelings and the facts that give rise to them and then generalizes on the importance of the daily mail, noting what it contains and the attention the woman gives it. The second description uses first person and identifies the woman as the author's mother, the words *I* and *mother* forming an emotional bond between reader and writer, overlaying with feeling the picture of the woman walking to the mailbox. On finishing the first passage, the reader understands the role an everyday event—the arrival of the mail—plays in the life of an old woman; on finishing the second, the reader knows and feels how old age has diminished a once vital person.

Organization and Ideas

All the details, all the comparisons are organized so that they add up to a single dominant impression. In descriptive essays, this single dominant impression may be implicit or explicit, and it stands as the **thesis.** An explicit thesis jumps off the page and is usually stated openly in one or two easily identifiable sentences. An implicit thesis is more subtle. As reader, you can come to understand what the thesis is even though you can't identify any single sentence that states it. If that process of deduction seems mysterious, think of reading a description of the ultimate pizza, a description that alluringly recounts its aroma, taste, texture. After reading about that pizza you would probably think, Wow, that's a really good pizza. And that's an implied thesis.

Whether implicit or explicit, the thesis is what the writer builds the essay around. It's the main point. The writer must select the most important details, create sentences and paragraphs around them, and then sequence the paragraphs so that everything not only contributes to but also helps create the thesis. In description, paragraphs can be arranged by **patterns of organization,** such as process and definition, and according to spatial, temporal, or dramatic relationships. The writer can describe a scene so that the reader moves from one place to another, from one point in time to another, or according to a dramatic order. If this last idea seems vague, think of how a film or novel builds to a high point, one that usually occurs just before the end.

The building block for that high point and for the essay itself is the paragraph. And just as the essay has a controlling idea, an assertion that is its thesis, so, too, does the paragraph, usually in the form of a **topic sentence.** Like the thesis, the topic sentence can be explicit or implied, and it can be found in one sentence or deduced from the statements made in several. Because paragraphs frequently cluster around a central idea, particularly in a longer essay, one over 600 words or so, a topic sentence often covers more than one paragraph.

There's no magic number for how many words make up a paragraph and no magic number for how many paragraphs make up an essay, but it is safe to say that all essays have a beginning, middle, and end. The same is true of a paragraph or group of paragraphs that function under one topic sentence. As you read, ask yourself why a given paragraph ends where it does and how it connects to the one that follows. You may discover that sometimes paragraph breaks are not set in cement, that they could occur in several different places and still be "right."

Useful Terms

Abstract words Words that stand for something that cannot be easily visualized and, therefore, may hold different meanings for different people. A box of cereal labeled "large" may be your idea of "small."

Allusion An indirect reference to a real or fictitious person, place, or thing.

Analogy A point-by-point comparison to something seemingly unlike but more commonplace and less complex than the subject. An analogy is also an extended metaphor.

Cliché A comparison, direct or indirect, that has been used so often that it has worn out its novelty, such as *cool as a cucumber* or *ice cold.*

Concrete details Words that stand for something that can be easily visualized and have fixed meaning. If you replaced the "large" on the cereal box with "8 ounces" or "two servings for moderately hungry people," you would be replacing the abstract with more definite, concrete details.

Exposition Writing that explains; also called expository writing.

Metaphor An implied but direct comparison in which the primary term is made more vivid by associating it with a quite dissimilar term. "Life is a roller coaster" is a metaphor.

Objective prose Writing that is impersonal.

Patterns of organization Paragraphs and essays are usually organized according to the patterns illustrated in this book: description, narration, example, division and classification, comparison, process, cause and effect, and definition. Although more than one pattern may exist in a paragraph or essay, often one predominates.

Persuasion Writing that argues a point, that attempts to convince the reader to adopt the writer's stand.

Simile A comparison in which the primary term is linked to a dissimilar one by *like* or *as* to create a vivid image. "Life is like a roller coaster" is a simile. Remove the linking word and you have a metaphor.

Subjective prose Writing that is personal.

Thesis A one-sentence statement or summary of the basic arguable point of the essay.

Tone A writer's attitude toward the subject and the audience.

Topic sentence A statement of the topic of a paragraph containing an arguable point that is supported by the rest of the paragraph.

POINTERS FOR USING DESCRIPTION

Exploring the Topic

1. **What distinguishes your topic?** What characteristics, features, or actions stand out about your subject? Which are most important? Least important?
2. **To what senses can you appeal?** What can you emphasize about your subject that would appeal to sight? Smell? Touch? Taste? Motion?
3. **What concrete details can you use?** What abstract words do you associate with each of the features or events you want to emphasize? How can you make those abstractions concrete?
4. **How can you vary your narrative?** Where might you use quotations? Where might you use dialogue?
5. **What can your audience identify with?** What comparisons can you use? What similes, metaphors, or allusions come to mind?
6. **What order should you use?** Is your description best sequenced by time? Place? Dramatic order?
7. **What is your tentative thesis?** What is the dominant impression you want to create? Do you want it to be implicit? Explicit?
8. **What is your relationship to your subject?** Given your tentative thesis, how objective or subjective should you be? Do you want to be part of the action or removed? What personal pronoun should you use?

Drafting the Paper

1. **Know your reader.** If you are writing about a familiar subject, ask yourself what your reader might not know about it. If you are writing about an unfamiliar subject, ask yourself what your reader does know that you can use for comparison.
2. **Know your purpose.** If you are writing to inform, make sure you are presenting new information and offering enough detail to bring your subject to life. If you are writing to persuade, make sure your details add up so that the reader is moved to adopt your conviction. Keep in mind that your reader may not share your values and indeed may even hold opposite ones.

3. **Vary sensory details.** Emphasize important details by appealing to more than just one sense.
4. **Show, don't tell.** Avoid abstract terms such as *funny* or *beautiful*. Instead, use concrete details, quotations, and dialogue. Don't settle for vague adjectives such as *tall;* replace them with sharper details such as *6 feet 7 inches*.
5. **Use comparisons.** Make your description vivid with an occasional metaphor or simile. If you are writing about something quite unfamiliar, use literal comparison to make your description clear.
6. **Arrange your details to create a single dominant impression.** If you are writing descriptive paragraphs, check the order of your sentences to make sure they follow each other logically and support the impression you wish to create. If you are writing an essay that relies heavily on description, check for the same points from one paragraph to another. Is your topic sentence or thesis implicit or explicit? Reexamine your first paragraph. Does it establish the scene? The tone?

A Sandwich

Nora Ephron

Journalist, essay writer, novelist, screenwriter, and director, Nora Ephron has been busy. She started her career working for the New York Post *as a reporter, then did freelance work before she became a member of the staff at* New York *and* Esquire. *Her essays have been collected in* Wallflower at the Orgy *(1970) and* Crazy Salad *(1975), but she is probably best known for* Heartburn *(1983), a thinly disguised and funny "novel" about her marriage. The daughter of screen writers, Ephron has written three scripts nominated for Oscars:* Silkwood *(1983),* When Harry Met Sally *(1989), and* Sleepless in Seattle *(1993). More recently, she directed* You've Got Mail *(1998) and* Bewitched *(2005). Her essay "A Sandwich" appeared in the August 2002 double issue (19 and 20) of the* New Yorker. *In it, you'll find she's quite familiar with Los Angeles and New York, to say nothing of pastrami.*

What to Look For   Not everyone knows about, much less likes, a hot pastrami sandwich, so when you read Ephron's essay, watch for the various ways she tries to get the reader's interest and attention.

1   The hot pastrami sandwich served at Langer's Delicatessen in downtown Los Angeles is the finest hot pastrami sandwich in the world. This is not just my opinion, although most people who know about Langer's will simply say it's the finest hot pastrami sandwich in Los Angeles because they don't dare to claim that something like a hot pastrami sandwich could possibly be the best version of itself in a city where until recently you couldn't get anything resembling a New York bagel, and the only reason you can get one now is that New York bagels have deteriorated.

2   Langer's is a medium-sized place—it seats a hundred and thirty-five people—and it is decorated, although "decorated" is probably not the word that applies, in tufted brown vinyl. The view out the windows is of the intersection of Seventh and Alvarado and the bright-red-and-yellow signage of a Hispanic neighborhood—bodegas, check-cashing storefronts, and pawnshops. Just down the block is a spot notorious

for being the place to go in L.A. if you need a fake I.D. The Rampart division's main police station, the headquarters of the city's second-most-recent police scandal, is a mile away. Even in 1947, when Langer's opened, the neighborhood was not an obvious place for an old-style Jewish delicatessen, but in the early nineties things got worse. Gangs moved in. The crime rate rose. The Langers—the founder, Al, now eighty-nine, and his son Norm, fifty-seven—were forced to cut the number of employees, close the restaurant nights and Sundays, and put coin-operated locks on the restroom doors. The opening of the Los Angeles subway system—one of its stops is half a block from the restaurant—has helped business slightly, as has the option of having your sandwich brought out to your car. But Langer's always seems to be just barely hanging on. If it were in New York, it would be a shrine, with lines around the block and tour buses standing double-parked outside. Pilgrims would come—as they do, for example, to Arthur Bryant's in Kansas City and Sonny Bryan's in Dallas—and they would report on their conversion. But in Los Angeles a surprising number of people don't even know about Langer's, and many of those who do wouldn't be caught dead at the corner of Seventh and Alvarado, even though it's not a particularly dangerous intersection during daytime hours.

3   Pastrami, I should point out for the uninitiated, is made from a cut of beef that is brined like corned beef, coated with pepper and an assortment of spices, and then smoked. It is characterized by two things. The first is that it is not something anyone's mother whips up and serves at home; it's strictly restaurant fare, and it's served exclusively as a sandwich, usually on Russian rye bread with mustard. The second crucial thing about pastrami is that it is almost never good. In fact, it usually tastes like a bunch of smoked rubber bands.

4   The Langers buy their pastrami from a supplier in Burbank. "When we get it, it's edible," Norm Langer says, "but it's like eating a racquetball. It's hard as a rock. What do we do with it? What makes us such wizards? The average delicatessen will take this piece of meat and put it into a steamer for thirty to forty-five minutes and warm it. But you've still got a hard piece of rubber. You haven't broken down the tissues. You haven't made it tender. We take that same piece of pastrami, put it into our steamer, and steam it for almost three hours. It will shrink twenty-five to thirty per cent, but it's now tender—so tender it can't be sliced thin in a machine because it will fall apart. It has to be hand-sliced."

5   So: tender and hand-sliced. That's half the secret of the Langer's sandwich. The other secret is the bread. The bread is hot. Years ago, in the nineteen-thirties, Al Langer owned a delicatessen in Palm Springs, and, because there were no Jewish bakers in the vicinity, he was forced to bus in the rye bread. "I was serving day-old bread," Al Langer says, "so I put it into the oven to make it fresher. Hot crispy bread. Juicy soft pastrami. How can you lose?"

6   Today, Langer's buys its rye bread from a bakery called Fred's, on South Robertson, which bakes it on bricks until it's ten minutes from being done. Langer's bakes the loaf the rest of the way, before slicing it hot for sandwiches. The rye bread, faintly sour, perfumed with caraway seeds, lightly dusted with cornmeal, is as good as any rye bread on the planet, and Langer's puts about seven ounces of pastrami on it, the proper proportion of meat to bread. The resulting sandwich, slathered with Gulden's mustard, is an exquisite combination of textures and tastes. It's soft but crispy, tender but chewy, peppery but sour, smoky but tangy. It's a symphony orchestra, different instruments brought together to play one perfect chord. It costs eight-fifty and is, in short, a work of art.

ORGANIZATION AND IDEAS

1. Ephron makes a claim in her first sentence and echoes it in the last two sentences of the final paragraph. Which of the two is the more valid and why?
2. What reasons can you think of for Ephron's delaying a definition of a pastrami sandwich till paragraph 3?
3. Paragraphs 4–6 describe how the restaurant creates a pastrami sandwich. What reasons can you give for Ephron's sequencing the paragraphs as she does?
4. What effect does Ephron achieve by contrasting the negative aspects of the restaurant with the positive ones of the sandwich?
5. To what extent does Ephron persuade you about the excellence of Langer's pastrami sandwiches?

TECHNIQUE AND STYLE

1. Ephron mentions New York City in paragraphs 1 and 2, along with Kansas City and Dallas. What does her mention of these other cities add to her image of Pastrami Expert?
2. The second sentence of paragraph 2 is quite long. Try breaking it up into two or more sentences. What is gained? Lost?
3. Ephron quotes Norm Langer in paragraph 4 and Al Langer in paragraph 5. What do the direct quotations add to the essay?

4. How effective is Ephron's concluding metaphor—the "symphony orchestra"?
5. To what senses does Ephron appeal? Which one predominates?

SUGGESTIONS FOR WRITING

Journal

1. Assuming you were in Los Angeles, explain why you would or wouldn't have a pastrami sandwich at Langer's.
2. Based on the essay, analyze the kind of person Ephron appears to be. Use examples from the essay to support your views.

Essay

1. Most people have a favorite food or restaurant that they regard as a "work of art." It may be the ultimate cheeseburger or BLT, and the restaurant may be a fast-food franchise or nondescript diner, but "It's the best!" Write your own essay in which you describe, explain, and analyze your choice. Possible topics:
   burger
   hot dog
   BLT
   fried chicken
   pizza
2. Sooner or later almost everyone is confronted with a vegetable or fruit or dish that challenges the imagination of the diner, perhaps an artichoke, avocado, kiwi, clam, or whole fish. Think about such a time and write an essay in which you describe the situation, explain how you dealt with it, and analyze what you thought about it.

The Bridge

Jason Holland

Almost everyone has a special place, either in the present or past, that represents any number of emotions, pleasure being first among them. For Jason Holland, that place was a bridge and the time was when he was in high school. At the time he wrote the essay, he was a student at Valley City State University in Valley City, North Dakota, having decided on attending VCSU because of the academic and athletic opportunities the university provided. When he began his first-semester composition course, he says that he was "somewhat skeptical of my writing skills, but began finding it was easy to write about memorable moments," particularly those spent with his friends in high school. He used "writing about these incidents as an outlet as well as a coping device" to accommodate himself to the difficulties of college life. One of the results is what he characterizes "a short, descriptive essay," "The Bridge." Noreen Braun, his instructor, reprinted the essay on a Web page devoted to what she titled as "Some Fine Student Writing from Composition I, Fall Semester, 1997."

What to Look For   If you are having a difficult time giving your reader a vivid picture of your scene, you might try writing down as many adjectives and adverbs about various objects or people as you associate with the place. After you have done this, then you can choose the most appropriate ones. That is what Jason Holland did when he was coming up with his descriptive essay about his adventures with his friends on a condemned bridge. As you read the essay look specifically at the detail he uses to enhance his essay.

1   I can see it now. The four of us sitting out on the wood bridge puffing on our cheap, Swisher cigars. The smoke rising above the rusty, cast iron sides and filtering up to the full moon above. As the moon reflects off the Goose River my friends and I sit and talk about everything from girls to UFO theories. We sit without a worry on our minds.

2   The bridge looks like it's something from a surreal movie with a midnight atmosphere. Located two miles out of town, it's hidden on a winding, gravel road that sometimes gets washed out if it rains heavily. Because of the lack of maintenance the bridge has old oak and maple trees leaning against it. The wood tiling on the bottom is spaced far apart, almost to the point where our feet could fall through.

3   When we were at the bridge we felt as though nothing could go wrong. We thought that all our problems and fears would go away if we stayed out there long enough. We felt as though our parents, teachers, and coaches had no control over us. We could

talk about anything and anyone without even thinking about the consequences. No one could touch us. We were like 1920 bootleg gangsters that the law couldn't catch up with. We were almost invincible as we smoked our cigars and talked about our dreams and aspirations.

4   As we sat and smoked it felt as though we were the only people on earth. The world revolved around us. It was like we could control the world while we were out at the bridge. It was a rickety, old bridge, but it seemed to empower us to the point where we felt as though we could control our own destiny. My friend who didn't do well in school was a smarter and more insightful person when he was at the bridge. My friend who wasn't good at athletics felt like he was as good an athlete as any professional. My friend who didn't have a girlfriend seemed like he was a savvy, babe magnet. The bridge had the power to give us confidence.

5   The bridge was county property, but my friends and I felt like we were the owners. It was a mutual relationship. We owned the bridge, and the bridge owned us. On the long, cool summer nights we knew that the bridge needed company so we would get our cigars and take a ride down the long, windy road and leave our problems behind. We sat out at the bridge for hours basking in the sounds of an occasional swat of a mosquito, the cooing of an owl in the distance, the splashing of a fish in the river, with the cool yet comfortable, windless night.

6   I haven't yet found a place where I could be so much in my own world and in my own element as I could when I was at the bridge. Having my best friends and cheap cigars made me enjoy it even more.

ORGANIZATION AND IDEAS

1. Paragraph 1 tells you where the scene takes place and who is there. What else does it do?

2. Examine paragraphs 2–5 and in one or two words list a subject or main idea for each one. What progression do you find?

3. Considering the ideas you identified in question 2, what does the bridge represent to the writer?

4. State the thesis of the essay in your own words. Where in the essay does the writer place the thesis? How effective do you find that placement?

5. How important is it to have a place where you can "be in [your] own world and in [your] own element"?

TECHNIQUE AND STYLE

1. In a handbook of grammar and style, look up *sentence fragment* and then reexamine Holland's second and third sentences. What are they missing? Explain whether the two sentences are acceptable fragments.
2. If you vary the length of your sentences, you'll find that your prose moves more smoothly and is apt to be of greater interest to the reader. What evidence can you find that Holland uses this technique?
3. Reread paragraph 2. Which sentence functions as a topic sentence? What words in the other sentences are related to it?
4. Repetition can be effective or ineffective. Explain how you judge Holland's similar sentence beginnings in paragraph 3.
5. Reread paragraph 5, looking for details that appeal to the senses. What are they?

SUGGESTIONS FOR WRITING

Journal

1. Imagine that you are the narrator of "The Bridge." What "problems and fears" would you be leaving behind?
2. Holland describes the bridge as looking like "something from a surreal movie with a midnight atmosphere." Think about places you know about that match that description and describe one of them.

Essay

1. Almost everyone has at least one "special place" that represents a particular mood or feeling, either positive or negative. To write an essay about such a place that holds meaning for you, think first about an emotion and then about the place you associate with it. Here's a list of emotions to consider, but others will probably occur to you as well:

   comfort
   fear
   happiness
   excitement
   curiosity

   Once you've decided on a topic, then you can start accumulating details that will make your scene and the way you feel about it come alive for the reader.
2. Holland's essay deals with two strong human bonds—to place and to a sense of community. Choose one of the two and analyze its importance to you. Try to distance yourself from your subject by limiting your use of the first person *I* so that what you write is a general thought-piece rather than a narrative or personal essay.

Countdown

Jonathan Franzen

For a novelist and nonfiction writer, Jonathan Franzen has a somewhat unusual background. While many a writer was born and raised in Missouri, and some even graduated from Swarthmore College, few have been awarded a Fulbright scholarship for study in Germany, to say nothing of having worked in the seismology lab at Harvard University in the Department of Earth and Planetary Sciences. Franzen is now creating his own planetary disturbances as a novelist, first with The Twenty-Seventh City *(1988), then with* Strong Motion *(1992), and finally with* The Corrections *(2001), which earned the National Book Award. More recently, he has turned to nonfiction with* How to be Alone *(2002) and* The Discomfort Zone, *a memoir published in 2006. Franzen is a frequent contributor to the* New Yorker, *where this essay appeared in the April 18, 2005, issue among a group of essays about trips. At the time Franzen took his, he was ten years old.*

What to Look For   One of Franzen's reviewers said, "His greatest inventiveness lies in his expressive detailing of sensation." As you read his essay, see if you can figure out what sensation the ten-year-old Franzen is "detailing."

1   In 1969, the drive from Minneapolis to St. Louis took twelve hours and was mostly on two-lane roads. My parents woke me up for it at dawn. We had just spent an outstandingly fun week with my Minnesota cousins, but as soon as we pulled out of my uncle's driveway these cousins evaporated from my mind like the morning dew from the hood of our car. I was alone in the back seat again. I went to sleep, and my mother took out her magazines, and the weight of the long July drive fell squarely on my father.

2   To get through the day, he made himself into an algorithm, a number cruncher. Our car was the axe with which he attacked the miles listed on road signs, chopping the nearly unbearable 238 down to a still daunting 179, bludgeoning the 150s and 140s and 130s until they yielded the halfway humane 127, which was roundable

down to 120, which he could pretend was just two hours of driving time even though, with so many livestock trucks and thoughtless drivers on the road ahead of him, it would probably take closer to three. Through sheer force of will, he mowed down the last twenty miles between him and double digits, and these digits he then reduced by tens and twelves until, finally, he could glimpse it: "Cedar Rapids 34." Only then, as his sole treat of the day, did he allow himself to remember that 34 was the distance to the *city center*—that we were, in fact, less than thirty miles now from the oak-shaded park where we liked to stop for a picnic lunch.

3   The three of us ate quietly. My father took the pit of a damson plum out of his mouth and dropped it into a paper bag, fluttering his fingers a little. He was wishing he'd pressed on to Iowa City—Cedar Rapids wasn't even the halfway point—and I was wishing we were back in the air-conditioned car. Cedar Rapids felt like outer space to me. The warm breeze was someone else's breeze, not mine, and the sun overhead was a harsh reminder of the day's relentless waning, and the park's unfamiliar oak trees all spoke to our deep nowhereness. Even my mother didn't have much to say.

4   But the really interminable drive was through southeastern Iowa. My father remarked on the height of the corn, the blackness of the soil, the need for better roads. My mother lowered the front-seat armrest and played crazy eights with me until I was just as sick of it as she was. Every few miles a pig farm. Another ninety-degree bend in the road. Another truck with fifty cars behind it. Each time my father floored the accelerator and swung out to pass, my mother drew frightened breath:

"Fffff!

"Ffff*ffff!*

"Fffff—*FFFFFFFF!*—OH! EARL!

OH! Ffff*fff!*"

5   There was white sun in the east and white sun in the west. Aluminum domes of silos white against white sky. It seemed as if we'd been driving steadily downhill for hours, careering toward an ever-receding green furriness at the Missouri state line. Terrible that it could still be afternoon. Terrible that we were still in Iowa. We had left behind the convivial planet where my cousins lived, and we were plummeting south toward a quiet, dark, air-conditioned house in which I didn't even recognize loneliness as loneliness, it was so familiar to me.

6   My father hadn't said a word in fifty miles. He silently accepted another plum from my mother and, a moment later, handed her the pit. She unrolled her window and flung the pit into a wind suddenly heavy with a smell of tornadoes. What looked like diesel exhaust was rapidly filling the southern sky. A darkness gathering at three in the afternoon. The endless downslope steepening, the tasselled corn tossing, and everything suddenly green—sky green, pavement green, parents green.

7   My father turned on the radio and sorted through crashes of static to find a station. He had remembered—or maybe never forgotten—that another descent was in progress. There was static on static on static, crazy assaults on the signal's integrity, but we could hear men with Texan accents reporting lower and lower elevations, counting the mileage down toward zero. Then a wall of rain hit our windshield with a roar like deep-fry. Lightning everywhere. Static smashing the Texan voices, the rain on our roof louder than the thunder, the car shimmying in lateral gusts.

8   "Earl, maybe you should pull over," my mother said, "Earl?"

9   He had just passed milepost 2, and the Texan voices were getting steadier, as if they'd figured out that the static couldn't hurt them: that they were going to make it. And, indeed, the wipers were already starting to squeak, the road drying out, the black clouds shearing off into harmless shreds. "The Eagle has landed," the radio said. We'd crossed the state line. We were back home on the moon.

ORGANIZATION AND IDEAS

1. Franzen presents the trip chronologically, condensing a 12-hour journey into a little over 800 words. What events does he highlight? What do they contribute to the essay?

2. Paragraph 2 brims with details about Franzen's father. How would you describe him?

3. What details does Franzen provide about his stay with his cousins? How would you describe that stay? How does it compare to what he implies about his life at home?

4. Compare the introduction, paragraph 1, to the conclusion in paragraph 9. In what ways are they related?

5. Franzen's thesis is implied rather than stated. Consider what he says about his cousins, his parents, and the trip he describes. What thesis can you deduce?

TECHNIQUE AND STYLE

1. Although Franzen organizes his essay chronologically, he uses his final three sentences to provide a dramatic ending. How effective is it?
2. Franzen quotes his mother in paragraphs 5 and 8. What do the quotations contribute to the essay as a whole?
3. In paragraphs 6 and 7, Franzen uses sentence fragments for dramatic effect. Rewrite the ones in paragraph 7 as complete sentences. What is gained? Lost?
4. What descriptive words stand out in paragraphs 3–7? What feelings and general atmosphere do they imply?
5. What is the other "descent" Franzen mentions in paragraph 7? In what ways can the essay as a whole be seen as describing a descent?

SUGGESTIONS FOR WRITING

Journal

1. Franzen's trip took place in 1969, a time when there were relatively few interstates and four-lane highways, but emotions are emotions. Explain why you think the essay is or is not dated.
2. What car trips have you taken with your parents? Select one, consider how you felt, and use your journal to explore the ways your trip differed or resembled Franzen's.

Essay

1. A journey can be long or short, exciting or boring, fun or dull, lonely or companionable, and a million other combinations. Think about a journey you have taken, defining "journey" in the broadest possible way so that the word could apply to a very short trip, a long one, or anything in between. With that journey in mind, what emotions did you feel? What events stick in your mind? What details stand out? What atmosphere did it have—exciting, strange, dangerous, what? If you're stuck, think about a
      journey into the unknown
      vacation trip
      train ride
      airplane flight
      frightening drive in a car
2. Consider the essay's title and also write down your ideas in response to question 5, above. Ask yourself questions as well. What is the "countdown" to? Why might Franzen have brought in "The eagle has landed"? What "moon" is he referring to? Is it significant that he is ten years old? That only his parents are with him on the trip? That he had been with his cousins for a week? Use your notes to develop an essay that analyzes what Franzen implies about "descent."

El Hoyo

Mario Suárez

Son of immigrants and the oldest of five children, Mario Suárez grew up in Tucson, Arizona, in the neighborhood known as "El Hoyo." Shortly after graduating from high school, Suárez joined the Navy and served his tour of duty during World War II. When he returned home, he enrolled at the University of Arizona and found himself taking freshman English. The essay that follows was written for that class and so impressed his teacher, Ruth Keenan, that she not only encouraged him to take other writing courses but also to submit "El Hoyo" to the Arizona Quarterly, *where it was published. That was a long time ago (1947), but it started Suárez on a successful writing career; it is a rare anthology of Chicano literature that doesn't include at least one of Suárez's works. Hailed as a "key figure in the foundation of Chicano literature," Suárez's stories have recently been collected and reissued as* Chicano Sketches, *published by the University of Arizona Press in 2004.*

What to Look For Like many writers, Suárez faces the problem of explaining the unfamiliar, but for Suárez the problem is compounded. Many of his readers do not know the meaning of *barrio,* nor are they familiar with Latino culture. Those who do know the terms may have negative associations with them. As you read his essay, note the techniques he uses to combat these problems. Also note how Suárez uses repetition effectively to lend emphasis to his description. Read Suárez's second paragraph out loud so you can hear the repetition more clearly.

1 From the center of downtown Tucson the ground slopes gently away to Main Street, drops a few feet, and then rolls to the banks of the Santa Cruz River. Here lies the section of the city known as El Hoyo. Why it is called El Hoyo is not very clear. In no sense is it a hole as its name would imply; it is simply the river's immediate valley. Its inhabitants are chicanos who raise hell on Saturday night and listen to Padre Estanislao on Sunday

morning. While the term chicano is the short way of saying Mexicano, it is not restricted to the paisanos who came from old Mexico with the territory or the last famine to work for the railroad, labor, sing, and go on relief. Chicano is the easy way of referring to everybody. Pablo Gutíerrez married the Chinese grocer's daughter and now runs a meat department; his sons are chicanos. So are the sons of Killer Jones who threw a fight in Harlem and fled to El Hoyo to marry Cristina Mendez. And so are all of them. However, it is doubtful that all these spiritual sons of Mexico live in El Hoyo because they love each other—many fight and bicker constantly. It is doubtful they live in El Hoyo because of its scenic beauty—it is everything but beautiful. Its houses are simple affairs of unplastered adobe, wood, and abandoned car parts. Its narrow streets are mostly clearings which have, in time, acquired names. Except for some tall trees which nobody has ever cared to identify, nurse, or destroy, the main things known to grow in the general area are weeds, garbage piles, dark-eyed chavalos, and dogs. And it is doubtful that the chicanos live in El Hoyo because it is safe—many times the Santa Cruz has risen and inundated the area.

2   In other respects living in El Hoyo has its advantages. If one is born with weakness for acquiring bills, El Hoyo is where the collectors are less likely to find you. If one has acquired the habit of listening to Octavio Perea's Mexican Hour in the wee hours of the morning with the radio on at full blast, El Hoyo is where you are less likely to be reported to the authorities. Besides, Perea is very popular and sooner or later to everyone "Smoke in the Eyes" is dedicated between the pinto beans and white flour commercials. If one, for any reason whatever, comes on an extended period of hard times, where, if not in El Hoyo, are the neighbors more willing to offer solace? When Teofila Malacara's house burned to the ground with all her belongings and two children, a benevolent gentleman carried through the gesture that made tolerable her burden. He made a list of 500 names and solicited from each a dollar. At the end of a month he turned over to the tearful but grateful señora $100 in cold cash and then accompanied her on a short vacation. When the new manager of a local store decided that no more chicanas were to work behind the counters, it was the chicanos of El Hoyo who, on taking their individually small but collectively great buying power elsewhere, drove the manager

out and the girls returned to their jobs. When the Mexican Army was en route to Baja California and the chicanos found out that the enlisted men ate only at infrequent intervals, it was El Hoyo's chicanos who crusaded across town with pots of beans and trays of tortillas to meet the train. When someone gets married, celebrating is not restricted to the immediate friends of the couple. Everybody is invited. Anything calls for a celebration and a celebration calls for anything. On Memorial Day there are no less than half a dozen good fights at the Riverside Dance Hall. On Mexican Independence Day more than one flag is sworn allegiance to amid cheers for the queen.

3   And El Hoyo is something more. It is this something more which brought Felipe Suárez back from the wars after having killed a score of Japanese with his body resembling a patchwork quilt to marry Julia Armijo. It brought Joe Zepeda, a gunner, . . . back to compose boleros. He has a metal plate for a skull. Perhaps El Hoyo is proof that those people exist, and perhaps exist best, who have as yet failed to observe the more popular modes of human conduct. Perhaps the humble appearance of El Hoyo justifies the indifferent shrug of those made aware of its existence. Perhaps El Hoyo's simplicity motivates an occasional chicano to move away from its narrow streets, babbling comadres and shrieking children to deny the bloodwell from which he springs and to claim the blood of a conquistador while his hair is straight and his face beardless. Yet El Hoyo is not an outpost of a few families against the world. It fights for no causes except those which soothe its immediate angers. It laughs and cries with the same amount of passion in times of plenty and of want.

4   Perhaps El Hoyo, its inhabitants, and its essence can best be explained by telling a bit about a dish called capirotada. Its origin is uncertain. But, according to the time and the circumstance, it is made of old, new or hard bread. It is softened with water and then cooked with peanuts, raisins, onions, cheese, and panocha. It is fired with sherry wine. Then it is served hot, cold, or just "on the weather" as they say in El Hoyo. The Sermeños like it one way, the Garcias another, and the Ortegas still another. While it might differ greatly from one home to another, nevertheless it is still capirotada. And so it is with El Hoyo's chicanos. While being divided from within and from without, like the capirotada, they remain chicanos.

ORGANIZATION AND IDEAS

1. Examine the essay using the standard journalistic questions. Which paragraph describes *where* El Hoyo is? What paragraphs describe *who* lives there? What paragraph or paragraphs describe *how* they live? *Why* they live there?
2. All of the questions above lead to a larger one: *What* is El Hoyo? Given the people and place, and how and why they live there, what statement is the author making about El Hoyo?
3. The essay ends with an analogy, and toward the end of paragraph 4, Suárez spells out some details of the analogy. What other characteristics of *capirotada* correspond to those of *chicanos?* Where in the essay do you find evidence for your opinion?
4. How would you describe the movement in the essay? Does it move from the general to the particular? From the particular to the general? What reasons can you give for the author's choice of direction?
5. It's obvious that Suárez likes and appreciates El Hoyo, but to what extent, if any, does he gloss over its negative qualities?

TECHNIQUE AND STYLE

1. The introductory paragraph achieves coherence and cohesion through the author's use of subtle unifying phrases. Trace Suárez's use of "it is doubtful." How often does the phrase occur? Rewrite the sentences to avoid using the phrase. What is lost? Gained?
2. What key words are repeated in paragraph 2? What is the effect of the repetition?
3. Paragraph 2 gives many examples of the advantages of living in El Hoyo. List the examples in the order in which they appear. The first two can be grouped together under the idea of El Hoyo as a sanctuary, a place where people aren't bothered. What other groupings does the list of examples suggest? What principle appears to have guided the ordering of the examples?
4. Why might the author have chosen not to use either first or second person? What is gained by using "one"?

SUGGESTIONS FOR WRITING

Journal

1. Write a journal entry explaining why you would or would not like to live in El Hoyo. Use examples from the essay to flesh out your reasons.

2. Suárez compares the dish capirotada to El Hoyo, developing it as a metaphor. Think of a metaphor that would work for your neighborhood or for one of your classes. Write a paragraph or two developing your comparison and you will probably discover that using metaphor may also make you see the familiar in a new way.

Essay

1. If you live in an ethnic neighborhood, you can use the essay as a close model. If you do not, you can still use the essay as a general model by choosing a topic that combines people and place. Suggestions:

    family ritual at Christmas, Hanukkah, or Ramadan

    family ritual at Thanksgiving

    dinner at a neighborhood restaurant

    busy time at the university student center

2. Write an essay analyzing and explaining why you would or would not like to live in El Hoyo. Use examples from the essay to flesh out your reasons.

Left Sink

Ellery Akers

Ellery Akers is a writer, naturalist, and poet who lives near San Francisco. Knocking on the Earth, *her first book of poems, was published in 1989 by Wesleyan University Press, and her poems have been published in the* American Poetry Review, *the* Harvard Review, *and* Ploughshares *as well as other poetry journals. She is also a contributor to* Stories From Where We Live—The California Coast, *published by Milkweed Editions in 2005. As you read the essay, you'll discover that her prose reflects a number of characteristics of poetry—imagery, concise language, and an acute eye for detail. You'll also see that the line between description and narration is a fine one. The essay won the 1990 Sierra Club Award for nature writing and was published the same year in* Sierra. *Although the essay is longer than most in this book, you'll find its length is deceptive. You'll read it quickly.*

Writers who deal with familiar subjects face the
challenge of making the familiar new or unusual, and to do that they
rely on concrete detail. Ellery Akers knows her readers are familiar
with bathrooms and frogs, but she goes on to individualize this particular bathroom and the frog she names Left Sink. Some writers
might be content to state "The frog was small." Akers, however, takes
the word *small* and gives it substance, "no bigger than a penny, and
his round, salmon-colored toes stuck out like tiny soupspoons."
Remember as you write that one person's idea of a general term,
such as *small,* may not be the same as another's, so it's best to use
concrete details to show just what you mean.

1   The first time I saw Left Sink, I was brushing my teeth and
almost spit on him by mistake. I wasn't expecting to find a frog in a
Park Service bathroom, but there he was, hopping out of the drain
and squatting on the porcelain as casually as if he were sitting
beside a pond.

2   He was a small green tree frog, no bigger than a penny, and his
round, salmon-colored toes stuck out like tiny soupspoons. For a
few minutes I stared into his gold eyes, each pupil floating in the
middle like a dark seed.

3   I was so close I could see his throat pulse, but I was probably too
close, for he looked at me fearfully and leaped onto the silver "C" of
the cold-water faucet.

4   Then he must have thought better of it, for he jumped down
again, and sat, hunched over, by the soap. He kept making nervous little hops toward the safety of the drain, but my looming
face was obviously in the way, so I ducked below the basin for a
moment, and when I looked again he was descending into the
hole, head first.

5   Feeling I'd disturbed his evening hunt, I decided to make amends.
I grubbed around the floor for a dead moth, found one (though it
was a little dried up), and offered it to the hole. The wing slanted
into the drain, but nothing happened. I thought perhaps he'd
hopped back down into the pipe. Trying to find something a little
more appealing, I picked around the window sills until I discovered
a really decent-looking moth, pushed it up to the drain, and
waited. After a few minutes, I got discouraged and walked away.

When I turned back to sneak one last look, I found both moths had vanished.

6   The next day was so hot I forgot Left Sink completely. It is always hot in the California chaparral in September, especially in the Gabilan Mountains. I spent the afternoon in the shade, lying on the cool pebbles of a dry wash and looking over my field notes. I had been camping for weeks, studying birds, and by now I had gotten used to the feeling of expectation in the landscape.

7   Everything seemed to be waiting for rain. The streambeds were dry, the fields were dry, and when the buckeye leaves hissed in the wind they sounded like rattlesnakes. Ravens flew overhead, croaking, their wings flapping loudly in the air, and the rocks baked. Once in a while a few thirsty finches fluttered up to a seep in a cliff and sipped from a damp clump of algae.

8   I leaned against the cool flank of a boulder and fanned myself with my hat. From far away I could hear the staccato drill of a Nuttall's woodpecker.

9   All the animals had some way of coping with the heat. The wrentits could last for several weeks without drinking. The deer found beds of shade and waited patiently until evening. Even the trees adapted. Though I couldn't see it, I knew that somewhere beneath my boots, 100 feet down, the root of a digger pine was twisting along a crevice in the bedrock, reaching far below the surface to tap into the permanent water.

10   And the frogs—the normal ones—were sleeping away the summer and fall, huddled in some moist spot in the ground in a kind of hot-weather hibernation.

11   That night, when I went back to the bathroom, I discovered Left Sink had a neighbor. Even before I turned on the water in the right-hand basin, I noticed a second frog, and when I stepped back to look at both of them in their respective sinks, I started to laugh: They reminded me of a couple of sober, philosophical old monks peering out of their cells.

12   Overhead was a third frog, puffy and well-fed, squatting on top of the fluorescent lights, surrounded by tattered moths. Light Buddha, I would call him.

13   In the world of the bathroom the light shelf was a delicatessen of the highest order. Light Buddha sat there night after glorious night, lazily snapping up moths as they fluttered past. The other two frogs seemed content to stake out the sinks, which weren't quite as

dependable a food source, though they weren't bad. Almost every night I found a damp moth thrashing around in one of the basins, one little flopping death after another, leaving a trail of scales behind.

14   Right Sink was extremely shy, and spent most of his time crouched far back in the pipe. Usually I saw his gold eyes shining in the darkness, but that was all. Left Sink was more of an adventurer, and explored the whole bathroom, darting behind the mirror, splatting onto the porcelain, hopping on the window sills, leaping on the toilet, and climbing the slippery painted walls toe pad by toe pad.

15   From time to time I was tempted to pick him up as he was climbing. But I didn't think it would be fair; I knew this geometrical universe, and he didn't. Besides, there was no place for him to hide on those smooth, painted bricks, so I let him be.

16   I was amazed at how few people noticed Left Sink, even when he was sitting on top of the faucet. Kids saw him right away, though, and I worried sometimes that one night a little girl would pop him into a jar and take him home to some confining terrarium.

17   Also, he stood out. Even though tree frogs can change color in ten minutes, there was nothing in Left Sink's repertoire that could possibly match white paint; the best he could do was a sickly pink.

18   I could always tell if he had just emerged from the drain because he would still be a murky gray-green. As the evening wore on he got paler and paler. Once I couldn't find him for half an hour. Finally I caught sight of him over my head. Plopped on a narrow ledge, he looked like a pale pebble in all that metal and paint. I climbed onto the toilet for a better look. To my horror he began hopping along the ledge, which was no wider than half an inch. It was a ten-foot fall to the floor—for a frog that small, an abyss. He bounded past me, his grainy throat quivering.

19   He headed toward a swarm of moths and flies that circled the fluorescent lights. A fly drifted down from the glare; Left Sink, his pink mouth flashing, snapped it up.

20   I was never quite sure just how skittish he really was. Sometimes he tolerated my watching him, sometimes he didn't. I got in the habit of sidling up to the plumbing, bent over so as not to be seen, and I must have looked pretty peculiar. One night a woman came into the bathroom and caught me hunched over like Quasimodo, staring intently at the drains, my hands full of dead moths.

21   "Left Sink! Right Sink!" I was saying. "Got a little treat for you guys!"

22   The woman bolted out the door.

23   For the next few weeks I checked on the frogs every morning and evening. Sometimes when I saw Left Sink skidding down a length of plastic, unable to hold on in spite of his adhesive toe pads, I worried. I couldn't help thinking there was something unnatural about a frog in a bathroom.

24   Of course, I knew there were a few oddballs that *had* managed to live with us in our artificial world, but they were mostly insects. One year in school I had learned about the larvae of petroleum flies: They lived in the gunk of oil fields, so numerous at times that, according to my textbook, they imparted "a shimmering effect to the surface of the oil." Their world was oil; if you deprived them of it, took them out and cleaned them off, they'd curl up and die in less than a day.

25   In that same class I'd learned that furniture beetles live in our table legs, and occasionally, in wooden spoons; drugstore beetles float happily in bottles of belladonna, mating, pupating, dying. We have cheese mites in our cheese, and flour mites in our flour.

26   As far as I knew no one had ever done any research on frogs and plumbing. Luckily, I always carried a trunkful of books and field guides in my car, and one night I flipped through every book I had to see if I could find any instances where humans and animals—wild ones—had actually gotten along. Arthur Cleveland Bent said that wrens nested in old clothes in barns, and swallows on moving trains. Edwin Way Teale said he had once read about a pigeon using rubber bands and paper clips in her nest on a window ledge off Times Square. One year, he wrote, a thrush spent the entire winter in a florist's shop on Madison Avenue, flitted about between the iced gladiolas and roses, and flew away in spring.

27   But no one mentioned anything about frogs.

28   Actually, considering the drought, Left Sink had a pretty good set-up. It was already October and still no rain. Once in a while a few drops would plop into the dirt and gravel, and I would catch a whiff of wet dust, soaked cheat grass, and buckwheat. But that was all.

29   All the other frogs were holed up in the dirt, huddled in a moist crack or an abandoned gopher hole, waiting for the first rains of winter to wake them up. There were probably a few hiding in the field next to Left Sink's bathroom, their eyelids closed, their toes pulled

under them to conserve moisture, unmoving, barely breathing, their heartbeats almost completely stilled. If I dug them up they would look like small stones.

30   One night just before I was about to leave, I had a nightmare. It was a dream I had had many times, a dream of a city so polluted the air rose in black plumes above the granite and cement. I was at the entrance of a tunnel. Inside I could hear a whoosh of air: Millions of butterflies were flashing in the dark, thousands of ducks, eagles, sparrows, their wings making a vast rustling as they flew off and vanished.

31   I heard a low shuffling. After a while I realized it was the sound of feet: the slow trudge of bears, the pad of badgers, the pattering of foxes, the rasp of a hundred million beetles, rabbits, ants, mice. I looked around, panicked, to see if any animals were left. There were still cockroaches scuttling over the window sills. There were pigeons, flies, starlings. I named them over and over in a kind of chant: the adaptable, the drab, the ones who could live with us, who had always lived with us.

32   A fox coughed close to my camp in the middle of the nightmare and woke me up. I unzipped the tent and looked out at the stars: Rigel, Algol, clear, cold, and changeless. A golden-crowned sparrow chirped from a nearby branch, then sputtered off into silence. For a while I tried to stay awake, but soon drifted off.

33   The next morning huge bluish clouds rolled across the sky. A couple of ravens sailed past the cliff in front of me. One of them jackknifed its wings, plummeted straight down, and then, at the last minute, unfolded them and flapped away. It was still early, but when I reached the bathroom it had already been cleaned. It reeked of ammonia, and a mop and bucket leaned against the door.

34   I rinsed off my face, brushed my hair, and looked sleepily into the drains. As usual, Right Sink was huddled far back into the dark pipe; he retreated still further when I bent over.

35   Left Sink, however, was gone. I wondered if he had slipped behind the mirror, or had come up in the world and was squatting above with Light Buddha. The shelf was empty. I looked on the window sill—not there either.

36   It was not until I opened the door to the toilet that I found him. There, in the center of the ammonia-filled bowl, his green bloated body turning gray, was Left Sink, splayed out in the milky liquid, dead.

Floating in front of him was a dead damselfly. I suppose he must have jumped in after his prey, convinced he was at the edge of a strange-looking pond, his toe pads gripping the cold, perfectly smooth surface of the porcelain.

37   His skin looked curdled, and it occurred to me he might have been there all morning waiting to die. Then I remembered that frogs breathe through their skin; it must have been a hard, stinging death, but a quick one.

38   I flushed him down, wishing I could think of something to say as he made his way through the pipes and rolled out to the septic tank, some acknowledgment of the link between my kind and his, but I couldn't think of anything except that I would miss him, which was true.

39   When I opened the door, a couple of nervous towhees blundered into the bushes. It was beginning to rain.

ORGANIZATION AND IDEAS

1. The story of Left Sink unfolds slowly. Which paragraphs provide the introduction? What reasons can you give for your choice?
2. An essay of this length tends to group paragraphs around a topic sentence or main idea rather than have a topic sentence for each paragraph. What groupings can you identify? What ideas tie those paragraphs together?
3. Paragraphs 30 and 31 stand out because they strike a very different note from the rest of the essay. What function do they serve?
4. Akers says "there was something unnatural about a frog in a bathroom" (paragraph 23). What does she imply in that paragraph and elsewhere about the relationship between humans and nature?
5. Many essays have an explicit thesis, one that you can spot in a complete sentence. Others, however, have an implied thesis, one that the writer suggests and the reader must deduce. That is the case with Akers' essay. What do you find to be its thesis?
6. Most people would find it difficult to cultivate affection for a frog, but that's what Akers tries to do. How well does she succeed?

TECHNIQUE AND STYLE

1. What does Akers think and feel about Left Sink? What details can you find to support your opinion?
2. What details can you find that lead to the conclusion that Akers is a naturalist?

3. Unlike many more formal essays, Akers uses lots of short paragraphs. Look up types of paragraphs in your handbook. What justification can you find for short paragraphs?

4. Akers' choice of verbs helps create the fast pace of the essay and its readability. Find a sentence that uses unusual verbs and rewrite it, substituting other verbs. What is gained? Lost?

5. At various places in the essay, Akers refers to rain or the lack of it. What does that contribute to the essay?

SUGGESTIONS FOR WRITING

Journal

1. The tone of an essay can be tricky, particularly if it appeals to emotion. To pinpoint Akers' tone, explain how you feel about the frog at the start of the essay, in the middle, and at the end.

2. Take a moment to jot down all the words you associate with the word *frog*. Looking at your list, mark the associations according to whether they are positive, negative, or neutral. Then make another list of the adjectives you think Akers would use for Left Sink. What differences do you find between your list and Akers'?

Essay

1. Day-to-day life is apt to be full of contrasts, though not usually so striking as a frog in a bathroom. See how many contrasts you can spot in the course of a day when you're looking for them. Jot down what you see, and then choose from your notes to work the contrast into a descriptive essay. Like Akers' essay, yours should have a thesis, either implied or explicit. Suggestions:

   at a beach, look for a fully dressed person
   in a library, look for someone who is nervous or loud
   at a film, look for someone who has brought a baby
   in a cafeteria, look for someone who is studying

2. Write an essay in which you analyze your response to "Left Sink." Use examples and quotations from the essay to support your points, but remember to analyze any quotation you use rather than letting it speak for itself.

ADDITIONAL WRITING ASSIGNMENTS

Using Description

1. Describe a person so that you convey the person's character: friend, family member, student, teacher, or coworker.
2. Describe a place so that you create a specific point about it: neighborhood, workplace, classroom, where you live, or restaurant.
3. Describe a job so that you communicate exactly what it's like: part-time, summer, indoors, outdoors, or household chore.
4. Describe a favorite article of clothing so that your attachment to it comes across to your reader: tee shirt, blue jeans, hat, running shoes, or top.

Evaluating the Essays

1. The authors of "A Sandwich" and "Countdown" rely on descriptive language to convince their readers about their subjects. Ephron wants you to lust after one of Langer's pastrami sandwiches, and Franzen wants you to feel that boredom and isolation. Write an essay in which you compare the two pieces to determine which is the more effective description. Use evidence from the essays to support your point.
2. Description is often used to bring scenes and events to life in such a way that the unfamiliar becomes familiar. That is the challenge facing the authors of "El Hoyo" and "Left Sink." Not many readers would know El Hoyo or a similar chicano neighborhood, nor have many observed the life of a small frog in a sink. Reread the two essays noting the ways the writers depict their subjects and what they think about them. Which does the better job of describing the unusual?
3. Think about the idea of community that is suggested by "The Bridge" and "El Hoyo." How would you define each writer's concept of community? How important is it? Who is involved in it? What values do those in that community share? What emotions are included? Which of the two is closer to your own idea of community? Write an essay in which you analyze your own

definition of the word *community* and how your concept differs from those of Holland and Suárez.

4. In terms of description, "Left Sink" and "Countdown" have a lot in common. Both authors appeal to the senses, amass details, and try to make their readers connect to their subjects emotionally. Go through each of the essays noting the words and phrases that carry emotional overtones. What feelings are described or implied? What atmosphere does the writer create? Of the two, which does the better job and why?

On Using Narration

2

Whether prompted by the child's "Tell me a story" or the adult's "What happened?" **narration** supplies much of our entertainment and information. But anyone who has asked "What happened?" only to be overwhelmed with every detail knows that telling everything can blunt the point and bore the listener. Effective narration is more than telling a story; it calls for compressing and reshaping experience so that the listener or reader relives it with you and is left with a particular point. Shaping narrative draws on some of the same skills used in description:

- keen observation
- careful selection of details
- coherent sequencing

But to turn description into narration, you have to add two other elements:

- conflict
- resolution

A story with no point is indeed pointless. One with no conflict is no kind of story at all, and one with no resolution leaves the reader up in the air.

Often the narrative and the subject are the same: if you are writing about what happened to you when lightning struck your house, what happened is the subject of your narrative. Frequently, however, a writer chooses narrative to introduce or to conclude an essay or perhaps to do both, thus building a narrative framework. Or perhaps you would opt for narrative to emphasize a particular point. An essay that explains the dangers of toxic waste may be made more effective if it starts with a brief narrative of what happens when pollution threatens an area and its residents; an essay on Los Angeles and its smog, for example, might begin with the story of an asthma attack. A paper on the same subject that argues for stricter federal and state controls may end by predicting what might happen without tougher regulation. The essays in this chapter, however, rely on narration for their primary structure. All present conflicts, build to a point, and spring from personal experience—from the something that happened.

Audience and Purpose

No one tells a story for the sake of telling a story, at least no one who wants to be listened to. Most of us will use a narrative to explain something, or to argue a point, or perhaps to entertain. If you think of a journal, the concepts of narration, audience, and purpose may become clearer. If you've ever kept a journal, then you realize that even though *you* are the audience, much of what you write may not make much sense later. It does, of course, right after you finish the journal entry, but two months or two years down the line, you can no longer supply the details from your memory. "Had a terrible argument," you might write, but unless you explain what the argument was about, you may be mystified when you reread that entry. And had you told the whole story behind the quarrel, you might have found that you could muster even more ammunition to support your side than you did in the heat of battle. In that case, you would not only have written about an argument, you would also have written one.

Much of what people write in journals, however, has explanation and entertainment as the goals. Writing in a journal helps many of us think through problems or events. Essentially, we are reliving the incident or situation so that we may examine and comprehend it more clearly: we retell our stories to understand them. A seemingly simple question (such as "Why did I feel so?") calls for a narrative that provides the context. Often, however, we record an event simply because it gave us pleasure, pleasure that we want to be able to relive, once as it is written and again and again as we reread it.

The need for details increases as the distance between the reader and the subject grows. Yet there are always general experiences held in common. Say, for example, you are writing an essay based on something that happened to you in high school. And say you went to a small, all-male Catholic high school in Chicago. You might well wonder how you can make your narrative speak to a general readership, people who attended public, private, or religious schools, schools large and small, rural and urban, some single sex but most coed. Big differences, yes, but when you start thinking about details, you may find yourself turning to description to tap into shared experience—the blurred hum and jangle of students gathered together before a bell rings, the stale, dusty smell of chalk, the squeal of rubber-soled shoes on a waxed floor.

Emotion also speaks across differences. Anyone who has ever been to school knows the panic of being called on by a teacher when you don't even know the question, much less the answer. Moments of praise are equally memorable, whether it be for a point scored on a test or on a basketball court. Joy, despair, fear, elation, anguish, frustration, boredom, laughter, embarrassment—all these and an almost infinite number of other emotions are interwoven in narratives, no matter what the topic, making the topic more interesting because the reader has experienced the same feeling.

Who, What, Where, When, How, Why

These are the standard questions used in journalism, and they are important in narrative essays as well. *What happened?* That's the essential question for narrative, and you'll probably find that the greater part of your essay supplies the answer. *How* and *why* will probably figure in as well, and *who* is obviously essential. But it's easy to neglect *where* and *when.*

If you think of both *where* and *when* as the **setting,** as ways to set the scene, you can remember them more easily and perhaps put them to good use. An essay that relates the tale of a job interview that began as a disaster and ended as a success, for example, might begin by describing the writer as a night person, barely human before 11 A.M. The time of the interview? Nine o'clock. Sharp. The office is impersonal to the point of being cell-like, and the interviewer is so buttoned into his three-piece suit that it looks like armor. Add to those descriptions so that the reader gets the impression that the interview itself will make the Spanish Inquisition look like the first Woodstock, and the writer will have set the tone for the essay as well as built up the readers' interest in what will happen next, the meat of the essay.

Conflict

Narratives are structured around a **conflict.** In its simplest form, conflict is *x* versus *y,* Superman versus the Penguin, the Roadrunner versus Wile E. Coyote. But rarely does conflict exist in such a clear-cut way. Put real people in place of any of those terms, and you begin to understand that what seemed so simple is not; the defense versus the prosecution, a Republican candidate versus a Democrat—these conflicts are complex. The issues become even more complex when you substitute ideas, such as reality versus illusion, a distinction that even a postcard can blur (how many of us have been disappointed when a scene didn't live up to its photograph?). Even distinguishing good from evil isn't always clear, as the debates over capital punishment and abortion constantly remind us. When a writer explores the complexity involved in a conflict, the essay gains depth and substance, making the reader think. That exploration can be direct, such as naming the opposing forces, or indirect, implying them.

The conflict that occurs in narrative essays is of two kinds and many layers. If, for instance, you were to write about leaving home for the first time—whether you were headed off to college, to the army, or just off—your initial conflict might have been **internal:** Should you go or should you stay? But it might have been **external** as well—what your parents wanted you to do versus what *you* wanted to do. And the conflict was probably also one of ideas—of freedom versus constraints, independence versus dependence.

And then if you generalize about your experience, using first person sparingly, you'll forge an even stronger link to your readers who have experienced similar conflicts. By minimizing first person, you'll also be writing the kind of prose expected in other college courses, prose that focuses more on the subject than the writer.

Point of View

A not-so-obvious question about any narrative you're about to write is, "Who tells it?" This question identifies the **point of view,** the perspective from which the narrative is related. Probably the first pronoun that comes to mind is *I,* first-person singular, and that's a good choice if you want your readers to identify with you and your angle on the narrative you're relating. When a reader sees first person, an automatic psychological identification takes place, one that allows the reader to look through the writer's eyes. That sort of identification is strongest if you, as narrator, are part of the action. Obviously, there's a huge difference between "I was there" and "I heard about it."

But using first person can be a hazard, and that's why at some point in some classroom, you have probably been warned off using *I.* There are at least three reasons: it's easy to overuse the pronoun; it can modify your purpose in a way you hadn't intended; and it can lead to an overly informal tone. If you were to take a look at your first draft for an essay you wrote using *I,* odds are you used it too frequently. The result is apt to be short, choppy sentences that are similar in structure—subject (*I*) followed by a verb and its complement (the word or words that complete the sense of the verb). That's fine for a first draft, and you can revise your way out of the problem. You *need* to revise because too many *I*'s can shift the aim of your essay away from exposition or argument to self-expression; what becomes important is you, not your subject. Your tone may also change, becoming more informal than the assignment calls for, which is why you don't see many research papers that use first person.

Choosing to relate the narrative from the position of *he* or *she* (rarely *they*) puts more distance between the subject and the reader. Think of the difference between "I fell out of the window" and "He fell out of the window." With the latter, the reader's sympathies are at one remove. That's not the case with the second person, *you. You* is direct and that's what makes it a somewhat slippery choice. If you're going to use a second-person point of view, make sure the reader understands exactly who is meant by *you.* Many a teacher has been stopped short when reading an essay that has a sentence such as "When you graduate, you'll start looking for a job that can turn into a career"; if that sentence occurred in an essay on surviving an important job interview, its author had too narrow an audience in mind, one composed only of classmates and ignoring everyone else interested in the topic—including the teacher. One way around that problem is to specify the audience in your paper. "All of us who are now in college worry about jobs" tells the reader just who the audience is, and the teacher then reads the essay from the perspective of a college student.

Organization and Ideas

Narratives often begin with the setting, which is the context for the conflict, then establish the nature of the conflict and move toward its resolution. Setting, conflict, and resolution all reinforce the essay's thesis, one that can be explicit or implicit. If the thesis is explicit, it's apt to occur in the introduction; sometimes, however, the writer will reserve it for the conclusion. That kind of placement puts an extra burden on the writer, in that everything in the essay must build to the conclusion. If the organization isn't tight, the reader wonders where the story is going; with a delayed thesis, the reader needs to have the feeling that the story is going somewhere, even though the final destination isn't apparent till the very end.

With narrative essays, as with short stories, the thesis is often implied and the reader must deduce it. If you opt for an implied thesis, make sure that the reader can easily identify your subject and then, without too much effort, move on to infer your thesis. The question that the reader needs to ask is "What is the writer saying about the subject?" The answer, phrased as a complete sentence, is the thesis.

One way to control what the reader infers is to work with the narrative's chronology. The sequence of events can be shaped to emphasize different elements. It may help to list the most important incidents in the narrative on a scrap of paper; then you can review them to check that each one is essential and to figure out the best order in which to present them. Writers often disrupt exact chronology, opting for dramatic placement over actual time sequence. The **flashback** is a technique that allows the writer to drop from the present into the past and bring in an event that occurred prior to the narrative's action. You may be most familiar with this device from seeing it in films, the moment when the camera fades out of a scene and then fades in to a past event.

You can also reinforce your thesis, implicit or explicit, by underscoring the relationship between what happens and where it happens. If the two are incongruous, for example, then the resulting irony will probably emphasize your main point. A narrative of the job interview that began badly but ended well, for example, may use the turn from bad to good to imply that "all's well that ends well."

Useful Terms

Conflict An element essential to narrative. Conflict involves pitting one force, a force that may be represented by a person or a physical object or an abstract concept, against another.

External conflict Conflict that is outside of a person in the narrative though it may involve that person, as in St. George versus the Dragon.

Internal conflict Conflict that takes place within a person, as in "Should I or should I not?"

Flashback A break in the narrative that takes the reader to a scene or event that occurred earlier.

Narration Narration tells a story, emphasizing what happened.

Point of view In essays, point of view usually refers to the writer's use of personal pronouns. These pronouns control the perspective flow from which the work is written. For example, if the writer uses *I* or *we* (first-person pronouns), the essay will have a somewhat subjective tone because the reader will tend to identify with the writer. If the writer depends primarily on *he, she, it,* or *they* (third-person pronouns), the essay will have a somewhat objective tone because the reader will be distanced from the writer. Opting for *you* (second person) can be a bit tricky in that *you* can mean you the reader, quite particular, or you a member of a larger group, fairly general. In both cases, *you* brings the reader into the text.

Setting The *where* and *when* in the narrative, its physical context.

POINTERS FOR USING NARRATION

Exploring the Topic

1. **What point do you want to make?** What is the subject of your narrative? What assertion do you want your narrative to make about the subject? Is your primary purpose to inform, to persuade, or to entertain?

2. **What happened?** What are the events involved in the narrative? When does the action start? Stop? Which events are crucial?

(*Continued*)

POINTERS FOR USING NARRATION (*Continued*)

3. **Why and how did it happen?** What caused the events? How did it cause them?

4. **Who or what was involved?** What does the reader need to know about the characters? What do the characters look like? Talk like? How do they think? How do others respond to them?

5. **What is the setting for your story?** What does the reader need to know about the setting? What features are particularly noteworthy? How can they best be described?

6. **When did the story occur?** What tense will be most effective in relating the narrative?

7. **What was the sequence of events?** What happened when? Within that chronology, what is most important: time, place, attitude?

8. **What conflicts were involved?** What levels of conflict exist? Is there any internal conflict?

9. **What is the relationship between the narrator and the action?** Is the narrator a participant or an observer? What is the attitude of the narrator toward the story? What feelings should the narrator evoke from the reader? What should be the attitude of the reader toward the narrative? What can be gained by using first person? Second person? Third person?

Drafting the Paper

1. **Know your reader.** Try to second-guess your reader's initial attitude toward your narrative so that if it is not what you want it to be, you can choose your details to elicit the desired reaction. A reader can be easily bored, so keep your details to the point and your action moving. Play on similar experiences your reader may have had or on information you can assume is widely known.

2. **Know your purpose.** If you are writing to inform, make sure you provide enough information to carry your point. If you are writing to persuade, work on how you present yourself and your thesis so that the reader will be favorably inclined to adopt your viewpoint. If you are writing to entertain, keep your tone in mind. A humorous piece, for instance, can and probably will

vary from chuckle to guffaw to belly laugh. Make sure you're getting the right kind of laugh in the right place.

3. **Establish the setting and time of the action.** Use descriptive details to make the setting vivid and concrete. Keep in mind the reaction you want to get from your reader, and choose your details accordingly. If, for instance, you are writing a narrative that depicts your first experience with fear, describe the setting in such a way that you prepare the reader for that emotion. If the time the story took place is important, bring it out early.

4. **Set out the characters.** When you introduce a character, immediately identify the person with a short phrase, such as "Anne, my sister." If a character doesn't enter the narrative until midpoint or so, make sure the reader is prepared for the entrance so that the person doesn't appear to be merely plopped in. If characterization is important to the narrative, use a variety of techniques to portray the character, but make sure whatever you use is consistent with the impression you want to create. You can depict a person directly—through appearance, dialogue, and actions—as well as indirectly—through what others say and think and how they act toward the person.

5. **Clarify the action.** Narration is set within strict time limits. Make sure the time frame of your story is set out clearly. Within that time limit, much more action occurred than you will want to use in your narrative. Pick only the high points so that every action directly supports your thesis. Feel free to tinker with the action, sacrificing a bit of reality for the sake of your point.

6. **Sharpen the plot.** Conflict is essential to narration, so be sure your lines of conflict are clearly drawn. Keeping conflict in mind, review the action you have decided to include so that the plot and action support each other.

7. **Determine the principle behind the sequence of events.** Given the action and plot you have worked out, determine what principle should guide the reader through the events. Perhaps time is the element you want to stress, perhaps place, perhaps gradual change. No matter what you choose, make sure that the sequence has dramatic tension so that it builds to the point you want to make.

(Continued)

POINTERS FOR USING NARRATION (*Continued*)

8. **Choose an appropriate point of view.** Your choice of grammatical point of view depends on what attitude you wish to take toward your narrative and your audience. If you can make your point more effectively by distancing yourself from the story, you will want to use *he, she,* or *they.* On the other hand, if you can make your point most effectively by being in the story, use first person and then decide whether you want to be *I* the narrator only or *I* the narrator who is also directly involved in the story.

9. **Make a point.** The action of the narrative should lead to a conclusion, an implicit or explicit point that serves as the thesis of the piece. If explicit, the thesis can appear in a single sentence or it can be inferred from several sentences, in either the introduction or conclusion of the essay. Ask yourself if everything in the narrative ties into the thesis.

Designer of Audio CD Packaging Enters Hell

Steve Martin

Anyone who has watched television or been to the movies in the last few years is familiar with the wacky world of Steve Martin. Best known as a comedian, he is also becoming a familiar name to the readers of the New Yorker, *where his writing often appears in the "Shouts & Murmurs" slot. Martin got his start in television as a writer, turning out material for Sonny and Cher and the Smothers Brothers, among many others. From there, he went on to stand-up comedy and made frequent and memorable appearances on* Saturday Night Live *as well as various talk shows. More recently, he starred in dramatic as well as comic films and is also the author of* Picasso at the Lapin Agile, *a play that opened off-Broadway in 1995,* Shopgirl *(2001) and* The Pleasure of My Company *(2003), both novellas, and* Pure Drivel *(1999), a collection of short pieces, some of which were published in the* New Yorker. *Firmly grounded in the absurd, his comic sense runs from slapstick to sophistication, both of which can be found in the essay that follows, one published in the April 19, 1999, issue of the* New Yorker.

What to Look For   Dialogue is often used in narrative writing because it adds a sense of realism and also provides variety. As you read Martin's essay, keep track of who is speaking and note how the dialogue matches the speaker. Also keep track of how Martin breaks up a quoted sentence so that the emphasis is right where he wants it. That's a technique that can work well any time you use dialogue.

1   The burning gates of Hell were opened and the designer of CD packaging entered to the Devil's fanfare. "We've been wanting him down here for a long time," The One of Pure Evil said to his infernal minions, "but we decided to wait, because he was doing such good work above, wrapping the CDs with cellophane and that sticky tape strip. Ask him to dinner and be sure to invite the computer-manual people too."

2   The Devil vanished, missing the warm display of affection offered the inventor. "Beelzebub himself opened a nasty cut on his finger trying to unwrap a Streisand best-of," whispered an imp. A thick snake nuzzled closer, and wrapped itself around the inventor's leg. "He used to be enamored of the remote-control people, with their tiny little buttons jammed together, and their enigmatic abbreviations," the snake said, "but now all he ever talks about is you, you, you. Come on, let's get you ready for dinner. We can talk about your assignment later."

3   As the snake led the way to the dressing halls of Hell, a yearning, searching look came over its face. "How did you do it?" the snake asked. "You know, invent the packaging? Everyone wants to know."

4   The inventor, his feet comfortably aflame, and flattered by all the recognition, relaxed into his surroundings. "The original plastic CD 'jewel box' was just too damn easy to get into," he explained. "I mean, if we're going to prevent consumer access, for God's sake, let's prevent it! I wanted a packaging where the consumer would run to the kitchen for a knife, so there was a chance to at least slice open his hand."

5   "Is that when you got the idea for shrink-wrap?" said the snake.

6   "Shrink-wrap was nice for a while. I liked that there was absolutely no place to tear into it with a fingernail, but I knew there was further to go. That's when I hit on cellophane, cellophane with the illusion of an opening strip, where really none exists."

7   That night, at the celebratory dinner held once an aeon to honor new arrivals, the inventor sat to the Devil's right. On his left sat Cerberus, the watchdog of Hades and noted designer of the pineapple. The Devil chatted with the inventor all night long, then requested that he open another bottle of wine, this time with a two-pronged, side-slip corkscrew. The inventor perspired, and an hour later the bottle was uncorked.

8   At first, no one noticed the muffled disturbance from above, which soon grew into a sustained clamor. Eventually, the entire gathering looked toward the ceiling, and finally the Devil himself noticed that their attention had shifted. He raised his head.

9   Hovering in the ether were three angels, each holding an object. The inventor knew clearly what the objects were: the milk carton, the Ziploc bag, and the banana, all three perfectly designed packages. He remembered how he used to admire them before he fell into evil. The three angels glided toward the dais. One held the Ziploc bag over the aspirin-bottle people, and bathed them in an otherworldly light. A yellow glow from the banana washed over the hellhound

Cerberus, designer of the pineapple, and the milk carton poured its white luminosity in the direction of the CD packager. The Devil stood up abruptly, roared something in Latin while succubae flew out of his mouth, and then angrily excused himself.

10 After the fiasco, the inventor went back to his room and fiddled with the five remotes it took to operate his VCR. Frustrated, he closed his eyes and contemplated the eternity to come in the bleakness of Hell, and how he would probably never again see a snowflake or a Fudgsicle. But then he thought of the nice meal he'd just had, and his new friends, and decided that snowflakes and Fudgsicles weren't that great anyway. He thought how the upcoming eternity might not be so bad after all. There was a knock at the door, and the snake entered.

11 "The Devil asked me to give you your assignment," the snake said. "Sometimes he gets powerful headaches. He wants you to be there to open the aspirin bottle."

12 "I think I could do that," the inventor replied.

13 "Just so you know, he likes a fresh aspirin every time, so you'll have to remove the tamper-resistant collar, the childproof cap, *and* the aluminum sealer," said the snake.

14 The inventor breathed easily. "No problem."

15 "Good," the snake said, and turned to go.

16 Just then a shudder rippled through the inventor's body. "Say"— his voice quavered with nervousness—"who will remove the cotton wad from the inside of the bottle?"

17 The snake turned slowly, its face contorted into the mask of Beelzebub. Then its voice deepened and transformed itself, as though it were coming from the bowels of Hell:

18 "Why, *you* will," he said. "HA HA HA HA HA!"

ORGANIZATION AND IDEAS

1. What paragraph or paragraphs introduce the essay? What reasons do you have for your choice?
2. Trace the essay's organization. What paragraphs mention articles that can be grouped with CD packaging? What articles are contrasted with it?
3. What paragraph or paragraphs make up the essay's conclusion? How effective do you find the conclusion?
4. Reread the essay keeping track of the various conflicts in it. How universal are they?
5. Unlike many essays, Martin's has an implied thesis. Think about the various conflicts in the essay and state his implied thesis in your own words.

TECHNIQUE AND STYLE

1. Jot down the various items Martin mentions. Why might he have presented them in the sequence he does?

2. The main person in the essay is never named but instead referred to as "the inventor." What does the essay gain by not naming him?

3. "Hot as Hell" is a common expression, so common that it has lost any freshness it might have had. How does Martin breathe life into what has become a cliché?

4. For a narrative as short as this one is, it has a surprisingly large cast of characters. How does Martin make them easy to keep track of?

5. Often, humor arises from the linking of unlikely objects. Where do you find Martin using this technique? How else does he create a comic effect?

SUGGESTIONS FOR WRITING

Journal

1. Write an entry in which you describe your own battle with a product or machine.

2. Think of a time when you expected one thing but got another. Perhaps you were dreading a particular event and then found it was fun, or perhaps you thought you had done badly on a test only to find you did well. The difference between expectation and reality can become the central conflict for a narrative in your journal.

Essay

1. Write your own narrative of Hell, either serious or comic, replacing "the inventor" with a choice of your own. The list below gives you some categories to think about:

   former friend
   political figure
   music group
   historical figure
   celebrity

   You can use Martin's essay as a fairly close model if you like, incorporating dialogue and using much the same devilish cast.

2. If you responded to the first suggestion for the journal entry, you have a rough draft of an essay. Given the mechanical and technological world we live in, it's likely that you have been frustrated by one of its products. Turn that frustration into an essay, either a fictional narrative similar to Martin's or a straightforward one that relates and analyzes the situation.

Learning, then College

Meg Gifford

When Meg Gifford was considering taking a year off before college, her peers and high school guidance counselor opposed the idea, but she had her parents' support. Her mother even suggested she write the essay that follows and send it in to her local newspaper, the Baltimore Sun. *Not only did the* Sun *publish it, but it was reprinted in the New Orleans* Times-Picayune *on April 10, 2002. After taking her year off, Gifford enrolled at the University of Maryland, majoring in Family Studies and spending one semester at the University of Edinburgh in Scotland. By the time you read this note, she will probably be enrolled in graduate school, working on a master's degree in public health. She reports, "I received several e-mails thanking me for speaking up on the issue—one from as far away as Mexico."*

What to Look For   A major flaw in some narratives that use first person is the failure to generalize about an individual experience. As you read Meg Gifford's essay, notice how often she uses *I* and how she broadens her experience so that it connects with the experience of others.

1   As my younger friends receive their college acceptance letters this time of year, I think about my senior year at Western High School in Baltimore City and the decision I made that changed my life forever: taking time off before college.

2   In Britain, it's called a gap year—the sabbatical that most students take between high school and college.

3   This is a time for young people to discover themselves before their devotion to another four years of intensive schoolwork. Not a bad idea, considering that a good number of college freshmen flunk out because of the overwhelming temptations of extracurricular college life.

4   Most gap year students take a job or an internship to get a better grasp on the real world and pick up some life skills along the

way. Some students understand that they are just not ready for college.

5   I chose to take a gap year for this very reason. I knew I wasn't ready to settle down and work. And because college is so expensive, I wanted to be sure that I would take that investment seriously.

6   I acknowledge that postponing college is not easy. Few people supported my decision, telling me that once I stopped my education I'd never get back on track. My classmates were especially doubtful, thinking that my time off was just an excuse for being lazy. It was infuriating to think that people could and would not associate my travels or internship as an extension of my education.

7   I learned more in my gap year than I have in two years of college. I discovered life skills that continue to help me through the hardest of times. I found independence and a new self-esteem. I learned the value of a dollar, and then I learned the value of not having a dollar. I learned that eggs are cheap and easy to cook.

8   Being 18 is wonderful. There's a whole world waiting to be discovered with a lifetime to do it. The average person doesn't retire until he is well into his 60s, and he probably has been working since he graduated from college. As I see my friends now settling down with careers and families, many of them express regrets at not having seen the world before taking on such unyielding responsibilities.

9   My advice to high school seniors is this: Now is your chance to explore. Do it before you have devoted your life to something else.

10   By the age of 20, I delivered three babies as part of my midwifery internship in Hyden, Ky., and learned how to cook a fine Kentucky rattlesnake. After teaching a 90-year-old-man the alphabet, he showed me how to make furniture.

11   I also have attended two years of college so far, making the dean's list every semester. What story will you be able to tell?

ORGANIZATION AND IDEAS

1. In what ways does paragraph 1 prepare you for what follows in the rest of the essay?
2. Work out a timeline for the essay, noting when each paragraph takes place. What happens when?

3. How effective is Gifford's use of time?
4. Consider the pros and cons Gifford outlines and summarize them in one sentence. What is her thesis?
5. To what extent does Gifford persuade you that a gap year is a good idea?

TECHNIQUE AND STYLE

1. Reread the essay, paying particular attention to Gifford's audience. Who is it? What reasons do you have for your choice?
2. Consider the tone of the essay, the author's attitude toward her audience and subject. Is she earnest? Supercilious? Know-it-all? Caring? What?
3. To what extent is Gifford someone you would like to know? Why?
4. In paragraph 7, Gifford uses a lot of repetition. How effective is it?
5. Paragraph 10 summarizes Gifford's experience by presenting the highlights of her year off. How effective are her examples?

SUGGESTIONS FOR WRITING

Journal

1. Did you consider taking a year off before entering college? Use your journal to explore why or why not.
2. Paragraph 7 summarizes what Gifford learned during her gap year. To what extent do you believe her and why?

Essay

1. One way to view Gifford's essay is to think of it as describing the kind of learning that is vital yet can take place out of the classroom. Consider what Gifford learned that she states in paragraph 7. Where have you gained knowledge that you value? Narrow down your choice to one example and write an essay in which you explore what you learned, where, and why. Suggestions:
   working part-time
   working full-time
   participating in a sport
   participating in an extracurricular activity
   being responsible for someone
2. Gifford cites the "overwhelming temptations of extracurricular college life" as a reason some students flunk out. Flunking out aside, consider the various "temptations" you face in college and write an essay in which you analyze the most hazardous one and how you dealt with it.

The Night of Oranges

Flavius Stan

Flavius Stan was 17 years old when this piece was published on Christmas Eve day, 1995, in the New York Times. *At the time, he was an exchange student at the Fieldston School in the Bronx, one of New York City's five boroughs. The time and place he writes about, however, is Christmas Eve in the city of Timisoara in the Romania of 1989, when the country was emerging from Communist rule. It had been an incredible month. On December 16, government forces opened fire on antigovernment demonstrators in Timisoara, killing hundreds. The president, Nicolae Ceausescu, immediately declared a state of emergency, but that did not stop antigovernment protests in other cities. Finally, on December 22, army units also rebelled, the president was overthrown, and civil war raged. The new government quickly won out, and Ceausescu was tried and found guilty of genocide. He was executed on December 25.*

What to Look For   Few of us reading this essay have had firsthand experience of a revolution, nor have many of us lived under Communism or a dictatorship, much less a government whose leader was not only overthrown but also executed. But all of us know oranges. What is familiar to us was strange to Stan, and what is strange to us was his everyday world. The resulting gap between Stan's society and ours is huge, yet in this essay he is able to bring his readers into the cold, postrevolution world of a city in Romania and make us see our familiar orange in a new way. Read the essay once for pleasure and then read it again, looking for the ways in which he makes the unfamiliar familiar and vice versa.

1   It is Christmas Eve in 1989 in Timisoara and the ice is still dirty from the boots of the Romanian revolution. The dictator Nicolae Ceausescu had been deposed a few days before, and on Christmas Day he would be executed by firing squad. I am in the center of the city with my friends, empty now of the crowds that prayed outside the cathedral during the worst of the fighting. My friends and I still hear shots here and there. Our cold hands are gray like the sky above us, and we want to see a movie.

2   There is a rumor that there will be oranges for sale tonight. Hundreds of people are already waiting in line. We were used to such lines under the former Communist Government—lines for bread, lines for meat, lines for everything. Families would wait much of the day for rationed items. As children, we would take turns for an hour or more, holding our family's place in line.

3   But this line is different. There are children in Romania who don't know what an orange looks like. It is a special treat. Having the chance to eat a single orange will keep a child happy for a week. It will also make him a hero in the eyes of his friends. For the first time, someone is selling oranges by the kilo.

4   Suddenly I want to do something important: I want to give my brother a big surprise. He is only 8 years old, and I want him to celebrate Christmas with lots of oranges at the table. I also want my parents to be proud of me.

5   So I call home and tell my parents that I'm going to be late. I forget about going to the movie, leave my friends and join the line.

6   People aren't silent, upset, frustrated, as they were before the revolution; they are talking to one another about life, politics and the new situation in the country.

7   The oranges are sold out of the back doorway of a food shop. The clerk has gone from anonymity to unexpected importance. As he handles the oranges, he acts like a movie star in front of his fans.

8   He moves his arms in an exaggerated manner as he tells the other workers where to go and what to do. All I can do is stare at the stack of cardboard boxes, piled higher than me. I have never seen so many oranges in my life.

9   Finally, it is my turn. It is 8 o'clock, and I have been waiting for six hours. It doesn't seem like a long time because my mind has been flying from the oranges in front of me to my brother and then back to the oranges. I hand over the money I was going to spend on the movie and watch each orange being thrown into my bag. I try to count them, but I lose their number.

10   I am drunk with the idea of oranges. I put the bag inside my coat as if I want to absorb their warmth. They aren't heavy at all, and I feel that it is going to be the best Christmas of my life. I begin thinking of how I am going to present my gift.

11   I get home and my father opens the door. He is amazed when he sees the oranges, and we decide to hide them until dinner. At dessert that night, I give my brother the present. Everyone is silent. They can't believe it.

12   My brother doesn't touch them. He is afraid even to look at them. Maybe they aren't real. Maybe they are an illusion, like everything else these days. We have to tell him he can eat them before he has the courage to touch one of the oranges.

13   I stare at my brother eating the oranges. They are my oranges. My parents are proud of me.

ORGANIZATION AND IDEAS

1. Paragraphs 1–3 introduce the essay. Explain how they do or do not fit the journalistic questions establishing *who, what, where, why, when, how.*

2. The central part of the essay takes the reader from the time Stan decides to buy the oranges to his presenting them to his brother. What is the effect of presenting the narrative chronologically?

3. The last paragraph functions as the essay's one-paragraph conclusion, a conclusion presented in three short sentences. Explain whether you find the ending effective.

4. On the surface, Stan's essay has a simple thesis—that finding the rare and perfect gift for his brother fills him with pride, pride also reflected by his family. If you dig a bit, however, you may also discover other less obvious theses. What, for instance, might Stan be implying about Christmas? About Romania's future?

5. How would you characterize the conflict or conflicts in this essay?

TECHNIQUE AND STYLE

1. Although the essay was written in 1995, it is set at an earlier time, 1989. Many writers would, therefore, opt for the past tense, but Stan relates his narrative in the present. What does he gain by this choice?

2. Trace the number of contrasts Stan has in his essay. What do you discover? How do they relate to the thesis?

3. Paragraphs 7 and 8 describe the clerk in charge of selling the oranges in some detail. What does this description add to the essay?

4. Why is it important that the money Stan spends on the oranges is the money he was going to spend on the movies?

5. Reread the first paragraph, one that sets not only the scene but also the atmosphere, the emotional impression arising from the scene. In your own words, describe that atmosphere.

SUGGESTIONS FOR WRITING

Journal

1. Choose a common object and describe it as though you were seeing it for the first time.

2. In a sense, Stan's essay is written from the perspective of an 11-year-old, the age he was at the time of the narrative. Leaf through your journal to find a short narrative and then try rewriting it from the perspective of a much younger person.

Essay

1. Sift through your memory to find several times when you felt proud. Choose one to turn into a narrative essay. Perhaps, like Stan, you may want to retell the event in the present tense, placing yourself in the position of reliving it. If you do, check your draft to see if you have an implied thesis that is larger than the apparent one, for you want your essay to have some depth to it. For ideas of what might have made you feel proud, consider something you

    did

    didn't do

    saw

    owned

    said

2. For a more generalized essay, consider the times you felt pride and list them. What were the occasions? What do they have in common? In what ways are those examples similar? Different? Write an essay in which you define *pride,* using your experiences as examples and keeping first person to a minimum so that you emphasize the subject, not yourself.

Time to Look and Listen

Magdoline Asfahani

Newsweek *runs a regular column called "My Turn," one that you can check out by going to www.newsweek.com. There on the left you'll see "My Turn Online" listed, and in the box below you'll find "Newsweek Columnists." If you were to click that, you'd turn up the "My Turn" columns that have been published in previous editions. Magdoline Asfahani's piece was published on December 2, 1996, when Asfahani was a student at the University of Texas at El Paso. Then, she was trying to balance her identity in ways that honored her parents' Syrian and Lebanese cultures while embracing her*

American-born values. It wasn't easy. Reflecting on what she wrote, Asfahani now finds "the piece is probably more meaningful now than it was when I wrote it." See if you agree.

What to Look For   If you have ever written about a painful experience, you know that it's hard to keep your emotions under control. Anger, resentment, pain can break through and overwhelm what you are trying to portray in a cool, rational manner. As you read Asafahani's essay, look for the ways she keeps her emotions from engulfing her ideas.

1   I love my country as many who have been here for generations cannot. Perhaps that's because I'm the child of immigrants, raised with a conscious respect for America that many people take for granted. My parents chose this country because it offered them a new life, freedom and possibilities. But I learned at a young age that the country we loved so much did not feel the same way about us.

2   Discrimination is not unique to America. It occurs in any country that allows immigration. Anyone who is unlike the majority is looked at a little suspiciously, dealt with a little differently. I knew that I was an Arab and a Muslim. This meant nothing to me. At school I stood up to say the Pledge of Allegiance every day. These things did not seem incompatible at all. Then everything changed for me, suddenly and permanently, in 1985. I was only in seventh grade, but that was the beginning of my political education.

3   That year a TWA plane originating in Athens was diverted to Beirut. Two years earlier the U.S. Marine barracks in Beirut had been bombed. That seemed to start a chain of events that would forever link Arabs with terrorism. After the hijacking, I faced classmates who taunted me with cruel names, attacking my heritage and my religion. I became an outcast and had to apologize for myself constantly.

4   After a while, I tried to forget my heritage. No matter what race, religion or ethnicity, a child who is attacked often retreats. I was the only Arab I knew of in my class, so I had no one in my peer group as an ally. No matter what my parents tried to tell me about my proud cultural history, I would ignore it. My classmates told me I came from an uncivilized, brutal place, that Arabs were by nature anti-American, and I believed them. They did not know the hours

my parents spent studying, working, trying to preserve part of their old lives while embracing, willingly, the new.

5   I tried to forget the Arabic I knew, because if I didn't I'd be forever linked to murderers. I stopped inviting friends over for dinner, because I thought the food we ate was "weird." I lied about where my parents had come from. Their accents (although they spoke English perfectly) humiliated me. Though Islam is a major monotheistic religion with many similarities to Judaism and Christianity, there were no holidays near Chanukah or Christmas, nothing to tie me to the "Judeo-Christian" tradition. I felt more excluded. I slowly began to turn into someone without a past.

6   Civil war was raging in Lebanon, and all that Americans saw of that country was destruction and violence. Every other movie seemed to feature Arab terrorists. The most common questions I was asked were if I had ever ridden a camel or if my family lived in tents. I felt burdened with responsibility. Why should an adolescent be asked questions like "Is it true you hate Jews and you want Israel destroyed?" I didn't hate anybody. My parents had never said anything even alluding to such sentiments. I was confused and hurt.

7   As I grew older and began to form my own opinions, my embarrassment lessened and my anger grew. The turning point came in high school. My grandmother had become very ill, and it was necessary for me to leave school a few days before Christmas vacation. My chemistry teacher was very sympathetic until I said I was going to the Middle East. "Don't come back in a body bag," he said cheerfully. The class laughed. Suddenly, those years of watching movies that mocked me and listening to others who knew nothing about Arabs and Muslims except what they saw on television seemed like a bad dream. I knew then that I would never be silent again.

8   I've tried to reclaim those lost years. I realize now that I come from a culture that has a rich history. The Arab world is a medley of people of different religions; not every Arab is a Muslim, and vice versa. The Arabs brought tremendous advances in the sciences and mathematics, as well as creating a literary tradition that has never been surpassed. The language itself is flexible and beautiful, with nuances and shades of meaning unparalleled in any language. Though many find it hard to believe, Islam has made progress in women's rights. There is a specific provision in the Koran that permits women to own property and ensures that their inheritance is protected—although recent events have shown that interpretation of these laws can vary.

9   My youngest brother, who is 12, is now at the crossroads I faced. When initial reports of the Oklahoma City bombing pointed to "Arab-looking individuals" as the culprits, he came home from school crying. "Mom, why do Muslims kill people? Why are the Arabs so bad?" She was angry and brokenhearted, but tried to handle the situation in the best way possible through education. She went to his class, armed with Arabic music, pictures, traditional dress and cookies. She brought a chapter of the social-studies book to life and the children asked intelligent, thoughtful questions, even after the class was over. Some even asked if she was coming back. When my brother came home, he was excited and proud instead of ashamed.

10   I only recently told my mother about my past experience. Maybe if I had told her then, I would have been better equipped to deal with the thoughtless teasing. But, fortunately, the world is changing. Although discrimination and stereotyping still exist, many people are trying to lessen and end it. Teachers, schools and the media are showing greater sensitivity to cultural issues. However, there is still much that needs to be done, not for the sake of any particular ethnic or cultural groups but for the sake of our country.

11   The America that I love is one that values freedom and the differences of its people. Education is the key to understanding. As Americans we need to take a little time to look and listen carefully to what is around us and not rush to judgment without knowing the facts. And we must never be ashamed of our pasts. It is our collective differences that unite and make us unique as a nation. It's what determines our present and our future.

ORGANIZATION AND IDEAS

1. In paragraphs 3–6, Asfahani recreates her experiences as a seventh-grader. How well does she do it?
2. It's possible to find a number of subjects in Asfahani's essay: discrimination, education, American values, stereotyping. Which is the most important? What evidence can you find to support your opinion?
3. What statement is Asfahani making about that subject?
4. How would you characterize the essay's aim: Is Asfahani trying to persuade the reader? Explain her position? Let off steam? If some combination, which dominates?
5. The essay was published in 1996 just after Thanksgiving. To what extent, if any, is it dated?

TECHNIQUE AND STYLE

1. Asfahani describes her "political education" (paragraphs 2–9). Which example is the most telling and why?
2. In paragraph 8, Asfahani asserts that she comes "from a culture that has a rich history." How well does she back up that claim?
3. Asfahani never told her parents what she was going through when she was in the seventh grade, keeping it to herself. How realistic is that reaction?
4. According to Asfahani, "Education is the key to understanding" (paragraph 11). What evidence does she present to back up that idea?
5. What examples can you find of Asfahani appealing to the reader's emotions? To reason? Which predominates?

SUGGESTIONS FOR WRITING

Journal

1. Use your journal to record the time you first recognized or experienced discrimination.
2. Think of how culture is expressed through language, food, celebrations, dress, gestures, relationships, and the like. Write a brief entry in which you tell of a time when you first experienced a culture different from your own.

Essay

1. "Know thyself" was a basic belief of the ancient Greeks, and it is as difficult to do today as it was then. You can define yourself, for example, in any number of ways by associating yourself with a group or belief or heritage, to name just a few. Think about the various ways in which you define yourself and write an essay in which you explain who you are. To generate some ideas, try thinking about who you are in relation to

    family
    ethnic heritage
    friends
    religion
    political beliefs

    Choose one of these ideas, or any other, and consider the conflicts you encountered in becoming who you are. The danger here is taking on too much so that you have the first chapter of your autobiography instead of an essay, so be sure you narrow down your topic.
2. Asfahani says that in high school, she reached a "turning point" and "would never be silent again" (paragraph 7). Think of such turning points in your own life and select one to explore in an essay. Like Asfahani, you should try to distance yourself from the time so that you can balance the emotional and the rational.

Footprints on the Flag

Anchee Min

Anchee Min's narrative will tell you a great deal about her earlier life under the rule of Mao Zedong, China's Chairman Mao. You will also discover that she is a painter, but she is also a photographer and musician. It is as a writer, however, that she is best known, and her books, whether fiction or nonfiction, explore life in China, her own and that of historical figures—an empress and the wife of Mao. Red Azalea *(1994) is a memoir in which she describes her own experiences under the Maoist regime. Min's first novel,* Katherine, *was published in 1995 and was followed by* Wild Ginger *(2002) and* Empress Orchid *(2004). Her most successful novel is* Becoming Madame Mao *(2000), based not only on personal experience but also on more than five years' worth of research. Madame Mao was known in China as "White-bone-demon," a name that gives you a good idea about her character. You'll find a lot about Min's character in her essay below. It was published in the October 15, 2001, issue of the* New Yorker, *where it was grouped with other essays under the title "American Encounter."*

What to Look For   The time frame for Min's essay extends from September 1984 to 2000. As you read her narrative, be thinking of how she covers that amount of time and how she compresses it.

1   I arrived in America on September 1, 1984, at the age of twenty-seven. Using the few English words I had memorized, I asked the immigration officer in Seattle for an opportunity to stay. "If I don't learn English in three months, I'll deport myself," I promised. After he stamped my passport, I flew to Chicago, where I had been accepted by the School of the Art Institute of Chicago, thanks to a friend who had helped me fill out the application. When the institute found out that I didn't speak English, I was sent to a language program at the University of Illinois. Over the next few months, I learned to speak English by watching "Sesame Street" and Oprah Winfrey, and I supported myself by working as a fabric painter—painting roses on women's underwear—and as a waitress in a Chinese restaurant.

2   My roommate, Alice, was a black pre-med student from Mississippi. She didn't mind that I was quiet, because she loved to talk. One day, when I was reading an article about President Reagan in the local paper, she exclaimed, "Ronald Reagan is a dog! Do you understand?" I sprang up from my chair and looked over my shoulder. In China, you would be imprisoned for saying something like that about Mao.

3   I had grown up during Mao's Cultural Revolution and had been in the Red Guard since I was nine years old, when I had joined to avoid being beaten. I had been taught to write Mao's name before I learned to write my own, and had painted hundreds of portraits of him for parades. In the nineteen-seventies, I spent three years in a labor camp, following Mao's teaching, until I was discovered by the Shanghai Film Studio. Because of my "proletarian look"—weather-beaten face and a solid body—I was chosen to play leading roles in Madame Mao's propaganda films. After her downfall, I was denounced as "political debris" and was given a job at the film studio, working fourteen-hour days as a set hand. By the end of eight years, I had seriously considered committing suicide.

4   Eight months after coming to America, I started my studies at the Art Institute. I continued working at the restaurant, and got a job at the institute's student gallery. One of the exhibits was an American flag laid flat on the floor. About three feet above it, mounted on the wall, was a notebook-size diary. I noticed that viewers had to step on the flag in order to read the diary. Footprints had started growing on the flag like blotches of mold.

5   I felt that I had neglected my duty. I quickly took off my jacket and used it to wipe the flag clean. When the next viewer came, I politely said, "Please be careful and do not step on the flag."

6   Two weeks later, the artist arrived to check on his work. When I told him that I had taken great pains to erase the footprints, he informed me, furiously, that he had intended to have people step on the flag. We argued. I said that I was grateful to America—if this country hadn't taken me in, I would not have survived.

7   The artist replied that I had no idea of the terrible things the American flag symbolized. I needed to get my English straight, he said, so I could begin to understand what this country had done to its people and to the world.

8   I couldn't find the words in English that were filling my head in Chinese. I wanted to tell him that twenty years earlier I had done

exactly what he was doing now. I had been taught to hate Americans, and I had burned the American flag. We had watched films in which Americans poked out the eyes of pregnant Vietnamese women. When I was eleven, I had denounced my beloved teacher as an American spy. As a teen-ager, I had taken a wooden stick and attacked a body made of straw with a United States Army helmet on its head. We were preparing for a war should the Americans dare to set foot on the soil of China.

9   When the professor in my twentieth-century-American-art class showed us Andy Warhol's Mao series, I thought, What's wrong with this country? I couldn't understand why a professor would project slides of Mao in an American classroom, when more than a billion Chinese were finally taking Mao buttons off their jackets, Mao portraits off their walls, and Mao quotations out of their speeches.

10   Most nights after class, I went to my waitressing job, where the owner of the restaurant used to say, "The house is not on fire!" if I walked fast, and "I didn't hire you to be lazy!" when I slowed down. One evening, I said, "I quit."

11   The awareness of myself as more than a screw in the Communist machine came slowly. This consciousness of the individual, I realized, was the essence of American art. Warhol's famous Mao series now seemed to say, "Who made Mao?"

12   A year ago, I was described in a *Times Magazine* article as an "American writer." When I showed the story to my father, he smiled splendidly. To him, it meant that his daughter was finally free of fear. He said, "Anchee, now you are ready to write about China".

ORGANIZATION AND IDEAS

1. The first paragraph sets out the scene but also depicts Min's words and actions. What do they tell you about her?
2. The most dramatic conflict is between Min and the artist. What other conflicts does the narrative present or imply?
3. Of those conflicts, which is the most important and why?
4. In paragraph 11, Min defines what she has learned about American art. What else did she learn from her experience? How can you turn what she learned into the essay's thesis?
5. In paragraph 7, Min describes the artist's intention behind his work and relates his view of America. Explain whether you find that part of her narrative realistic, exaggerated, or some place in between?

TECHNIQUE AND STYLE

1. Reread paragraph 3, Min's account of her life in China. How would you characterize her description? On a scale from objective to subjective, where would you put it and why?
2. Min's life under the Maoist regime was cruel, hard, unjust, unfree. To what extent do you think she feels sorry for herself?
3. Reexamine the details Min chooses to use in paragraph 8. Explain whether you find them effective. What emotions do they arouse?
4. In paragraph 10, Min recounts her boss's comments at work and her response. How does that paragraph relate to the rest of the essay?
5. Reread the essay looking for comparisons. What do you find? What do they contribute to the essay's organization? To its thesis?

SUGGESTIONS FOR WRITING

Journal

1. Use your journal to record the emotions you felt when you read Min's narrative. What were they? What in the essay triggered them?
2. Look up *patriotism* in an unabridged dictionary. Use your journal to explore how the term might apply to Min.

Essay

1. The artist Min encountered saw the American flag as a symbol of all he thought wrong about the country, and indeed the flag is a potent symbol. Think about other objects that have symbolic value within our culture and write a narrative in which you relate an experience you had with one. To find a suitable subject, consider anything that can be thought of as absolutely American:
   the hamburger
   hot dog
   baseball caps
   blue jeans
   fast food
2. The Art Institute of Chicago owns the Mao series and operates a web site called "Art Access." Use it to learn more about the series. You can find it at http://www.artic.edu/artaccess/AA_Modern/pages/MOD_9 .shtml. Given that information and anything else you turn up in your research, write an essay that analyzes Min's interpretation of Warhol's portrait and how "it seemed to say, 'Who made Mao?'" What does she mean?

ADDITIONAL WRITING ASSIGNMENTS

Using Description

1. Write a narrative about an event that changed your opinion about a product, music group, person, place, or political candidate.
2. Write a narrative explaining a conflict: parent vs. child, brother vs. sister, boss vs. worker, human vs. animal, or human vs. nature.
3. Write a narrative about a crucial decision that you made: going to college, choosing a major, getting married (or divorced), joining an organization or club, getting a job, or leaving home.
4. Write a narrative about confronting prejudice. Perhaps it was based on gender, age, race, ethnic background, or looks.

Evaluating the Essays

1. The essays by Flavius Stan and Anchee Min use material objects as symbols to represent something greater than the objects themselves and thus provide greater meaning as well as dramatic effect. For Stan, it's the oranges; for Min it's the flag and the portraits of Mao. Which of the two writers uses symbol more effectively? Quote from both essays to support your opinion.
2. Reread Meg Gifford's "Learning, then College" and Magdoline Asfahani's "Time to Look and Listen," paying particular attention to what each of the writers values. Which of the two comes closer to what you value? Write an essay in which you explain your answer and use evidence from the essays to support your thesis.
3. Dialogue and characterization add to the essays by Steve Martin and Anchee Min, though the essays differ greatly in tone and purpose. Martin tells a fictional story to satirize a technological "advance"; Min recounts an experience to explain her first understanding of individuality and being "free from fear." Martin is humorous; Min is serious. Focus on either dialogue or characterization to explore how it operates in the narratives and argue for its more effective use.
4. Flavius Stan and Magdoline Asfahani grew up in cultures that differ from mainstream America, and their essays explore some of those differences and their effects. Both writers deal with conflict, external and internal. Which of the two writers do you identify with and why? Quote both to make your point.

On Using
Definition

3

"When I use a word," said Humpty Dumpty, "it means just what I choose it to mean—neither more nor less." To that Alice replied, "The question is whether you can make words mean so many different things." Humpty Dumpty then pronounced, "The question is which is to be the master—that's all." Writers are the masters of their words, although not to the extent that Humpty Dumpty would like, and often a discussion or argument boils down to the meaning of a crucial word. *Liberty, justice, civil rights, freedom,* and other similar concepts, for example, are all abstractions until they are defined.

If you had to write a paper on what *freedom* means to you, you might be tempted first off to look up the word in a dictionary, but you will discover more to say if you put aside the dictionary and first think about some basic questions, such as "Whose freedom?" If it's your freedom you are writing about, who or what sets limits on your freedom? The law? The church? Parents? Family responsibilities? After you mull over questions such as these, you are in a better position to make use of a dictionary definition. The dictionary is the most obvious place to find what the word means, but what you find there is only explicit meaning, the word's **denotation.** Look up *freedom* in a collegiate dictionary, and you'll see the different ways in which the word can be used, and also its etymology, but that won't convey the rich layers of meaning that the word has accumulated through the years.

What the dictionary does not reveal is the word's associative or emotional meanings, its **connotation.** One way to discover connotation is to ask yourself questions about the word, questions similar to those above that get at how the concept of freedom touches your life. The more specific your examples, the more concrete your definition can be, and the less the danger of slipping into clichés. Unless the word you are defining is quite unusual, most readers will be familiar with its dictionary definition; your own definition and your speculations on the word's connotation are of much greater interest.

A paper that defines a familiar word can hold just as much interest as one that examines an unfamiliar word or a word that is particularly powerful. "What does boredom mean?" "Why is synergism a useful concept?" "What does it mean to be called disabled?" Questions such as these can be explored through almost any mode of thinking and writing. You can use those that you have already studied both to probe your subject as you think about it and to develop your ideas as you write.

> *Description* What details best describe it? What senses can you appeal to?
> *Narration* What story might best illustrate it? What kind of conflict might the word involve?

And even though you may not have read essays that use the other modes discussed in this book, they are already familiar to you as ways of thinking and can, therefore, also be useful to you as you think and write about your central term.

> *Example* What sorts of examples illustrate it? What different times and sources can you use to find examples?
> *Comparison and contrast* What is it similar to? What is it different from?
> *Analogy* What metaphor would make it vivid? What might the reader be familiar with that you can draw an analogy to?
> *Division and classification* How can it be divided? What types or categories can it be broken into?
> *Process* What steps or stages are involved in it? Which are crucial?
> *Cause and effect* What are the conditions that cause it? What effect does it have?

When questions such as these are tailored to the particular word or concept under scrutiny, they will help you develop your ideas.

Audience and Purpose

Unless your subject is unusual, you can assume that your audience has a general understanding of the word or phrase to be defined. The nature of that general understanding, however, differs. For instance, the word *spinster* most often raises an image of "little old lady," a picture possibly fleshed out with a cat or two and fussy furnishings. Short of those associations, a spinster is an unmarried woman of a certain age, but that age varies from one decade to another. Forty years ago, a single woman who was 26 might well have been considered a spinster. These days, the term—when used at all—would be applied to someone considerably older. Even so, the negative image remains, and those who use the word probably assume that the spinster leads a lonely, narrow life. Such an image, however, is a far cry from the likes of Diane Keaton, who has never married but is known for close relationships with the likes of Woody Allen and Warren Beatty. Still single, she has said, "I don't think that because I'm not married it's made my life any less. That old maid myth is garbage." Were you to write an essay arguing against the stereotype and focusing on the Diane Keatons of our time, you might introduce your subject by reminding your readers of the word's usual connotations.

Sometimes you not only want to change the reader's understanding but also want to make the reader aware of how the meaning of a word has changed, a change that has an effect on our society. In that case you may choose to argue for a redefinition of the word or go a step further and attack the effects of the term's changed meaning. Words such as *amateur*, *dilettante*, and *gay* have all undergone major shifts in meaning within a relatively short period of time, at least short in the linguistic sense. *Amateur* used to refer to someone engaged in an activity for pleasure, not pay, but it now has the common meaning of inexperienced, unskilled. *Dilettante* also had a positive connotation, someone who was a lover of the arts; now it is more likely associated with someone who dabbles at them. As for *gay*, today it is associated with the word *homosexual*, which puts a very different spin on the nineteenth century and its Gay Nineties.

Definition can also be used to explore what people know and don't know about a place. If you were to write an essay that explains what your neighborhood means to you, you would essentially be presenting a personal definition of it. The same would be true if you were to write about any favorite spot, whether it be a tree house from your childhood or a park bench. To some, a park bench may be an eyesore or a necessity or a plain park bench, whereas to you it may hold particular meaning as the place where you find peace and quiet.

Perhaps you merely want your readers to reexamine a term and consider its importance. *Education* is a word familiar to all, and you and your classmates have had years of experience with it, but it may well mean different things to different people. Were you to write about the word within the context of your college education, you might begin by chasing down its etymology, which would bring you to the Latin *educatus*, meaning brought up, taught. From there you might speculate on how the meaning of education has shifted, slipping from the general—conveying general knowledge and developing reason and judgment—to the particular—emphasizing skills and preparation for a profession. At that point, you would have the makings of a good argument against or in favor of the change.

Using Other Modes

Definition, perhaps more than any other rhetorical pattern, depends on other modes to serve its purpose. Were you to write an essay on *honesty*, for example, you might begin your discussion with a narrative, a brief story about a friend who bought a magazine at a newsstand and received too much change for a 20-dollar bill. The narrative can then lead to comparison and contrast, making a distinction between honest and dishonest. And if the friend kept the money but feels guilty about it, then you would be dealing with cause and effect. Make your reader feel that guilt, and you'll be using description.

While an essay that depends primarily on definition can be developed as a personal narrative, one that is organized as straightforward exposition will also involve other patterns of organization. If you were writing a short research paper on the common cold, comparison would help you distinguish it from the flu and process would enable you to trace its progress from first sore throat to last sniffle. In between you might discuss possible ways to relieve symptoms, which would bring in classification. Although you may use many different modes, your primary one would still be definition.

To flesh out the definition of a term, you can draw on a number of sources. You might make a quick connection with your reader's experience, for instance, by drawing examples from the world of athletics. An essay defining *grace* can cite Michael Jordan's drive to a basket, just as one on *bizarre* might well put Dennis Rodman at the head of the list for his habit of dyeing his hair different colors and cross-dressing. Citing examples of well-known figures from film, television, the arts, and politics is also a quick way to remind your readers of what they know and to make use of that to explain the unfamiliar. Contemporary figures are probably the first to come to mind, but historical ones will serve just as well with the additional advantage of broadening the base of your information and adding to your credibility, your **persona,** the image of self that you create and then present through the prose in your essay. A brief mention of the grace of a Donatello bronze or the bizarre world of Hieronymus Bosch extends the range of your definition while also revealing the depth of your knowledge, portraying you as someone who knows the fine arts. Combining those references with a formal vocabulary, varied sentence structure, and wit, you will create a sophisticated, informed persona.

Organization and Ideas

Although a definition can play a key role in an essay, it is not the essay's thesis. The thesis rises from the author's assertion about the definition. Sometimes your title can serve as your thesis or at least hint at it, as in "Honesty Isn't Easy" or "No Cure for the Common Cold." The explicit thesis is also obvious, usually found in one sentence in the introduction. Sometimes, however, you want the reader to infer the thesis by combining the ideas in two or more sentences. Far more subtle is the implied thesis, which is what you have here:

> Pile on onions, lettuce, tomato, cheese, even mushrooms and jalapeño peppers, douse it with ketchup, mustard, mayonnaise, and still you can't hide the classic American hamburger—a quarter pound or so of relatively lean grilled beef snuggled into a soft but not spongy round roll. If the meat's too lean, the hamburger's too dry, but if it's not lean enough, the juice soaks the bun and the whole creation falls apart.

The thesis? Several are possible but two come quickly to mind, variations on "You can't spoil the classic American hamburger" and "The classic American hamburger is a splendid creation." Either way, what you have is a definition and an implied assertion about it.

Like the thesis, an essay's organization can be straightforward or somewhat complex. At times, you may want to use a roughly chronological pattern of organization, starting at one point in time and moving forward to another. Structuring an essay so that it moves from the least to the most important point is another obvious pattern, one used by several of the writers in this chapter. You might also consider organizing your paper by question/answer, the introduction posing a question and the body of the essay answering it. A variation on that pattern is one in which one part of the essay poses a problem that is then discussed and analyzed in terms of possible solutions. Both those ways of organizing an essay are relatively uncomplicated. Perhaps the hardest to handle successfully is the organization that goes from the particular to the general. Were you to write a paper on the American flag, for example, you might start with the particular—a description of the modern flag—and then discuss the general—what it means as a symbol.

Useful Terms

Connotation The associations suggested by a word that add to its literal meaning. *Home* and *domicile* have similar dictionary meanings, but they differ radically in their connotation.

Denotation The literal meaning of a word, its dictionary definition.

Persona The character of the writer that comes through from the prose.

POINTERS FOR USING DEFINITION

Exploring the Topic

1. **What are the denotations of your term?** You should consult an unabridged dictionary and perhaps a more complete or specialized one, such as the *Oxford English Dictionary* or a dictionary of slang.

2. **What are the connotations of your term?** What emotional reactions or associations does it elicit from people? What situations evoke what responses and why?

3. **What other words can be used for your term?** Which are similar?

4. **What are the characteristics, qualities, or components of your term?** Which are most important? Are some not worth mentioning?

5. What other modes are appropriate? What modes can you draw on to help support your definition and the organization of the essay? Where can you use description? Narration? What examples can you use to illustrate your term?

6. Has your word been used or misused? If so, might that misuse be turned into an introductory narrative? A closing one?

Drafting the Paper

1. Know your reader. Review your lists of denotations and connotations together with the characteristics related to your term to see how familiar they are to your reader. Check to see if your reader may have particular associations that you need to redirect or change. Or if your reader is directly affected by your topic, make sure your definition does not offend.

2. Know your purpose. Unless your term is unusual, one of your biggest problems is to tell the reader something new about it. Work on your first paragraph so that it will engage the reader from the start. From that point on, keep your primary purpose in mind. If you are writing a paper that is basically self-expressive or persuasive, make sure you have an audience other than yourself. If your aim is informative, consider narration, example, cause and effect, and analogy as possible ways of presenting familiar material in a fresh light.

3. Use evidence. Provide examples as evidence to illustrate what your key term means. Also consider using negative examples and setting out distinctions between the meaning of your word and other, similar words.

4. Draw on a variety of sources. Define your term from several perspectives. Perhaps a brief history of the word would be helpful, or maybe some statistical information is in order. See if a brief narrative might provide additional meaning for the term.

5. Make a point. Don't mistake your definition for your thesis. The two are certainly related, but one is an assertion; the other is not. Perhaps your definition is a jumping-off place for a larger point you wish to make or a key part of that point. Or perhaps your term evokes a single dominant impression you want to convey. Whatever purpose your definition serves, it needs to support your thesis.

Chocolate Equals Love

Diane Ackerman

As an undergraduate at Boston University and then Pennsylvania State University, Diane Ackerman studied both science and literature, twin interests she would pursue as a writer while earning an MFA and PhD. A staff writer for the New Yorker, *Ackerman often writes on nature and its inhabitants.* The Moon by Whale Light *(1991) examines the threats to endangered animals. Another nonfiction book,* A Slender Thread *(1997), grew out of her volunteer work as a counselor at a suicide prevention and crisis center. Three of her books are* Natural Histor[ies] . . . of The Senses *(1990), of* Love *(1995), and of* My Garden *(2001). Her most recent nonfiction work is* An Alchemy of Mind: The Marvel and Mystery of the Brain *(2004). The essay below was published in* Parade Magazine *on February 9, 2003. Reading it, you will be able to tell that Ackerman is also a well-respected poet, for in "Chocolate Equals Love" she manages to combine the vivid detail and compression characteristic of poetry with the precise detail and keen observation associated with science.*

What to Look For Good writers have a way of listening to words so that they are aware of a word's sound as well as sense. If you read Ackerman's second paragraph out loud, for instance, you'll hear a lot of *s* sounds that help make the prose flow smoothly. Reading your own work out loud will help you develop your own ear for the sound of good writing.

1 What food do you crave? Add a hint of mischief to your desire, and the answer is bound to be chocolate, Dark, divine, sense-bludgeoning chocolate. A wooer's gift. A child's reward. A jilted lover's solace. A cozy mug of slumber. Halloween manna. A gimme-more that tantalizes young and old alike. Almost every candy bar. Chocolate.

2 We can thank the Indians of Central and South America for chocolate's bewitching lusciousness. As the Spanish explorer Hernán Cortés found, the Aztecs worshiped chocolate (which they

named *cacahuatl*) as a gift from their wise god Quetzalcoatl. Aztec soldiers and male members of court drank as many as 2000 pitchers of chocolate every day. They spiked their drink with vanilla beans and spices, then drank it bubbly thick from golden cups. Adding chili peppers gave it bite. The Aztec leader Montezuma required a chocolate ice, made by pouring syrup over snow that runners brought to him from the nearest mountain.

3   Invigorating and dangerously sublime, chocolate dominated every facet of Aztec life, from sexuality to economy. Cocoa beans even served as currency: You could buy a rabbit for 10 beans, a slave for 100 beans.

4   At first, Cortés hated chocolate's shocking taste, which mingled bitter, spicy, pungent, silky, dank and dusty flavors. But in time its magic seduced him, and it is said that he introduced it to Spain, flavoring it with sugar instead of hot chili peppers.

5   By the 17th century, chocolate was thrilling Europeans with its sensory jolt—less devilish than liquor but still stimulating, luxurious and pleasantly addictive. Those who could afford it drank it thick and hot, as the Indians did, sometimes adding orange, vanilla or spices. Society ladies sipped several cups a day and even insisted on drinking it during church services. Doctors prescribed chocolate as a flesh-and-bone rejuvenator that could lift the spirits, hasten healing and raise a flagging libido.

6   Forget Viagra. Think bonbons.

7   Casanova, it is said, swore by chocolate and ate it as a prelude to lovemaking. The French King Louis XV's principal mistress Madame du Barry, served exquisitely refined but essentially drug-level chocolate to her various suitors. Unknowingly, they were following the custom of Montezuma, who was believed to have consumed extra chocolate before visiting his harem.

8   A liquid treasure until the 19th century, chocolate suddenly changed shape and personality when a Dutch chemist discovered how to separate cocoa butter, leaving powdered cocoa. The public clamored for portable, ever-ready chocolate, and confectioners obliged with pyramids of chocolate bars. Joining the chocolamania, the Cadbury brothers introduced chocolate in heart-shaped boxes in 1868. Milk chocolate appeared in Switzerland in 1875, thanks to Peter Daniel and Henri Nestlé. Then American mass-production provided cheap chocolates for the multitudes, thanks to the foresight of Milton Hershey. And the rest is history.

9   Is chocolate a health food? Chocolate is chemically active—a mind-altering drug that's good for you in moderation. The higher the cocoa content, the more antioxidants and other nutritious bonuses. Cocoa powder contains the most antioxidants, followed by dark chocolate and milk chocolate.

10   What delivers the chocolate buzz? Chocolate contains more than 300 chemicals, including tiny amounts of anandamide, which mimics the active ingredient in marijuana, plus such stimulants as theobromine and phenylethylamine. A 1.4-ounce bar of chocolate also can provide 20 milligrams of caffeine. That's jitters away from the 140 milligrams of an average cup of coffee, not to mention a thimbleful of espresso. But it's rousing enough, combined with the rest of chocolate's chemical bag of tricks. And the full sensory and nostalgic saga of eating chocolate— the mouth feel, the aroma, the taste, the memories—can calm the brain or lighten one's thoughts, for a while anyway.

11   If we luxuriate in a memory framed by the heaven of chocolate— say, eating s'mores around a campfire with a giggling Girl Scout troop or receiving a box of chocolates from a sappy beau and then sampling them with him—a small constellation of pleasure will attach itself to the idea of chocolate lifelong. That happens early on to nearly everyone.

12   For example, when I was a child, each year my mother and I would choose a colossal chocolate Easter rabbit with pink candy dot eyes. Together, we would sit on the floor in the aptly named "den" and devour most of the hollow rabbit—always starting with the ears and working our way down—until we went way beyond sated and started to feel a little sick. We would laugh with shared delight as we gobbled and afterward lounged about in a chocolate haze.

13   It was a cherished bonding ritual more visceral than verbal, reminding me how much we adore our senses. They're our house-guests, our explorers, our pets—and we love to give them treats. So how do you reward the sense of taste? For ages, the delicacy of choice has been rich, sensuously inviting chocolate.

ORGANIZATION AND IDEAS

1. Paragraph 1 announces the subject and describes it with quick images, all to interest the reader. How well does it succeed?
2. Ackerman chooses to begin the body of the essay (paragraphs 2–8) with a brief history of chocolate. How does that history help define it?

3. Paragraphs 9 and 10 provide a scientific view of chocolate. What information surprises you and why?
4. Think of the ideas Ackerman presents in paragraphs 2–10 and how chocolate can cause an emotional attachment, as described in paragraphs 11–13. State her thesis in one sentence.
5. To what extent does Ackerman's account of and appreciation for chocolate mesh with your own?

TECHNIQUE AND STYLE

1. Consult a handbook of grammar and usage for what it says about a sentence fragment, and then take another look at paragraph 1. To what extent, if any, are those fragments effective?
2. You are probably used to paragraphs as units that extend an idea, but Ackerman's sixth paragraph is quite different. What is its function?
3. In the last paragraph, Ackerman uses several metaphors for our senses. Which do you prefer and why?
4. In paragraphs 1, 9, 10, and 13, Ackerman uses questions. What purpose do they serve?
5. Most of the essay can be categorized as expository and objective, but in paragraphs 12 and 13, Ackerman switches to the personal. Why might she have chosen to do that and what effect does it have?

SUGGESTIONS FOR WRITING

Journal

1. Use your journal to explore how the senses can be viewed as pets.
2. Write a description that defines the kind of chocolate you like or dislike the most.

Essay

1. Think of the senses as possible topics for an essay that explains and defines the one you depend on the most: sight, smell, hearing, touch, or taste. Like Ackerman, you will want to include some scientific information, so you should do some research to be able to explain how that sense functions (a medical encyclopedia or medical Web page would be a good source). And, of course, use your own experience to explain why that sense is important to you.
2. Think about a kind of snack or food that you like a great deal, and write an essay that defines it. Like Ackerman, you can point out its history, how it is produced, the various forms it comes in, and your experiences with it. No matter what your topic, you can find a great deal of information about it from the Web by using a search engine.

I Was a Member of the Kung Fu Crew

Henry Han Xi Lau

New York City is still in many ways a city of neighborhoods, many of which are ethnic ones. The Chinatown that Henry Han Xi Lau writes about is one of the oldest, and it's where you can still walk down the street and not hear a word of English. To Lau, it's also home, even though he and his family have moved to Brooklyn, which, like Manhattan, is one of the city's five boroughs or districts. A sophomore at Yale University at the time he wrote this essay, Lau describes the people and places of Chinatown, defining it as "ghetto." The piece was published in the New York Times Magazine *on October 19, 1997. After the essay came out, Lau objected to the way it had been edited, and in a later piece he wrote for* Discourses, *an undergraduate journal at Yale, he called it a "warped presentation." If you'd like to read his critique, you can find it by typing his name into a search engine; it was reprinted in* Microcosm, *a Web journal published by Rice University. What's missing in the* Times *version, according to Lau, is the "resource-fulness and hard-working side of ghettoness." See if you agree.*

What to Look For   Lau relies heavily on definition to convey what it's like to be a member of the Kung Fu Crew and to be "ghetto." Many of the techniques he uses are ones that can carry over to your own writing, so be on the lookout for the details that define the Crew's physical prowess, hair, pants, attitudes, accessories, and language, all of which add up to being "cool."

1   Chinatown is ghetto, my friends are ghetto, I am ghetto. I went away to college last year, but I still have a long strand of hair that reaches past my chin. I need it when I go back home to hang with the K.F.C.—for Kung Fu Crew, not Kentucky Fried Chicken. We all met in a Northern Shaolin kung fu class years ago. Our *si-fu* was Rocky. He told us: "In the early 1900's in China, your grand master was walking in the streets when a foreigner riding on a horse disrespected him. So then he felt the belly of the horse with his palms and left. Shortly

thereafter, the horse buckled and died because our grand master had used *qi-gong* to mess up the horse's internal organs." Everyone said, "Cool, I would like to do that." Rocky emphasized, "You've got to practice really hard for a long time to reach that level."

2   By the time my friends and I were in the eighth grade, we were able to do 20-plus pushups on our knuckles and fingers. When we practiced our crescent, roundhouse and tornado kicks, we had 10-pound weights strapped to our legs. Someone once remarked, "Goddamn—that's a freaking mountain!" when he saw my thigh muscles in gym class.

3   Most Chinatown kids fall into a few general categories. There are pale-faced nerds who study all the time to get into the Ivies. There are the recent immigrants with uncombed hair and crooked teeth who sing karaoke in bars. There are the punks with highlighted hair who cut school, and the gangsters, whom everyone else avoids.

4   Then there is the K.F.C. We work hard like the nerds, but we identify with the punks. Now we are reunited, and just as in the old days we amble onto Canal Street, where we stick out above the older folks, elderly women bearing leaden bags of bok choy and oranges. As an opposing crew nears us, I assess them to determine whether to grill them or not. Grilling is the fine art of staring others down and trying to emerge victorious.

5   How the hair is worn is important in determining one's order on the streets. In the 80's, the dominant style was the mushroom cut, combed neatly or left wild in the front so that a person can appear menacing as he peers through his bangs. To gain an edge in grilling now, some kids have asymmetrical cuts, with long random strands sprouting in the front, sides or back. Some dye their hair blue or green, while blood red is usually reserved for gang members.

6   Only a few years ago, examination of the hair was sufficient. But now there is a second step: assessing pants. A couple of years ago, wide legs first appeared in New York City, and my friends and I switched from baggy pants. In the good old days, Merry-Go-Round in the Village sold wide legs for only $15 a pair. When Merry-Go-Round went bankrupt, Chinatown kids despaired. Wide-leg prices at other stores increased drastically as they became more popular. There are different ways of wearing wide legs. Some fold their pant legs inward and staple them at the hem. Some clip the back ends of their pants to their shoes with safety pins. Others simply cut the bottoms so that fuzzy strings hang out.

7   We grill the opposing punks. I untuck my long strand of hair so that it swings in front of my face. Nel used to have a strand, but he chewed it off one day in class by accident. Chu and Tom cut their strands off because it scared people at college. Jack has a patch of blond hair, while Tone's head is a ball of orange flame. Chi has gelled short hair, while Ken's head is a black mop. As a group, we have better hair than our rivals. But they beat us with their wide legs. In our year away at college, wide legs have gone beyond our 24-inch leg openings. Twenty-six- to 30-inch jeans are becoming the norm. If wide legs get any bigger, they will start flying up like a skirt in an updraft.

8   We have better accessories, though. Chi sports a red North Face that gives him a rugged mountain-climber look because of the jungle of straps sprouting in the back. Someone once asked Chi, "Why is the school bag so important to one's cool?" He responded, "Cuz it's the last thing others see when you walk away from them or when they turn back to look at you after you walk past them." But the other crew has female members, which augments their points. The encounter between us ends in a stalemate. But at least the K.F.C. members are in college and are not true punks.

9   In the afternoon, we decide to eat at the Chinatown McDonald's for a change instead of the Chinese bakery Maria's, our dear old hangout spot. "Mickey D's is good sit," Nel says. I answer: "But the Whopper gots more fat and meat. It's even got more bun." Nel agrees. "True that," he says. I want the Big Mac, but I buy the two-cheeseburger meal because it has the same amount of meat but costs less.

10   We sit and talk about ghettoness again. We can never exactly articulate what being ghetto entails, but we know the spirit of it. In Chinatown toilet facilities we sometimes find footprints on the seats because F.O.B.'s (fresh off the boats) squat on them as they do over the holes in China. We see alternative brand names in stores like Dolo instead of Polo, and Mike instead of Nike.

11   We live by ghettoness. My friends and I walk from 80-something Street in Manhattan to the tip of the island to save a token. We gorge ourselves at Gray's Papaya because the hot dogs are 50 cents each. But one cannot be stingy all the time. We leave good tips at Chinese restaurants because our parents are waiters and waitresses, too.

12   We sit for a long time in McDonald's, making sure that there is at least a half-inch of soda in our cups so that when the staff wants to

kick us out, we can claim that we are not finished yet. Jack positions a mouse bite of cheeseburger in the center of a wrapper to support our claim.

13   After a few hours, the K.F.C. prepares to disband. I get in one of the no-license commuter vans on Canal Street that will take me to Sunset Park in Brooklyn, where my family lives now. All of my friends will leave Chinatown, for the Upper East Side and the Lower East Side, Forest Hills in Queens and Bensonhurst in Brooklyn. We live far apart, but we always come back together in Chinatown. For most of us, our homes used to be here and our world was here.

ORGANIZATION AND IDEAS

1. The essay is set out in chronological order. What paragraphs cover what times?
2. What categories of kids does Lau describe? Where does the Crew fit?
3. Lau describes "grilling" in paragraphs 4–8. What is his point?
4. Lau may have moved away from Chinatown, but he is still very much a part of its community. How would you characterize that community and its values?
5. Is Lau's thesis explicit or implicit? How can you phrase it in your own words?

TECHNIQUE AND STYLE

1. Look up the term *comma splice* in a handbook of grammar and usage, and check what you find against Lau's first sentence. Why is it a legitimate comma splice?
2. Lau uses dialogue in paragraphs 8 and 9. What does it add to the essay?
3. The essay piles on details and information that lead up to a definition of *ghetto*. State that definition in your own words.
4. *Ghetto* usually has a negative connotation. How does Lau make it positive?
5. The essay is written in standard American English. Why might Lau have chosen to write it that way instead of in "ghetto"?

SUGGESTIONS FOR WRITING

Journal

1. If you met the Kung Fu Crew on the street, you might find yourself ignoring them, "grilling" them, admiring them, but no matter what, you'd have some sort of reaction. Describe how you would react.

2. Look up the word *intimidation* in an unabridged dictionary, and think about times in your experience when you were intimidated or when you intimidated someone else. Use your journal to define how you felt.

Essay

1. People spend a lot of time analyzing what's in and what's out. For some, those in advertising or fashion, for instance, it's a business, but all of us are affected by it. Perhaps you would find a lot to say in an essay about what it means to be "in" or "cool" or the opposite. Think about a category (some suggestions are listed below), choose a subject, and then start jotting down details such as the particulars of language (spoken and body), appearance, attitudes, and likes and dislikes that define your central term.

> music
> films or television shows
> dates
> schools
> cars

As you draft your essay, try to keep your focus on definition. It's natural to lean toward comparisons, but, like Lau, make sure you use them to support what you are defining.

2. Each generation usually ends up with at least one label or tag—the Baby Boomers, Gen X, or some such. What label works for your generation? Write an essay that explains your choice, providing examples to prove your point.

The Handicap of Definition

William Raspberry

William Raspberry left the small and segregated town in Mississippi where he grew up to take a summer job with the Indianapolis Reporter, *moving on in 1962 to the* Washington Post. *Although he now teaches at Duke University, where he is the Knight Chair in Communications and Journalism, he is better known as a writer for the* Washington Post *and as the author of a syndicated column that runs in more than 200 newspapers. His commentary on issues such as rap music, crime, and AIDS earned him a Pulitzer Prize in 1994. In the essay that follows, he writes about the terms* black *and* white, *words that have connotations we don't often think about. Raspberry shows us that if we stop to think about* black, *we'll see that it has so narrow a definition that it is "one of the heaviest burdens black Americans—and black children in particular—have to bear." Not much has changed since 1982, when this essay first appeared in Raspberry's syndicated column.*

What to Look For   Somewhere along the line, we've all been warned never to begin a sentence with a conjunction such as *and, but,* and the like. But as long as you know how to avoid the trap of a sentence fragment, beginning a sentence with a conjunction can lend a conversational tone to your essay. As you read Raspberry's essay, notice how often he uses this technique.

1   I know all about bad schools, mean politicians, economic depriva-tion and racism. Still, it occurs to me that one of the heaviest bur-dens black Americans—and black children in particular—have to bear is the handicap of definition: the question of what it means to be black.

2   Let me explain quickly what I mean. If a basketball fan says that the Boston Celtics' Larry Bird plays "black," the fan intends it—and Bird probably accepts it—as a compliment. Tell pop singer Tom Jones he moves "black" and he might grin in appreciation. Say to Teena Marie or The Average White Band that they sound "black" and they'll thank you.

3   But name one pursuit, aside from athletics, entertainment or sex-ual performance in which a white practitioner will feel compli-mented to be told he does it "black." Tell a white broadcaster he talks "black," and he'll sign up for diction lessons. Tell a white reporter he writes "black" and he'll take a writing course. Tell a white lawyer he reasons "black" and he might sue you for slander.

4   What we have here is a tragically limited definition of blackness, and it isn't only white people who buy it.

5   Think of all the ways black children can put one another down with charges of "whiteness." For many of these children, hard study and hard work are "white." Trying to please a teacher might be criticized as

acting "white." Speaking correct English is "white." Scrimping today in the interest of tomorrow's goals is "white." Educational toys and games are "white."

6   An incredible array of habits and attitudes that are conducive to success in business, in academia, in the nonentertainment professions are likely to be thought of as somehow "white." Even economic success, unless it involves such "black" undertakings as numbers banking, is defined as "white."

7   And the results are devastating. I wouldn't deny that blacks often are better entertainers and athletes. My point is the harm that comes from too narrow a definition of what is black.

8   One reason black youngsters tend to do better at basketball, for instance, is that they assume they can learn to do it well, and so they practice constantly to prove themselves right.

9   Wouldn't it be wonderful if we could infect black children with the notion that excellence in math is "black" rather than white, or possibly Chinese? Wouldn't it be of enormous value if we could create the myth that morality, strong families, determination, courage and love of learning are traits brought by slaves from Mother Africa and therefore quintessentially black?

10   There is no doubt in my mind that most black youngsters could develop their mathematical reasoning, their elocution and their attitudes the way they develop their jump shots and their dance steps: by the combination of sustained, enthusiastic practice and the unquestioned belief that they can do it.

11   In one sense, what I am talking about is the importance of developing positive ethnic traditions. Maybe Jews have an innate talent for communication; maybe Chinese are born with a gift for mathematical reasoning; maybe blacks are naturally blessed with athletic grace. I doubt it. What is at work, I suspect, is assumption, inculcated early in their lives, that this is a thing our people do well.

12   Unfortunately, many of the things about which blacks make this assumption are things that do not contribute to their career success—except for that handful of the truly gifted who can make it as entertainers and athletes. And many of the things we concede to whites are the things that are essential to economic security.

13   So it is with a number of assumptions black youngsters make about what it is to be a "man": physical aggressiveness, sexual prowess, the refusal to submit to authority. The prisons are full of people who, by this perverted definition, are unmistakably men.

14   But the real problem is not so much that the things defined as "black" are negative. The problem is that the definition is much too narrow.

15   Somehow, we have to make our children understand that they are intelligent, competent people, capable of doing whatever they put their minds to and making it in the American mainstream, not just in a black subculture.

16   What we seem to be doing, instead, is raising up yet another generation of young blacks who will be failures—by definition.

ORGANIZATION AND IDEAS

1. Examine paragraphs 1–4, 5–7, and 8–11. Each functions as a unit. What sentence is the major assertion for each group of paragraphs?

2. Examine paragraphs 12–16 as a concluding paragraph block. What is the relationship between paragraph 12 and the preceding paragraphs?

3. Consider the controlling ideas that guide the paragraph blocks and the conclusions Raspberry draws from the examples that support those assertions. Stated fully, what is Raspberry's thesis?

4. A militant who read this essay would argue that Raspberry is trying to make blacks "better" by making them white. Is there any evidence to support this view? Explain.

5. A feminist who read the essay might argue that it is sexist. Is there any evidence to support this view? Explain.

TECHNIQUE AND STYLE

1. This essay was one of Raspberry's syndicated columns; as a result, it appeared in a large number of newspapers with equally large readerships, mostly white. What evidence can you find that Raspberry is trying to inform his white audience and persuade his black readers?

2. How and where does Raspberry establish his credibility as a writer on this subject? What grammatical point of view does he use?

3. Where in the essay does he qualify or modulate his statements? What is the effect of that technique?

4. Paragraphs 3, 7, 13, and 14 all begin with a conjunction. What effect does this technique achieve? Consult a handbook of grammar and usage for a discussion of this device. To what extent does Raspberry's usage conform to the handbook's advice?

5. Paragraph 16 is an example of a rhetorical paragraph, a one-sentence paragraph that gives dramatic emphasis to a point. If you eliminate the dash or substitute a comma for it, what happens to the dramatic effect? What does the pun add?

Journal

1. Raspberry's essay was published in 1982. Write a journal entry explaining whether his point holds true today.
2. Write down any examples you can think of that can substitute for those Raspberry uses, but focus on women. In a paragraph or two, explain how the substitutions would add to or detract from his point.

Essay

1. Find a word that has accumulated broad connotations and then see what definitions have evolved and their effect. Like Raspberry, you may want to consider two terms but emphasize only one. Possibilities:

   man
   hero
   student
   woman
   worker
   lover
   politician

2. Raspberry says "we have to make our children understand that they are intelligent, competent people, capable of doing whatever they put their minds to . . . " (paragraph 15). But *intelligent* and *competent* mean different things to different people. Select one of the words and write an essay in which you define what the word means to you. As you think about your topic, remember that it can be useful to define something by what it is not, by comparisons.

Where Nothing Says Everything

Suzanne Berne

A writer of both nonfiction and fiction, Suzanne Berne has taught at Harvard University and Wellesley College. Her first novel, A Crime in the Neighborhood (*1997*), *was hailed as "remarkable" by the* New York Times Book Review, *and it went on to be chosen as a* Times

"Notable Book." In 1999, it received the United Kingdom's Orange Prize, a singular honor. To be eligible, a novel must be written by a woman and written in English, for the prize "aims to celebrate novels of excellence, originality and accessibility, and to promote women writers to as wide a range of male and female readers as possible." Berne's next novel was A Perfect Relationship *(2001), and her new one,* The Last of Mark Twain's Daughters, *should be published by the time you read this note. When not working on fiction and teaching, Berne contributes to the travel section of the* New York Times, *where this essay appeared on April 21, 2002.*

What to Look For Berne has a difficult job in trying to define Ground Zero, as so many readers have vivid images of both the disaster and the site. As you read, notice how she uses description, contrast, narration, example, and cause and effect to define her subject.

1   On a cold, damp March morning, I visited Manhattan's financial district, a place I'd never been, to pay my respects at what used to be the World Trade Center. Many other people had chosen to do the same that day, despite the raw wind and spits of rain, and so the first thing I noticed when I arrived on the corner of Vesey and Church Streets was a crowd.

2   Standing on the sidewalk, pressed against aluminum police barricades, wearing scarves that flapped into their faces and woolen hats pulled over their ears, were people apparently from everywhere. Germans, Italians, Japanese. An elegant-looking Norwegian family in matching shearling coats. People from Ohio and California and Maine. Children, middle-age couples, older people. Many of them were clutching cameras and video recorders, and they were all craning to see across the street, where there was nothing to see.

3   At least, nothing is what it first looked like, the space that is now ground zero. But once your eyes adjust to what you are looking at, "nothing" becomes something much more potent, which is absence.

4   But to the out-of-towner, ground zero looks at first simply like a construction site. All the familiar details are there: the wooden scaffolding; the cranes, the bulldozers and forklifts; the trailers and construction workers in hard hats; even the dust. There is the pound of

jackhammers, the steady beep-beep-beep of trucks backing up, the roar of heavy machinery.

5   So much busyness is reassuring, and it is possible to stand looking at the cranes and trucks and feel that mild curiosity and hopefulness so often inspired by construction sites.

6   Then gradually your eyes do adjust, exactly as if you have stepped from a dark theater into a bright afternoon, because what becomes most striking about this scene is the light itself.

7   Ground zero is a great bowl of light, an emptiness that seems weirdly spacious and grand, like a vast plaza amid the dense tangle of streets in lower Manhattan. Light reflecting off the Hudson River vaults into the site, soaking everything—especially on an overcast morning—with a watery glow. This is the moment when absence begins to assume a material form, when what is not there becomes visible.

8   Suddenly you notice the periphery, the skyscraper shrouded in black plastic, the boarded windows, the steel skeleton of the shattered Winter Garden. Suddenly there are the broken steps and cracked masonry in front of Brooks Brothers. Suddenly there are the firefighters, the waiting ambulance on the other side of the pit, the police on every corner. Suddenly there is the enormous cross made of two rusted girders.

9   And suddenly, very suddenly, there is the little cemetery attached to St. Paul's Chapel, with tulips coming up, the chapel and grounds miraculously undamaged except for a few plastic-sheathed gravestones. The iron fence is almost invisible beneath a welter of dried pine wreaths, banners, ribbons, laminated poems and prayers and photographs, swags of paper cranes, withered flowers, baseball hats, rosary beads, teddy bears. And flags, flags everywhere, little American flags fluttering in the breeze, flags on posters drawn by Brownie troops, flags on T-shirts, flags on hats, flags streaming by, tied to the handles of baby strollers.

10   It takes quite a while to see all of this; it takes even longer to come up with something to say about it.

11   An elderly man standing next to me had been staring fixedly across the street for some time. Finally he touched his son's elbow and said: "I watched those towers being built. I saw this place when they weren't there." Then he stopped, clearly struggling with, what for him, was a double negative, recalling an absence before there was an absence. His son, waiting patiently, took a few photographs. "Let's get out of here," the man said at last.

12   Again and again I heard people say, "It's unbelievable." And then
they would turn to each other, dissatisfied. They wanted to say
something more expressive, more meaningful. But it is unbelievable, to stare at so much devastation, and know it for devastation,
and yet recognize that it does not look like the devastation one has
imagined.

13   Like me, perhaps, the people around me had in mind images
from television and newspaper pictures: the collapsing buildings,
the running office workers, the black plume of smoke against a
bright blue sky. Like me, they were probably trying to superimpose
those terrible images onto the industrious emptiness right in front of
them. The difficulty of this kind of mental revision is measured,
I believe, by the brisk trade in World Trade Center photograph
booklets at tables set up on street corners.

14   Determined to understand better what I was looking at, I decided
to get a ticket for the viewing platform beside St. Paul's. This proved
no easy task, as no one seemed to be able to direct me to South
Street Seaport, where the tickets are distributed. Various police officers whom I asked for directions, waved me vaguely toward the East
River, differing degrees of boredom and resignation on their faces.
Or perhaps it was a kind of incredulousness. Somewhere around the
American Stock Exchange, I asked a security guard for help and he
frowned at me, saying, "You want tickets to the disaster?"

15   Finally I found myself in line at a cheerfully painted kiosk,
watching a young juggler try to entertain the crowd. He kept
dropping the four red balls he was attempting to juggle, and having to chase after them. It was noon; the next available viewing
was at 4 p.m.

16   Back I walked, up Fulton Street, the smell of fish in the air, to
wander again around St. Paul's. A deli on Vesey Street advertised
a view of the World Trade Center from its second-floor dining area.
I went in and ordered a pastrami sandwich, uncomfortably aware
that many people before me had come to that same deli for pastrami sandwiches who would never come there again. But I was
here to see what I could, so I carried my sandwich upstairs and sat
down beside one of the big plate-glass windows.

17   And there, at last, I got my ticket to the disaster.

18   I could see not just into the pit now, but also its access ramp,
which trucks had been traveling up and down since I had arrived
that morning. Gathered along the ramp were firefighters in their

black helmets and black coats. Slowly they lined up, and it became clear that this was an honor guard, and that someone's remains were being carried up the ramp toward the open door of an ambulance.

19   Everyone in the dining room stopped eating. Several people stood up, whether out of respect or to see better, I don't know. For a moment, everything paused.

20   Then the day flowed back into itself. Soon I was outside once more, joining the tide of people washing around the site. Later, as I huddled with a little crowd on the viewing platform, watching people scrawl their names or write "God Bless America" on the plywood walls, it occurred to me that a form of repopulation was taking effect, with so many visitors to this place, thousands of visitors, all of us coming to see the wide emptiness where so many were lost. And by the act of our visiting—whether we are motivated by curiosity or horror or reverence or grief, or by something confusing that combines them all—that space fills up again.

ORGANIZATION AND IDEAS

1. The essay is organized by the time of the day, from the morning to the late afternoon. Why might Berne have chosen that organization and how effective is it?
2. Arguably the most important newspaper in the United States, the *New York Times* has a very broad and general readership. Even so, writers often have specific readers in mind. To whom is Berne's essay addressed?
3. To what extent would you call Berne's account objective? Subjective? What evidence can you find to support your view?
4. Reread the conclusion, paragraphs 18–20. What does it imply about the site? What is the essay's thesis?
5. What kind of effect do you think Berne is trying to have on the reader? Does it work? Why or why not?

TECHNIQUE AND STYLE

1. Berne uses the pronoun *you* in the essay. Reread the piece, keeping track of where the word occurs. Who is the *you?*
2. Look up the word *paradox* in an unabridged dictionary. Where do you find examples of it in Berne's essay? How effective are they?
3. Take another look at the essay's title. To what extent is it appropriate?
4. Paragraphs 3, 10, and 17 function as transitions. Choose one and explain whether it succeeds.

5. Look up the word *understatement* in an unabridged dictionary or dictionary of literary terms. To what extent does it describe Berne's tone?

SUGGESTIONS FOR WRITING

Journal

1. Explain why you would or would not have visited the site of the World Trade Center.

2. Berne uses the word *absence* in paragraphs 3, 7, and 11. What does her use of the word contribute to the essay as a whole?

Essay

1. Think of the times when you have made a visit to an important place. When did you go? What did you do? Who else was there? What effect did it have on you? Write an essay in which you define the meaning of such a visit. Suggestions:

cemetery
historic site
tourist attraction
museum
house you grew up in

2. It's almost impossible to avoid the emotional associations one has of 9/11. Think about your reactions at that time or now in retrospect, and list the emotions you felt—shock, horror, anger, despair, incredulity, and so on. Choose one of the words as the subject of an essay in which you define the word, using 9/11 as a starting point but also use examples from your own experience, including what you have seen or read.

Crippled By Their Culture

Thomas Sowell

As one would expect of a senior fellow at Stanford University's Hoover Institution, Thomas Sowell's academic credentials are impressive: AB (magna cum laude) from Harvard, AM from Columbia University, and PhD from the University of Chicago, all in the field of economics. Author of more than 20 books, Sowell notes, "I write only when I have something to say." And as his books attest, he has lots to say and on various topics, among them justice, law, culture, ethnicity, race, and affirmative action. He also has a lot to say about writing, and you might enjoy reading what he has to say about it at his web site, http://www.tsowell.com/About_Writing.html. Sowell's most recent books are On Classical Economics *(2006) and* Black Rednecks and White Liberals *(2005). The essay that follows defines "black rednecks" and was published by the* Wall Street Journal *on April 26, 2005.*

What to Look For   As you read Sowell's essay, look for the ways he bolsters his ideas by using the results of his research. Like Sowell, you can strengthen your points and make yourself credible by researching your subject. Your readers will be apt to find your essay more interesting and your point more believable.

1   For most of the history of this country, differences between the black and the white population—whether in income, IQ, crime rates, or whatever—have been attributed to either race or racism. For much of the first half of the 20th century, these differences were attributed to race—that is, to an assumption that blacks just did not have it in their genes to do as well as white people. The tide began to turn in the second half of the 20th century, when the assumption developed that black-white differences were due to racism on the part of whites.

2   Three decades of my own research lead me to believe that neither of those explanations will stand up under scrutiny of the facts. As one small example, a study published last year indicated that most of the black alumni of Harvard were from either the West Indies or Africa, or were the children of West Indian or African immigrants. These people are the same race as American blacks, who greatly outnumber either or both.

3   If this disparity is not due to race, it is equally hard to explain by racism. To a racist, one black is pretty much the same as another. But, even if a racist somehow let his racism stop at the water's edge, how could he tell which student was the son or daughter of someone born in the West Indies or in Africa, especially since their

American-born offspring probably do not even have a foreign accent?

4   What then could explain such large disparities in demographic "representation" among these three groups of blacks? Perhaps they have different patterns of behavior and different cultures and values behind their behavior.

5   There have always been large disparities, even within the native black population of the U.S. Those blacks whose ancestors were "free persons of color" in 1850 have fared far better in income, occupation, and family stability than those blacks whose ancestors were freed in the next decade by Abraham Lincoln.

6   What is not nearly as widely known is that there were also very large disparties within the white population of the pre–Civil War South and the white population of the Northern states. Although Southern whites were only about one-third of the white population of the U.S., an absolute majority of all the illiterate whites in the country were in the South.

7   The North had four times as many schools as the South, attended by more than four times as many students. Children in Massachusetts spent more than twice as many years in school as children in Virginia. Such disparities obviously produce other disparities. Northern newspapers had more than four times the circulation of Southern newspapers. Only 8% of the patents issued in 1851 went to Southerners. Even though agriculture was the principal economic activity of the antebellum South at the time, the vast majority of the patents for agricultural inventions went to Northerners. Even the cotton gin was invented by a Northerner.

8   Disparities between Southern whites and Northern whites extended across the board from rates of violence to rates of illegitimacy. American writers from both the antebellum South and the North commented on the great differences between the white people in the two regions. So did famed French visitor Alexis de Tocqueville.

9   None of these disparities can be attributed to either race or racism. Many contemporary observers attributed these differences to the existence of slavery in the South, as many in later times would likewise attribute both the difference between Northern and Southern whites, and between blacks and whites nationwide, to slavery. But slavery doesn't stand up under scrutiny of historical facts any better than race or racism as explanations of North-South

differences or black-white differences. The people who settled in the South came from different regions of Britain than the people who settled in the North—and they differed as radically on the other side of the Atlantic as they did here—that is, before they had ever seen a black slave.

10   Slavery also cannot explain the difference between American blacks and West Indian blacks living in the United States because the ancestors of both were enslaved. When race, racism, and slavery all fail the empirical test, what is left?

11   Culture is left.

12   The culture of the people who were called "rednecks" and "crackers" before they ever got on the boats to cross the Atlantic was a culture that produced far lower levels of intellectual and economic achievement, as well as far higher levels of violence and sexual promiscuity. That culture had its own way of talking, not only in the pronunciation of particular words but also in a loud, dramatic style of oratory with vivid imagery, repetitive phrases and repetitive cadences.

13   Although that style originated on the other side of the Atlantic in centuries past, it became for generations the style of both religious oratory and political oratory among Southern whites and among Southern blacks—not only in the South but in the Northern ghettos in which Southern blacks settled. It was a style used by Southern white politicians in the era of Jim Crow and later by black civil rights leaders fighting Jim Crow. Martin Luther King's famous speech at the Lincoln Memorial in 1963 was a classic example of that style.

14   While a third of the white population of the U.S. lived within the redneck culture, more than 90% of the black population did. Although that culture eroded away over the generations, it did so at different rates in different places and among different people. It eroded away much faster in Britain than in the U.S. and somewhat faster among Southern whites than among Southern blacks, who had fewer opportunities for education or for the rewards that came with escape from that counterproductive culture.

15   Nevertheless the process took a long time. As late as the First World War, white soldiers from Georgia, Arkansas, Kentucky and Mississippi scored lower on mental tests than black soldiers from Ohio, Illinois, New York and Pennsylvania. Again, neither race nor racism can explain that—and neither can slavery.

16   The redneck culture proved to be a major handicap for both whites and blacks who absorbed it. Today, the last remnants of that culture can still be found in the worst of the black ghettos, whether in the North or the South, for the ghettos of the North were settled by blacks from the South. The counterproductive and self-destructive culture of black rednecks in today's ghettos is regarded by many as the only "authentic" black culture—and, for that reason, something not to be tampered with. Their talk, their attitudes, and their behavior are regarded as sacrosanct.

17   The people who take this view may think of themselves as friends of blacks. But they are the kinds of friends who can do more harm than enemies.

ORGANIZATION AND IDEAS

1. What paragraph or paragraphs provide the essay's introduction? Its conclusion? What reasons do you have for your choices?
2. The essay poses a question in paragraph 4. What is Sowell's answer?
3. Where in the essay does Sowell use comparisons? What do they add?
4. How does Sowell define "redneck culture"? What examples does he use and how effective are they?
5. In paragraph 16, Sowell states: "The counterproductive and self-destructive culture of black rednecks in today's ghettos is regarded by many as the only 'authentic' black culture—and, for that reason, something not to be tampered with. Their talk, their attitudes, and their behavior are regarded as sacrosanct." How true do you find these statements?

TECHNIQUE AND STYLE

1. Paragraph 11 consists of three words. Rewrite paragraph 10 to include them. What is lost? Gained?
2. How does Sowell take some of the sting out of the word *redneck?* What, if anything, is positive about that "redneck culture"?
3. Paragraphs 12–16 trace the evolution of "redneck culture." What does that explanation add to Sowell's main point?
4. Sowell spends the first ten paragraphs arguing that neither race nor racism explains the disparities between blacks and whites but only six paragraphs on "redneck culture." What reasons can you think of for that decision?
5. Race and racism are explosive subjects, and anyone writing about them must tread carefully. How careful is Sowell? To what extent does his caution or lack of it hurt or strengthen the essay?

Suggestions for Writing

Journal

1. Use your journal to record your responses to Sowell's ideas. What do you agree or disagree with and why? Cite examples to support your opinion.

2. At no point in the essay does Sowell mention that he is black. Use your journal to explore whether that fact is relevant to his argument. How would including it change the essay?

Essay

1. In paragraph 16, Sowell states that a culture is expressed in a person's "talk . . . attitudes . . . and behavior." Use your library or a web resource to dig deeper into what is meant by *culture*. For the web, you might start by looking up the word in Wikipedia (www.en.wikipedia.org) or the Encyclopedia Brittanica (www.eb.com). Given a broader definition of *culture*, choose a subject whose culture you can analyze. Suggestions:
   sports fans
   poker players
   cheerleaders
   video game players
   celebrities

2. Though Sowell focuses on "redneck culture" as it applies to urban blacks, he sees it at work in the white world as well. Write an essay in which you define "redneck culture" as it exists in the white population. You will probably want to narrow down that population by age group, location, occupation, or some other characteristic. Make sure you give examples to illustrate your points and keep in mind that your readership may include someone in the group you select. As in the first suggestion above, you would do well to start by looking up the key word.

ADDITIONAL WRITING ASSIGNMENTS

Using Definition

1. Define an abstract term: morality, honor, courage, humility, or friendship.
2. Define your taste in: music, art, film, books, television, or friends.
3. Define the qualities you most admire in a person: parent, teacher, religious leader, sibling, or political figure.
4. Define an article of clothing that operates as a symbol: jeans, baseball hat, tee shirt, bandanna, or athletic shoes.

Evaluating the Essays

1. The essays by Henry Han Xi Lau and William Raspberry deal with identifiable groups and the conflicts both within and outside of them. Lau defines his group in terms of "ghettoness," and Raspberry defines young black children in terms of what it means to be a "man." Which conflict is the more difficult and why? Use both essays to back up your opinion.
2. Diane Ackerman and Suzanne Berne rely heavily on description and observation to define their subjects and bring them to life. Which one does the better job? Cite examples and quote material from both essays to prove your point.
3. William Raspberry and Thomas Sowell address sensitive issues of race from an African American perspective. Of the two, which one makes the more compelling argument? Again, quote from both essays to provide evidence for your choice.
4. Look up *symbol* in a dictionary of literary terms and then consider the essays by Henry Han Xi Lau and Suzanne Berne. Lau's hair, walk, clothing, and accessories are all symbols of his membership in the Kung Fu Crew (as is the name of the crew itself). Berne, however, concentrates on the site of the World Trade Center as symbol. Reread the essays, noting the larger meanings of what the symbols represent. Which author uses symbolism more effectively? What evidence supports your opinion?

On Using
Example

4

Any time you encounter *for instance, such as,* or *for example,* you know what will follow: an **example** that explains and supports the generalization. Used with general statements, examples fill in the gaps. If you are writing on the subject of violent crime and want to show that the facts contradict what many people believe, you might write "Many people believe most crime is violent and that crime is increasing." Then you might continue by citing statistics as examples that show the rate of crime peaked in the seventies but then ceased to rise in the eighties and actually fell in the nineties. You would have supported the idea that crime rates have fallen, but you would still need to provide evidence for the idea that many people believe the opposite. Readers also need to know what evidence supports your claim that crime, to many people, means violent crime. That evidence is apt to come in the form of an example. Examples

- develop
- illustrate
- clarify
- support
- emphasize

a main point. The most basic building block of all, examples pin down generalizations, supporting them with specifics.

To use examples well, you first need to know when to use them, then which ones to select, and finally, how to incorporate them. If you read actively, responding to the words on the page as you would to a person talking to you, odds are you will spot where examples are needed. On reading the sentence above about crime, you might think to yourself, "Hey, wait a minute! How about that violent crime statement?" Often it helps to read your own work belligerently, ready to shoot down any generalization with a "Says who?" The response to "Says who?" will vary according to your audience. A sociology paper will call for statistics; a personal narrative will draw on your own experience. Other good sources are the experiences of others and those of authorities whose work you can quote. The skill here is to match the example not only to the generalization it supports but also to the readers to whom it is addressed.

After you have found good examples, you need to sequence them logically, while at the same time you avoid overusing terms such as "for example." Where you use multiple examples, you can use **transitions.** It's possible to group transitions by their functions.

- addition: *and, also, again, besides, moreover, next, finally*
- for a turn or concession: *but, yet, however, instead, in contrast, of course, certainly,* or *granted*
- for a result or summary: *therefore, thus, as a result, so, finally, in conclusion, hence,* or *in brief*

Less obvious and, therefore, apt to be more effective are transitions that don't call attention to themselves, such as the repetition of a key word from the previous sentence or the use of a personal or demonstrative pronoun. If you use pronouns, however, make sure that what they refer to is clear. The demonstrative pronoun *this*, for instance, should usually be followed by a noun, as in *this sentence* or *this idea*. A *this* standing by itself may force your reader to go back to the previous sentence to understand exactly what it refers to.

Audience and Purpose

In general, the less familiar your audience is with your subject, the more important it is to have examples, and lots of them. If you find yourself writing about a sport, for instance, you would do well to think about what your audience may or may not know about it. If the sport is ice hockey and your readers are your classmates most of whom live in Mississippi, you'll know that most of them won't know much about your topic, so you will have to use lots of examples. And if you are arguing that ice hockey is an underrated sport, you can draw on your readers' experience with more familiar games such as basketball. You might use the example of the pace of a basketball game to make the point that ice hockey is even faster, so fast that at times the crowd can't even see the puck.

If your readers are relatively familiar with your topic, then your job is to make that familiarity come to life and shape it to your purpose. If you are writing an essay that explores the various levels of anxiety experienced by a first-year college student, you will probably cite a number of instances. You might start with the example of registering by telephone or on-line and the mild concern that the machine on the other end of the line will send your course requests to electronic heaven, then the fear of not finding the right classroom and turning up, if at all, late for class; next the uneasiness that occurs with the first look at the course syllabus, followed by the apprehension over the speed of a lecture; and then you might end with the sheer terror of the first test. If you provide enough examples, at least one is bound to remind a reader of a similar response.

The examples get harder to come by if your subject is a controversial or sensitive one. On familiar topics such as abortion, capital punishment, and prayer in public schools, your readers are not only apt to have opinions but very set ones, so set that you might do well to steer clear of the topic. Even less touchy subjects are difficult to write about because you have to be sensitive to views that differ from yours so that you don't alienate those readers. When dealing with a topic on which there has been much debate, it often helps to list the opposing arguments so you can find examples to support your points and to defeat the opposite ones.

Now and then, you may also find yourself writing an essay that tackles a subject that isn't controversial but still requires some caution on your part. You might, for example, want to write about what you find to be our culture's "throwaway" mentality and how it is adversely affecting the environment. When you start listing the more obvious throwaway items you can think of, you find you have fast-food wrappings and boxes, ball-point pens, paper napkins and towels, and plastic coverings for CDs, all items your readers probably use and throw away without thinking. Your problem then becomes one of educating your readers without insulting or blaming them, which isn't easy. Recognizing the problem, however, is halfway to solving it, and you'll read essays in this chapter that do just that.

Types of Examples

Examples generally fall into two categories, extended and multiple. An essay that rests its assertion on only one example is relatively rare, but you will run across one now and then. When you do, the example often takes the form of a narrative in support of the author's thesis. To show that a minimum-wage job can be a fulfilling one (or a demeaning one—take your pick), you might support your thesis by telling about a typical day on the job. While you are relying on only one example, you will have developed it in considerable depth, and you probably will have included a sentence or two to indicate that other experiences may contradict yours, so your readers will accept your extended example as valid.

Far more frequent, however, are multiple examples. They add clarity, support, and emphasis, and save you from having to make the kind of disclaimer mentioned above. Sometimes the examples will be drawn from your own experience and the experiences of others, but often you will find you want more generalized sources, so you consult books, magazines, the Internet, interviews, reports, and so on. You may well find that examples drawn from outside sources give your essay a more objective, reasoned **tone.** If you think of that term as similar to tone of voice, you will realize that it means the writer's attitude toward the subject and audience. Examples drawn from personal experience are apt to create an informal, conversational tone; those drawn from outside sources often provide a cooler, more formal tone. No matter where you find your examples, however, you can present them with some variety, summarizing some, quoting others.

Examples not only illustrate generalizations, they also expand and develop them. After you have written a draft of an essay, you may find it useful to double-check each of your examples by asking several questions: How does the example support the generalization? Is the source of the example clear? How does it connect to the readers' experiences? If the example is an extended one, is it sufficiently developed so that it can support the thesis by itself? Then you might think about the examples as a whole: Do they draw on a variety of sources? Do they incorporate both summary and quotation?

Details

In presenting an example, the writer uses many of the same techniques that come into play in description. Descriptive details can come from unlikely places, such as the pushers and products Michiko Kakutani cites as examples to support her claim that advertising has saturated our lives.

> The dead, including Marilyn Monroe (Chanel No. 5), Gene Kelly (Gap khakis) and Fred Astaire (Dirt Devil vacuum cleaners), have been hired as pitchmen, and so have New Delhi paraplegics, who now hawk Coca-Cola under bright red-and-white umbrellas. Even bananas have been colonized as billboard space, with stickers promoting the video release of "Space Jam" and the "Got Milk?" campaign turning up on the fruit. (136)

Drawing on the familiar and unfamiliar, Kakutani's examples catch our attention.

As with description, details are used to make the abstract concrete. If you were writing about an abstract principle such as freedom, for example, you might find yourself writing about one kind of freedom that you particularly value, the freedom that your parents allowed you to make mistakes. You would probably provide a number of examples, and each one might be in the form of a short narrative, but the effectiveness of those narratives will lie in the details you use. Your parents might not have wanted you to go out with a particular person, for instance, but merely stated their reasons and left the decision up to you. You decided not to take their advice, and the result was a "disaster." Spell out the details so that the reader concludes it was a disaster, and you will have made your point effectively.

Organization and Ideas

Whether an essay is developed by multiple examples or a single extended example, it has a major assertion. In your first draft, you may want to state your thesis in one sentence and in an obvious place, such as the end of your introduction. When you revise, however, you may want to play with the placement of the thesis, delaying it until the conclusion. If that's where you decide you want it, check to make sure that everything that precedes the conclusion leads up to it and that the reader has a clear focus on your subject all the way.

You might also try weaving your thesis into the introduction in a subtle way, taking the thesis apart so that it is in bits and pieces, each in its own sentence. If you try that idea, check to make sure that someone reading your introduction will come up with a thesis that closely matches the one-sentence assertion you had in your first draft.

Delaying your thesis or weaving it into your introduction is a subtle way of treating your major assertion. If you are worried these techniques are so subtle that the reader may miss your point, consider getting some mileage out of a title. An imaginative title can serve several purposes: arouse the reader's curiosity, set the tone, highlight the subject, reveal the essay's organization, or pave the way for the thesis. Good titles serve more than one purpose.

When examples are used as the primary mode for an essay, they are usually arranged in chronological or dramatic order, moving from what came first and ending with what came last or beginning with the least dramatic and finishing with the most. To decide which example is the most dramatic, all you need to do is ask some obvious questions: Which is the most important? Which is most likely to affect the reader? Which carries the most impact? You'll probably come up with the same answer for each question. That's the example you should use to cap your essay, the one that all the others should lead up to.

Although all the essays in this chapter have a thesis developed by examples, the examples themselves often cross over into other categories. You will discover that is also the case with your own writing. You may well find yourself using an example that is also a narrative, or, to put it more precisely, a narrative that functions as an example. Other patterns of organization such as a description, an analysis of causal relationships, a comparison, a definition, or an analysis of a process can also serve as examples. The function—to support and develop an assertion—is more important than the label.

Useful Terms

Example An illustration that supports a generalization, usually an assertion, by providing evidence that develops or clarifies it.

Tone A writer's attitude toward the subject and the audience. An author's tone can be contemplative, intense, tongue-in-cheek, aloof, matter of fact—as many kinds as there are tones of voice.

Transition A word, phrase, sentence, or paragraph that carries the reader smoothly from point A to point B. Some transitions, such as time markers (*first, next,* and the like) are obvious; others are more subtle, such as a repeated word or phrase or a synonym for a key term.

POINTERS FOR USING EXAMPLE

Exploring the Topic

1. **What examples can you think of to illustrate your topic?** Are all of them from your own experience? What examples can you find from other sources?
2. **Are your examples pertinent and representative?** Do they fit? Do they illustrate?
3. **Are your examples of equal weight?** Which are relatively unimportant?
4. **How familiar is your audience with each of your examples?**
5. **Which examples best lend themselves to your topic?** In what order would they best be presented?
6. **What point do you want to make?** Do your examples all support that point? Do they lead the reader to your major assertion?
7. **What is your purpose behind your point?** Is your primary aim to express your own feelings, to inform, to persuade, or to entertain?

Drafting the Paper

1. **Know your reader.** It may be that your audience knows little about your subject or that the reader simply hasn't thought much about it; on the other hand, maybe the reader knows a great deal and holds a definite opinion. Once you have made an informed guess about your audience's attitude toward your topic and thesis, reexamine your examples in light of that information. Some may have to be explained in greater detail than others, and the more familiar ones will need to be presented in a new or different light. Use the techniques you would employ in writing descriptive papers.
2. **Know your purpose.** Self-expressive papers are often difficult to write because you are so close to being your own audience. If you are writing with this aim in mind, try making yourself conscious of the personality you project as a writer. Jot down the characteristics you wish to convey about yourself and refer to this list as you revise your paper. While this is a highly self-conscious way to revise, when it is done well, the result appears natural.

Also double-check your examples, making sure that you present them in sufficient detail to communicate fully to your audience. That warning serves as well for informative and persuasive papers. Again, use description to make your examples effective: use sensory detail, compare the unfamiliar to the familiar, be concrete. If you are writing a persuasive paper, use these techniques to appeal to emotions.

3. **Consider extended example.** If an essay rests on one example, choose and develop that illustration with great care. Make sure your example represents its class and that you provide all relevant information. Make as many connections as you can between your example and the class it represents. During revision, you may eliminate some of these references, but at first it's best to have too many.

4. **Consider multiple examples.** Most essays rely on multiple examples to support their points; nevertheless, some examples will be more developed than others. Figure out which examples are particularly striking and develop them, reserving the others for mere mention. To lend breadth and credibility to your point, consider citing statistics, quotations, authorities, and the experience of others. Comment on what you take from other sources in order to make it more your own.

5. **Arrange your examples effectively.** Most essays move from the less dramatic, less important to the most, but examples can also be arranged chronologically or in terms of frequency (from least to most frequent). Like the essay itself, each paragraph should be developed around a central assertion, either stated or implied. In longer papers, groups of paragraphs will support a unifying statement.

6. **Check your transitions.** Take a hard look at what links one example and paragraph to another. The transitions should perform the appropriate function, so you might also check them against the list on p. 109.

7. **Make a point.** Examples so obviously need to lead up to something that it's not hard to make a point. But your point may not be an assertion. Test your thesis by asking whether your point carries any information. If it does, it's an assertion. Say you come

(Continued)

POINTERS FOR USING EXAMPLE *(Continued)*

up with, "We live in a world of time-saving technology." You can think of lots of examples and even narrow down the "we" to "anyone who cooks today." The setting is obviously the kitchen, but is the revised thesis an assertion? Given the information test, it fails. Your audience knows what you are supposedly informing them about. But if you revise and come up with "Electronic gizmos have turned the kitchen into a laboratory," you've given the topic a fresher look, one that does contain information.

Sweatin' for Nothin'

Michael Barlow

Unlike many students at the University of New Orleans, Michael Barlow went straight on to college after graduating from high school. As his essay implies, he is not a fitness freak, although he is engaged in a number of college activities. An education major concentrating in teaching English at the secondary level, he may soon turn up in the classroom on the other side of the desk. No matter what he does, he will try not to emulate Mimi.

What to Look For   Starting and ending an essay are often the most difficult parts of writing. One technique that works well is the one Barlow uses. You'll see that he sets up a framework by first setting out the image of the hamster in the cage and then, in his conclusion, returning to it. The effect is a sense of closure. You can use the same technique by ending your essay with a reference to an idea you bring out in your introduction.

1   During spring break, I visited my family in Fort Worth. It was a pleasant visit, but my, how things have changed. My mother has purchased a Stairmaster and joined a fitness club. My father now jogs at 6:00 every morning, and my sister is contemplating aerobics as one of her first electives when she goes off to college this August. This was not the group of people I last saw in January. These were not the laid-back complacent folks I've known so well. This was not *my* family.

2   One night around 2 a.m., after partying with some friends from high school, I was lying in bed watching Mimi, my pet hamster, crank out revolutions on an exercise wheel. I should have gone to sleep but I was captivated. The creaking of the wheel made me think of the strenuous exercise that seems to have plagued everyone at 301 Lake Country Drive. What was it? What was going on? So I asked myself whether or not Mimi knew that sprinting in a metal cylinder wouldn't get her out of the cage. She probably didn't know—her brain is smaller than a kernel of corn.

117

3   But what about humans? What about my family? I see millions of Americans, like my family, in Spandex outfits and gel-cushioned shoes trying to get out of their cages. Something is wrong with the fitness mania that has swept the Western World, and from watching Mimi I know what it is. Entropy.

4   Entropy is the measure of the amount of energy unavailable for useful work in a system—metaphorically speaking, it is a measure of waste. In our throwaway society, we waste energy at a maddening pace. Coal is lit to make a fire, which produces a lot of carbon dioxide, while heating a small amount of water to make steam, which produces electricity, which lights an incandescent bulb in a room in a house where nobody's home. Basic waste.

5   Exercise mania has crippled our culture. It is no coincidence that we are running out of cheap and available energy while at the same time polluting the air, land, and sea with our waste. According to the laws of physics, entropy diminishes in a closed system, meaning that eventually everything will be reduced to an amorphous, undifferentiated blob. The universe is a closed system. There are some parallels to a hamster cage, and Mimi creates entropy at a noisy rate.

6   What did we do for exercise in those past centuries when people did not act like captive hamsters? If a person chopped down wood or ran a long way, it was because he or she needed fuel or wanted to get somewhere. Now we do such things to fit into new pants or to develop our biceps. We have treadmills, rowing machines, Stairmasters, stationary bikes, NordicTracks, butt busters, and wall climbers, and we labor at them while going nowhere. Absolutely nowhere! We do work that is beyond useless; we do work that takes energy and casts it to the wind like lint. And we don't even enjoy the work. Look at people in a health club. See anybody smiling?

7   There is nothing magical about fitness machines. We can get the exact same result by climbing up stairs in our homes or offices. Take a look at any set of stairs in any building. Anybody in Spandex headed up or down? No. People ride elevators all day, then drive to their fitness centers where they pay to walk up steps.

8   When I was looking at Mimi, I was thinking of Richard Simmons, the King of Entropy, who wants everybody to exercise all the time and has made insane amounts of money saying so. Simmons says that he has raised his metabolism so high that he can eat more without gaining weight. Working out to pig out—an entropy double whammy.

9 I have a solution for such gratuitous narcissism and I think Simmons might find a tearful video in it. Let people on the machines create useable energy as they burn off their flabby thighs and excess baggage. Hook up engines and cams and drive shafts that will rotate turbines and generate electricity. Let exercisers light the health club itself. Let them air condition it. Let the clubs store excess energy and sell it to nearby shop owners at low rates.

10 Better yet, create health clubs whose sole purpose is the generation of energy. Pipe the energy into housing projects. Have energy nights where singles get together to pedal, chat, and swap phone numbers. Build a giant pony wheel that operates a flour mill, a rock crusher, a draw bridge, a BMW repair shop. Have the poles protrude from the wheel with spots for a couple hundred joggers to push the wheel around. Install magazine racks on the poles. Have calorie collections and wattage wars. Make it "cool" to sweat for the betterment of mankind, not just for yourself.

11 We cannot afford much more entropy. If we forget that, we might as well be rodents in cages, running into the night. Just like Mimi.

ORGANIZATION AND IDEAS

 1. The essay has a problem–solution structure. In your own words, what does Barlow describe as the problem?

 2. Paragraphs 5–7 give examples of kinds of exercise. What distinctions does Barlow draw among them?

 3. The solution appears in paragraphs 9–10 and is a humorous one. Summarize it.

 4. What do you find to be the main subject of the essay? Exercise? Fads? Waste? Entropy? American culture? What reasons can you find for your choice?

 5. To what extent, if any, do you agree with Barlow's thesis?

TECHNIQUE AND STYLE

 1. Look up *analogy* in an unabridged dictionary. What analogy does Barlow draw? What does the analogy contribute to the essay?

 2. Paragraph 4 defines *entropy*. How necessary is that definition? What does it add to the essay?

 3. What does the essay gain with the example of Richard Simmons?

 4. Imagine you are one of the people filling up the fitness club. Would you be offended by this essay? Why or why not?

 5. The person behind the words always comes through in an essay, sometimes more clearly than others. Explain why you would or would not want Michael Barlow as a classmate or friend.

SUGGESTIONS FOR WRITING

Journal

1. Take a few minutes to write down what you think about the exercise craze or to record your reaction to a television commercial advertising an exercise product.
2. How does exercise make you feel? Write about why you do or do not enjoy exercising.

Essay

1. Try your own hand at a problem–solution essay, giving detailed examples of both the problem and the solution. Like Barlow, you may want your tone to be humorous, sugarcoating a serious point. As for the problem, you're apt to be surrounded with choices:

   getting enough hours into the day
   scraping tuition together
   keeping up with schoolwork
   deciding which pleasure to indulge
   sorting out family loyalties

   Illustrate the problem by using examples. You may find examples for the solution harder to come by, in which case, like Barlow, you may want to propose something fantastic.

2. If you responded to the first suggestion for a journal entry, then you are already on your way to a rough draft. Think of all the ways people participate in America's fitness craze. What do they do? How do they do it? What do they get out of it? What are its hazards? Benefits? To what extent are you involved? Write an essay in which you explore what you think about the subject, providing examples to support your thesis.

Stop Ordering Me Around

Stacey Wilkins

Like many students, Stacey Wilkins worked in a restaurant waiting on tables, a job that helped her pay off a student loan but one that also extracts a price of its own, as her essay points out. The essay appeared in the January 4, 1993, issue of Newsweek *in a regular feature, the "My Turn" column. Wilkins' serving days are now in the past, though her experiences and memories of those days linger. At present, she is teaching English at a school in Connecticut and has the pleasure of being on the other side of the table. She now belongs to the same group as her* Newsweek *audience—educated, middle-class Americans more likely to patronize the kind of restaurant where Wilkins worked than the local fast-food place.*

What to Look For   The narrative that opens Wilkins' essay serves as the primary example in the essay, and one that sets the essay's tone as well. As you read the essay, try to hear it so that you can identify her tone more exactly. At times, the tone may strike you as angry, hurt, bitter, sarcastic, and any number of other variations. How would you characterize it?

1   I had just sat an extra hour and a half waiting for some country-club tennis buddies to finish a pizza. They came in 15 minutes after the restaurant closed—they hadn't wanted to cut short their tennis match. The owner complied and agreed to turn the oven back on and make them a pizza. The cook had long since gone home.

2   The customers had no problem demanding service after I explained that the restaurant had closed. They had no problem sitting there until well after 11 o'clock to recount the highlights of their tennis game (the restaurant closed at 9:30 p.m.). And, most important, they had no problem making me the brunt of their cruel little post-tennis match. What fun it was to harass the pathetic little waitress. "Oh, it's just so nice sitting here like this," one man said. After getting no response, he continued: "Boy, I guess you want us to leave." I was ready to explode in anger. "I am not going to respond to your comments," I said, and walked away.

3   He was geared up for a fight. The red flag had been waved. The man approached me and asked about dessert. A regular customer, he had never made a practice of ordering dessert before. You know, the '90s low-fat thing. But that night he enjoyed the power. He felt strong, I felt violated.

4   Three dollars and 20 cents later, I went home. Their tip was my payment for this emotional rape. As I drove, tears streamed down my face. Why was I crying? I had been harassed before. Ten years of waitressing should have inured me to this all-too-common situation. But this was a watershed: the culmination of a decade of abuse.

5   I am now at the breaking point. I can't take being the public's punching bag. People seem to think abuse is included in the price of an entree. All sense of decency and manners is checked with their coats at the door. They see themselves in a position far superior to mine. They are the kings. I am the peasant.

6   I would like them to be the peasants. I am a strong advocate of compulsory restaurant service in the United States. What a great comeuppance it would be for the oppressors to have to work a double shift—slinging drinks, cleaning up after kids and getting pissed off that a party of 10 tied up one of their tables for three hours and left a bad tip. Best of all, I would like to see that rude man with tomato sauce on his tennis shorts.

7   Eating in a restaurant is about more than eating food. It is an opportunity to take your frustrations out on the waiter. It is a chance to feel better than the person serving your food. People think there is nothing wrong with rudeness or sexual harassment if it is inflicted on a waiter.

8   Customers have no problem with ignoring the wait staff when they go to take an order. Or they won't answer when the waiter comes to the table laden with hot plates asking who gets what meal. My personal pet peeve is when they make a waiter take a separate trip for each item. "Oh, I'll take another Coke." The waiter asks, "Would anyone else like one?" No response. Inevitably when he comes back to the table someone will say, "I'll have a Coke, too." And so on and so on.

9   I find it odd because no matter what an insolent cad someone might be, they generally make an effort to cover it up in public. The majority of people practice common etiquette. Most individuals won't openly cut in line or talk throughout a movie. People are cognizant of acceptable behavior and adhere to the strictures it demands. That common code of decency does not apply while eating out.

10   Food-service positions are the last bastion of accepted prejudice. People go into a restaurant and openly torment the waiter, leave a small tip and don't think twice about it. Friends allow companions to be rude and don't say a word. The friends of this man did not once tell him to stop taunting me. They remained silent.

11   It doesn't cross their minds that someone has just been rotten to another human being. I have yet to hear someone stick up for the waitress, to insist a person stop being so cruel. This is because people don't think anything wrong has occurred.

12   However, if this man had shouted obscenities at another patron about her ethnicity, say, it would have rightly been

deemed unacceptable. Why don't people understand that bad manners are just as unacceptable in a restaurant? Why do they think they have license to mistreat restaurant personnel?

13   I believe it is because food-service workers are relegated to such a low position on the social stratum. Customers have the power. Food-service employees have none. Thus we are easy targets for any angry person's pent-up frustrations. What better sparring partner than one who can't fight back? Most waiters won't respond for fear of losing their jobs. Consequently, we are the designated gripe-catchers of society, along with similar service workers.

14   If people stepped down from their spurious pedestals, they might see how wrong they are. We have dreams and aspirations just like everyone else. Our wages finance those dreams. Even an insulting 10 percent tip helps us to move toward a goal, pay the rent, feed the kids.

15   I'm using my earnings to pay off an encumbering graduate-school debt. Our bus girl is financing her education at the University of Pennsylvania. My manager is saving for her first baby. Another waitress is living on her earnings while she pursues an acting career. The dishwasher sends his pay back to his children in Ecuador.

16   Our dreams are no less valid than those of someone who holds a prestigious job at a large corporation. A restaurant's flexible working hours appeal to many people who dislike the regimen of a 9-to-5 day. Our employment doesn't give someone the right to treat us as nonentities. I deserve respect whether I remain a waitress or move on to a different career. And so do the thousands of waiters and waitresses who make your dining experience a pleasant one.

ORGANIZATION AND IDEAS

1. How does the opening narrative set the scene? Where else in the essay do you find references to that narrative? Do they unify the essay or distract you? Why?
2. At what point in the essay does the author move from the particular to the general? Which gets the most emphasis?
3. Reexamine the essay as one that poses a problem and a solution. What is the problem? The solution?
4. To what extent does Wilkins' experience coincide with your own? That of your friends?
5. Where do you find Wilkins' thesis? Explain whether you find that placement effective.

TECHNIQUE AND STYLE

1. How would you characterize the author's tone?
2. Does the opening narrative enlist your sympathies? Why or why not?
3. Some readers may find the essay's aim is more expressive than expository or persuasive, that the author is more concerned with venting her feelings than explaining the problem or persuading her readers to resolve it. Make a case for your interpretation of the author's aim.
4. In paragraph 2, Wilkins repeats variations on "they had no problem." Explain whether you find the repetition effective.
5. At various times in the essay, Wilkins uses words that suggest she is really writing about issues of power and class, as in her use of "peasant" (paragraphs 5 and 6) and "low position on the social stratum" (paragraph 13). What other examples can you find? Would the essay be stronger or weaker if these issues were discussed more openly?

SUGGESTIONS FOR WRITING

Journal

1. We live in a service society, yet as Wilkins points out, sometimes we demand too much of those who provide the services. Record a few examples of rudeness that you have observed.
2. Write an entry recording your reaction to Wilkins' essay. Do you think her complaints are justified?

Essay

1. More than likely you have or have had a job similar to Wilkins', if not waiting on tables then some other low-paying job that is also low on the totem pole of status. Like Wilkins, you may have found you were (or are) not treated with respect. On the other hand, your experience may be quite the opposite. Write an essay in which you use examples from your own experience or the experiences of others to explain how you were (or are) treated on your job. You will want to narrow your subject so that you can cover it thoroughly in three to five pages, so you might focus on a specific category of people:
   customers
   co-workers
   supervisor(s)
2. Wilkins raises the issues of power and class in her essay (see paragraphs 5, 6, and 13), but as Americans we like to think we live in a classless society. Think about the idea of class and write an essay in

which you test the validity of the claim of classlessness. Make sure you define what you mean by class, and use examples from the news and any other sources to support your thesis.

A Black Fan of Country Music Finally Tells All

Lena Williams

Lena Williams started her career in journalism as a reporter for a radio station while she was a student at Howard University. After earning her BA at Howard, she entered the Columbia University Graduate School of Journalism, from which she received an MSc. She worked as a reporter while she was an intern at the Washington Post, *then as an associate editor at* Black Sports Magazine, *and has been on the staff of the* New York Times *since 1974, first as a clerk, then trainee, and now senior writer. She has written on civil rights, lifestyles, metropolitan news, and sports, winning various publishing awards along the way. An article she originally wrote for the* Times *in 1997 is now a book,* It's the Little Things: The Everyday Interactions That Get under the Skin of Blacks and Whites *(2000). Since 1998, she has moved from being a lifestyles writer to sports. The essay that follows appeared on Sunday, June 19, 1994, in the* Times' *"Arts and Leisure" section's coverage of "Pop Music." The column was titled "Pop View."*

What to Look For   At times, you may find yourself writing an essay on a subject that you're somewhat embarrassed about, which is the position Lena Williams found herself in when she wrote the essay that follows. In that case, you'll need to make a decision about your tone, the attitude you take toward your subject and your audience. Williams, as you will see, takes an unapologetic stance, almost daring her readers to challenge her. Yet the overall tone of the essay is not antagonistic because she takes the edge off of her "challenge" with humor and personal narrative, techniques that you can incorporate into your own writing.

1   I heard that Reba McEntire's new album, "Read My Mind," shot to No. 5 on the Billboard chart the first weekend of its release.

2   Well, she got my $11.95.

3   I'm a 40-something black woman who spent her youth in Washington, lip-syncing to the Supremes and slow dancing to the Temptations. Now I often come home to my Manhattan apartment and put on Vince Gill, Randy Travis or Reba. Consider me a fan of country music. So there. Deal with it.

4   For most of my adult life, I was a closet country music fan. I'd hide my Waylon Jennings and Willie Nelson albums between the dusty, psychedelic rock. I'd listen to Dolly Parton on my earphones, singing along softly, afraid my neighbors might mistake my imitation twang for a cry for help. I'd enter a music store, looking over my shoulder in search of familiar faces and flip through the rhythm-and-blues section for about five minutes before sneaking off to the country aisle where I'd surreptitiously grab a Travis Tritt tape off the rack and make a beeline for the shortest cashier's line.

5   Just when I'd reached for my American Express card, I'd spot a tall, dark, handsome type in an Armani suit standing behind me with a puzzled look. What's he going to think? "The sister seems down, but what's she doing with that Dwight Yoakum CD?"

6   So now I'm publicly coming out of the closet and proclaiming my affection for country perennials like Ms. McEntire.

7   When I told a friend I was preparing this confessional, he offered a word of caution: "No self-respecting black person would ever admit to that in public."

8   I thought about his comment. As a child growing up in the 1950's, in a predominantly black community, I wasn't allowed to play country-and-western music in my house. Blacks weren't supposed to like country—or classical for that matter—but that's another story. Blacks' contribution to American music was in jazz, blues and funk. Country music was dismissed as poor white folks' blues and associated with regions of the nation that symbolized prejudice and racial bigotry. Even mainstream white America viewed country as lower class and less desirable, often poking fun at its twangy chords and bellyaching sentiments.

9   But I was always a cowgirl at heart. I liked country's wild side; its down-home, aw-shucks musicians with the yodel in their voices and the angst in their lyrics. I saw an honesty in country and its universal

tales of love lost and found. Besides, the South didn't have a monopoly on racial hatred, and country artists, like everybody else, were stealing black music, so why should I hold it against country?

10   And while snickering at country, white America also demonstrated a similar cultural backwardness toward black music, be it gospel, ragtime or the blues. So I allowed country to enter my heart and my mind, in spite of its faults. Indeed, when prodded, some blacks who rejected country conceded that there was a spirituality that resounded in the music and that in its heartfelt sentiment, country was a lot like blues. Yet they could never bring themselves to spend hard-earned dollars on Hank Williams Jr.

11   The 1980's saw country (western was dropped, much to my chagrin) become mainstream. Suddenly there was country at the Copa and at Town Hall. WYNY-FM radio in New York now claims the largest audience of any country station, with more than one million listeners. Dolly Parton and Kenny Rogers became movie stars. Garth Brooks became an American phenomenon.

12   Wall Street investment bankers bought cowboy boots and hats and learned to do the two-step. And black and white artists like Patti LaBelle and Lyle Lovett and Natalie Cole and Ms. McEntire now sing duets and clearly admire one another's music.

13   Perhaps the nation's acceptance of country has something to do with an evolutionary change in the music. Country has got edge. It has acquired an attitude. Womens' voices have been given strength. Oh, the hardship and misery is still there. But the stuff about "standing by your man" has changed to a more assertive posture.

14   In "I Won't Stand in Line," a song on Ms. McEntire's new album, she makes it clear to a skirt-chasing lover that "I'd do almost anything just to make you mine, but I won't stand in line." That line alone makes me think of Aretha Franklin's "Respect."

15   One other thing: I don't like sad songs. I've cried enough for a lifetime. Country makes me laugh, always has. Maybe because it never took itself so seriously. Think about it. "Drop-Kick Me, Jesus, Through the Goal Posts of Life." "A Boy Named Sue."

16   Ms. McEntire serves up a humorous touch in "Why Haven't I Heard From You." "That thing they call the telephone/ Now there's one on every corner, in the back of every bar/ You can get one in your briefcase, on a plane or in your car/ So tell me why haven't I heard from you, darlin', honey, what is your excuse?" Call it Everywoman's lament.

17   Well it's off my chest; and it feels good.

18   I will no longer make excuses for my musical tastes. Not when millions are being made by performers exhorting listeners to "put your hands in the air and wave 'em like you just don't care."

19   Compare that with the haunting refrain of Ms. McEntire's "I Think His Name Was John," a song about a woman, a one-night stand and AIDS: "She lays all alone and cries herself to sleep/ 'Cause she let a stranger kill her hopes and her dreams/ And in the end when she was barely hanging on/ All she could say is she thinks his name was John."

ORGANIZATION AND IDEAS

1. What paragraph or paragraphs introduce the essay?
2. Paragraphs 4 and 5 detail a short narrative. What is Williams' point?
3. Paragraphs 8–12 sketch the evolution of country-and-western music. Trace the chronology and the changes in attitude toward the genre.
4. The essay ends with a comparison in paragraphs 18 and 19, one that Williams doesn't spell out. What is it? How does it relate to her thesis?
5. Williams maintains that since the 1980s, country music has "become mainstream" (paragraph 11). How accurate is that assertion?

TECHNIQUE AND STYLE

1. Paragraphs 2 and 17 consist of one sentence each. What effect does Williams achieve with a one-sentence paragraph?
2. Is the essay addressed primarily to a black or white audience or both? What evidence can you find to support your view?
3. Although the essay expresses Williams' personal opinion and is subjective, she achieves a balance between the personal and the general. How does she do that?
4. Williams supports her thesis with examples from popular music, both country-western and black. Explain whether you find her examples sufficient evidence for her thesis.
5. Analyze the effectiveness of the essay's title. What other titles can you think of? Which is the more effective and why?

SUGGESTIONS FOR WRITING

Journal

1. Taste in music, as in most everything else, is apt to be idiosyncratic. Think of a band or song or type of music that represents your particular taste and explain why you like it, using examples to support your ideas.

2. Make a list of the names and titles Williams uses as examples. What examples can you provide to update that list?

Essay

1. If you look back on your tastes, you will probably find that they change over time. Perhaps a type of music that you liked some years ago you would now have a hard time listening to. Or perhaps you were disappointed in a film you recently saw again or a book that you reread, one that had impressed you in the past and belonged to a particular genre such as horror films or adventure stories. You might start by drawing up two columns—*Then* and *Now*—and jotting down examples representing your earlier tastes and your present ones. Like Williams, you may want to write about how your taste has evolved or explain why you like what you like. For a general category, you might think about

> music
> food
> films
> books
> heroes
> sports

2. Williams' essay is an assertive defense of her taste in music. Write an essay in which you evaluate the essay's effectiveness. You might start by asking yourself questions such as, "Does she present enough evidence?" "Are her examples apt?" "Does she provide enough background for her explanations?"

Step Away from the Bear

Laura Lee

> *Armed with a degree in theatre from Oakland University and a good sense of humor, Laura Lee started off in radio by writing commercials, then moved on to reporting, conducting interviews, and writing for shows, finally becoming the morning announcer and program director at a Leesburg, Virginia, station. She now devotes herself full-time to her own writing, and her articles have*

appeared in magazines such as Smithsonian *and* Preservation. *She has written nine books and appears to have an encyclopedic knowledge about almost everything. A sampling of Lee's titles gives you some idea of her varied interests:* The Pocket Encyclopedia of Aggravation *(2001),* The Elvis Impersonator Kit: A Step by Step Guide to Becoming the King *(2006), and* 100 Most Dangerous Things in Everyday Life and What You Can Do About Them *(2004). The essay that follows is from the latter and was reprinted in the* Week *on August 6, 2004.*

What to Look For   You may have been warned to choose one grammatical point of view and stick to it. But it's possible, and often effective, to use more than one as long as you have a good reason to make the switch. As you read Lee's essay, note the personal pronouns she uses and consider why she makes those choices.

1   Fact: More people are killed each year by teddy bears than by grizzly bears.

2   The assertion above defies conventional wisdom, but it's true nonetheless. Grizzlies may have knives for teeth and claws like razors, but they're seldom found in the bedroom. A teddy bear's primary habitat, on the other hand, is under the covers. Particularly sinister ones have been known to sneak in button eyes that can be swallowed, loose fur that can be choked upon, and a host of debilitating viruses and bacteria that were picked up at the nursery school.

3   Human beings, in general, tend to overestimate the dangers of rare events while dismissing the dangers of everyday ones. In fact, everyday events are more likely to cause you harm if for no other reason than they happen every day.

4   We're also much more likely to fear man-made problems than natural ones. Some risk consultants believe our level of fear tends to correspond more to our level of "outrage" than to our actual level of risk. This is why, for example, we're more worried about getting AIDS from a blood transfusion than about being struck by lightning—when, in fact, the latter is 30 times more likely to occur than the former.

5   We travel less by plane than we do by car, so we fear it more, even though we're much more likely to die in an automobile. We

worry about engineered chemicals even though many foods contain far more natural carcinogens. We worry about being assaulted in the streets but not about being injured in the kitchen (where, in America, for example, 1 million people are seriously hurt each year), the living room (where 400,000 are injured annually), or the bathroom (site of more than 150,000 serious accidents each year).

6   So what's one to do? Never climb out of bed? (Not a good idea; see below.) The truth is, you can't create a risk-free environment no matter how hard you try. Protecting against one thing often leads to another unintended consequence.

7   Consider the following:

8   **Books:** If you think you can avoid injury by shunning sports and curling up with a good book, think again. If there were a manual on the proper use of books, quite a few people would cut their fingers on its pages, then trip over the cover on the way to get a bandage. Books are an often overlooked hazard, sending more people to emergency rooms than many common sports. In the United Kingdom, more people are hurt by books each year (2,707) than by training weights (1,884) or trampolines (1,902). And lest you think only British books are hazardous, you should know that in an average year, 10,683 U.S. citizens lose their battles with what the U.S. Consumer Product Safety Commission's National Electronic Injury Surveillance System categorizes as "books, magazines, albums, or scrapbooks," and that another 1,490 are clobbered by magazine racks or bookends.

9   What are so many people doing wrong? "From working with books for many years," said Karen Miller of the American Library Association, "I could offer up things like broken toes when books fall, losing one's balance when reaching for books, and repetitive stress from shelving them. Magazines could also be dangerous if the staples are loose and scrape the skin."

10   The heft of books is a special problem. Back injuries from moving overloaded boxes of books are common. Heavy school bags are also a concern. In 2003, a Hong Kong schoolboy was killed when his heavy book bag pulled him over the railing of his high-rise apartment.

11   **Chairs:** *The Texas Chair Massacre.* Okay, so it doesn't have quite the ring to it that *The Texas Chainsaw Massacre* has, but the fact of the matter is, chairs are more than 13 times as likely to cause injuries as chain saws.

12   Each year, more than 410,000 Americans have seating mishaps. Most of these injuries come from falls. You lean back too far in that office chair and *whoo-aaa-ahh!*

13   But there are other risks as well. The U.S. Consumer Product Safety Commission recently announced the voluntary recall of 142,000 zippered beanbag chairs because children can unzip the bags, then crawl inside and suffocate. At least five children have met their deaths this way.

14   Meanwhile, according to *The Wall Street Journal*, most of the lower-back pain in America is caused by long stretches of chair sitting. Back pain costs the U.S. economy $70 billion a year.

15   **Clothing:** It hangs in your closet and lurks in your drawers. Next thing you know, it is wrapped around your body, where it can maim or kill.

16   Yes, your clothing can be the death of you. In England, 9,635 people are injured in an average year by socks, 3,965 by trousers, 1,573 by coats, 1,353 by sweaters, and 311 by underwear. In the U.S. each year, an estimated 110,463 people are hurt by clothes and accessories. This is about 100,000 more people than are injured each year by fireworks, and almost 96,000 more than are hurt by nail guns.

17   **Cotton swabs:** With their soft cushions of cotton at either end, cotton swabs appear perfectly safe. But don't let them fool you. Those simple little bathroom tools send more people to the hospital than razor blades or shavers—more than twice as many.

18   Why are so many people walking into the hospital after bouts with these soft, white swabbers? For the most part, it is because they do not follow the directions. Boxes of these fearsome items contain stern warnings in many countries. Do not, under any circumstances, put cotton swabs into your ears, they advise. Sure, they may look like they were designed to clean out your ears, but the people who make them insist they were not. Clean your ears at your own risk.

19   In fact, the experts say, using cotton swabs to remove earwax is a bit like using a broom on a dirt floor. It just moves things around. Instead of making your ears cleaner, it pushes the gunk farther down the ear canal, where it makes things worse. Between 1992 and 1997, more than 100 people in the United States experienced a serious eardrum injury as a result of cleaning their ears with swabs.

20   A torn eardrum, however, is a mild injury compared with the damage that can be done by the hapless swabber who gets distracted and trips or bangs his arm, forcing the stick so far into the ear canal that it hits the small bones in the middle ear.

21   Fortunately, there are safety measures you can adopt. The ear canals are self-cleaning. Actions of the jaw, such as talking and chewing, help to "massage" the wax out of the ear canal. Instead of swabbing, then, simply have a conversation. Here's a starter: "What does the Q in Q-Tip stand for, anyway?" (The answer, by the way, is "quality.") Another: Q-Tips were originally marketed as Baby Gays. Discuss.

22   In any event, remember to keep cotton swabs out of your ears and use them for the many other tasks for which you buy them.

23   **Hospitals:** What kills the most Americans each year? Hospital visits. In fact, deaths attributable to hospital-acquired infections kill more people each year than car crashes and homicides combined. One out of every 20 people who enter a hospital leaves with an infection he did not have when he arrived. Hospital infections are common enough to have their own name: nosocomials. They affect nearly 2 million people each year; between 20,000 and 90,000 people die from them.

24   Hospitals are big, often poorly ventilated buildings filled with people who have germs of every description. Patients share close quarters and often come into contact with the same hospital equipment. This gives microbes ample opportunity to travel. Meanwhile, new medical technologies are increasing the risk of serious infection, because the various catheters and implants probe ever deeper into the body and stay there longer.

25   Yet one of the most common ways that germs travel from patient to patient is also the most preventable. According to the American Medical News Service, 34 separate studies have shown that doctors are not washing their hands regularly between patients. The Hospital of Saint Raphael's Hand Hygiene Resource Center, in New Haven, Conn., estimates that professionals only wash their hands thoroughly about 40 percent of the time.

26   **Natural Foods:** Warning—the following foods contain chemicals that have been proven to cause cancer in laboratory animals: apples, broccoli, carrots, bread, celery, grapes, lettuce, tomatoes, sweet potatoes, parsley, onions, mangoes.

27   In 1996, according to the American Cancer Society, there were approximately 555,000 deaths from cancer in the United States.

Many health-conscious people try to reduce their odds of developing the disease by avoiding food that contains "chemicals." They're out of luck. There is no such thing. The only difference between processed and organic foods is that processed foods have synthetic chemicals and organic foods get their chemicals from nature.

28 Healthy fruits and vegetables, even when grown without pesticides, still contain cancer-causing nitrates. The National Academy of Sciences estimates that 72 percent of nitrate exposure to the mouth and esophagus comes from vegetables and only about 9 percent comes from oft-maligned cured meats.

29 **Stairs:** There is a method of transportation that produces more nonfatal injuries each year than motor vehicle accidents. It can produce twice the G-forces of a roller coaster doing a loop. This deadly method of locomotion is, of course, the staircase. Every year, an estimated 1,091 American stair climbers are killed and 769,400 are injured.

30 What is it about a simple step that can be so deadly? The answer is, nothing—but the missteps will kill you. An extensive 1995 study of stair use (someone has to do it) revealed that a noticeable misstep occurred every 2,222 steps. While people usually say they "slip" on the stairs, the fact is they fall so fast they don't really know what happened. Generally, people misjudge the distance and plant one of their feet wrong. It only takes one-quarter of an inch difference between where the stair is and where you expect it to be to throw you off balance.

31 **Staying in bed:** Sorry, you're not safe there either. In the United States, 411,689 people a year experience injuries related to beds, mattresses, and pillows.

32 If you want extra security, you could trade in your bed for a safety model with side rails, the kind used in hospitals and nursing homes. But be forewarned: From 1985 to 2001, the U.S. Food and Drug Administration received 479 reports of patients becoming trapped in hospital beds; 297 of them died.

33 But you can't say you haven't been warned about hospitals.

ORGANIZATION AND IDEAS

1. What paragraph or paragraphs provide Lee's introduction? Her conclusion? How are the two connected?
2. Lee builds her essay around eight examples. What reasons can you find for the order in which she presents them?
3. Paragraph 3 presents Lee's working thesis. What do paragraphs 4 and 5 add to it?

4. Consider your answers to question 3 and combine those ideas with the ones in paragraph 3. In your own words, state the essay's full thesis.
5. Which of the examples is the most interesting? Why?

TECHNIQUE AND STYLE

1. Lee has chosen to set off her examples by using boldface type and full colons. How effective is that choice?
2. Though Lee's essay depends primarily on examples, she also employs comparisons and considers causes and effects. To what extent do these other patterns add to or detract from the essay?
3. Lee begins with *we* (paragraphs 4–5), switches to *one* and *you* in paragraph 6, and then sticks with *you* for much of what follows. What reasons can you think of for her choices of point of view?
4. Though some of Lee's facts seem preposterous, she has obviously done a lot of research. What does it contribute to the essay? To her persona?
5. The essay takes a humorous look at serious problems—injury and death. How would you characterize Lee's tone? What sort of humor is this?

SUGGESTIONS FOR WRITING

Journal

1. Given the brief biography of Lee and what you know about her from her essay, what sort of person does she seem to be? Write a brief description of her.
2. Lee writes about what we should fear that we don't, though we should. Set a timer for ten minutes and use your journal to write what you associate with the word *fear*. After the ten minutes is up, reread your entry and sum it up in one sentence. The result can be a thesis for an essay.

Essay

1. Think about the times you felt fear. Where were you? What caused it? Which incident was worse? Why? If nothing comes to mind, consider one of these suggestions:
   heights
   dogs (or cats)
   public speaking
   snakes (or spiders)
   the unknown
   Use your ideas to write an essay in which you depend on examples to support your main point.

2. Lee maintains we are "much more likely to fear man-made problems than natural ones" (paragraph 3). Analyze the degree to which her statement is true by jotting down examples of problems that are man-made—such as ID theft, terrorist attacks, transmission of AIDS—versus those that are natural—such as lightning, flood, forest fire. Add to those examples and then select the most appropriate ones to use in an essay that tests Lee's claim.

Bananas for Rent

Michiko Kakutani

Anyone who reads the book reviews in the New York Times *is familiar with Michiko Kakutani's byline, for she's the lead reviewer for the newspaper, covering both fiction and nonfiction, bestowing both praise and punches. As you might suspect, that sort of extensive analytical reading makes her an astute critic of the contemporary scene, so it was only fitting that she also contributed to the column "Culture Zone" in the* New York Times Magazine, *a column in which Ms. Kakutani takes a tough view of popular culture. Her wide range of interests is reflected in her book* Poet at the Piano: Portraits of Writers, Filmmakers, and Other Artists at Work *(1988). In 1998, Ms. Kakutani was awarded the Pulitzer Prize for Criticism. Her essay "Bananas for Rent" was a "Culture Zone" piece published on November 9, 1997.*

What to Look For   If you are writing about the contemporary scene and using examples to back up your points, you may find that some of your readers may not be familiar with the examples you use. One way out of that bind is to use lots. That is what Kakutani does in her essay, so be on the lookout for multiple examples as you read. It's easiest to think of multiple examples when you are making notes for an essay. If you were writing about blue jeans, for instance, you might be tempted to just name Levi's, but at that point, it's also easy to think of other brand names as well—Guess, Gap, Gloria Vanderbilt, and the like.

1   They are as pervasive as roaches, as persuasive as the weather, as popular as Princess Diana. They adorn our clothes, our luggage, our sneakers and our hats. They are ubiquitous on television, unavoidable in magazines and inevitable on the Internet. The average American, it is estimated, is pelted by some 3,000 advertising messages a day, some 38,000 TV commercials a year.

2   Not so long ago, it was only race cars, tennis stars and sports stadiums that were lacquered head-to-toe with ads. Nowadays, school buses and trucks rent out advertising space by the foot. There are entire towns that have signed exclusive deals with Coke or Pepsi. The dead, including Marilyn Monroe (Chanel No. 5), Gene Kelly (Gap khakis) and Fred Astaire (Dirt Devil vacuum cleaners), have been hired as pitchmen, and so have New Delhi paraplegics, who now hawk Coca-Cola under bright red-and-white umbrellas. Even bananas have been colonized as billboard space, with stickers promoting the video release of "Space Jam" and the "Got Milk?" campaign turning up on the fruit.

3   As the scholar James Twitchell observes, advertising has become "our cultural literacy—it's what we know." Twitchell, author of a book called *Adcult USA* and a professor at the University of Florida, says his students share no common culture of books or history; what they share is a knowledge of commercials. When he questions them at random about concepts from "The Dictionary of Cultural Literacy," he says he is likely to draw a blank. When, however, he recites a commercial jingle, his students "instantaneously know it, and they're exultant," he says. "They actually think Benetton ads are profound. To them, advertising is high culture."

4   Schoolchildren around the country avidly collect Absolut ads, and college students decorate their walls with poster-size reproductions of ads that are available from a four-year-old company called Beyond the Wall. Forget Monet and Van Gogh. Think Nike, BMW and Calvin Klein. As Brian Gordon, one of the company's founders, sees it, kids regard ads as "a form of self-expression." In today's "short-attention society," he reasons, ads are something people can relate to: they provide "insights into current culture," and they provide them in 30 seconds or less.

5   No doubt this is why entire "Seinfeld" episodes have been built around products like Pez and Junior Mints. The popularity of Nick at Nite's vintage commercials, Rosie O'Donnell's peppy renditions

of old jingles, the almost nightly commercial spoofs by Letterman and Leno—all are testaments to the prominent role advertising has assumed in our lives. A whole school of fiction known as Kmart realism has grown up around the use of brand names, while a host of well-known songs (from Nirvana's "Smells Like Teen Spirit" to Oasis' "Shakermaker") satirize old commercials. It used to be that advertisers would appropriate a hit song (like the Beatles' "Revolution") to promote a product; nowadays, the advertising clout of a company like Volkswagen has the power to turn a song (even an old song like "Da Da Da," by the now defunct German band Trio) into a hit.

6   So what does advertising's takeover of American culture mean? It's not just that the world has increasingly come to resemble the Home Shopping Network. It's that advertising's ethos of spin— which makes selling a means *and* an end—has thoroughly infected everything from politics (think of Clinton's "permanent campaign") to TV shows like "Entertainment Tonight" that try to pass off publicity as information. It's that advertising's attention-grabbing hype has become, in our information-glutted age, the modus operandi of the world at large. "Advertising is the most pervasive form of propaganda in human history," says the scholar Mark Crispin Miller. "It's reflected in every esthetic form today."

7   Miller points out that just as commercials have appropriated techniques that once belonged to avant-garde film—cross-cutting, jump cuts, hand-held camera shots—so have mainstream movies and TV shows begun to ape the look and shape of ads, replacing character and story with razzle-dazzle special effects. For that matter, more and more film makers, including Howard Zieff, Michael Bay, Adrian Lyne and Simon West, got their starts in advertising.

8   Advertising has a more insidious effect as well. Advertisers scouting TV shows and magazines are inclined to select those vehicles likely to provide a congenial (and therefore accessible or upbeat) backdrop for their products, while a public that has grown up in a petri dish of ads has grown impatient with any art that defies the easy-access, quick-study esthetic of commercials—that is, anything that's difficult or ambiguous. "People have become less capable of tolerating any kind of darkness or sadness," Miller says. "I think it ultimately has to do with advertising, with a vision of life as a shopping trip."

9   There are occasional signs of a backlash against advertising— the Vancouver-based Media Foundation uses ad parodies to fight

rampant consumerism—but advertising implacably forges ahead like one of those indestructible sci-fi monsters, nonchalantly co-opting the very techniques used against it. Just as it has co-opted rock-and-roll, alienation (a Pontiac commercial features an animated version of Munch's painting "The Scream") and Dadaist jokes (an ad campaign for Kohler featured interpretations of bidets and faucets by contemporary artists), so it has now co-opted irony, parody and satire.

10 The end result of advertising's ability to disguise itself as entertainment and entertainment's willingness to adopt the hard-sell methods of advertising is a blurring of the lines between art and commerce. Even as this makes us increasingly oblivious to advertising's agenda (to sell us stuff), it also makes us increasingly cynical about everything else—ready to dismiss it, unthinkingly, as junk or fluff or spin, just another pitch lobbed out by that gigantic machine called contemporary culture.

ORGANIZATION AND IDEAS

1. Kakutani's opening sentence announces qualities that unify the essay that follows. What paragraph or paragraphs focus on ads as "pervasive"? As "persuasive"? As "popular"?
2. Which paragraphs emphasize the effect of ads? What effect do they have?
3. Reread the first and last paragraphs. What is the thesis of the essay? What evidence can you cite to back up your opinion?
4. To what extent do you agree with Kakutani's thesis?
5. Kakutani maintains that advertising "disguise[s] itself as entertainment" (paragraph 10). How accurate do you find that assertion?

TECHNIQUE AND STYLE

1. Kakutani violates a principle of usage in her first paragraph in that the pronoun "they" has no antecedent. What effect does she achieve by not initially specifying to whom the "they" refers?
2. Ads and the culture within which they exist come in for much negative criticism in this essay. How would you characterize Kakutani's tone—negative, reasoned, thoughtful, strident, what?
3. Describe what you perceive to be Kakutani's persona. What evidence can you find to support your view?
4. In a handbook of grammar and usage, look up the uses of the dash. You'll note that Kakutani uses dashes frequently, as in paragraphs 3, and 5–10.

What other punctuation could she have used? What reasons can you think of for her choice of the dash?

5. Kakutani uses three similes in her first sentence. Choose one of them and make up three or four of your own. Which do you prefer and why?

SUGGESTIONS FOR WRITING

Journal

1. Anyone who watches television learns to hate certain ads. Take a minute to write down the ads you dislike the most and then, for each, put down the reasons. You'll end up with the working notes for an essay.

2. Kakutani states that thanks to ads we are becoming "increasingly cynical about everything else—ready to dismiss it, unthinkingly, as junk or fluff or spin, just another pitch lobbed out by that gigantic machine called contemporary culture" (paragraph 10). Write an entry in which you agree or disagree with Kakutani's statement, citing examples to support your views.

Essay

1. Whether or not you agree with Kakutani, there's no arguing about the prevalence of advertisements. To test Kakutani's points or simply to analyze advertisements on your own, flip through a popular magazine noting various categories of advertisements—cars, liquor, clothes, perfumes, and the like. Choosing a group of ads for a type of product, examine it as though it were a window into our culture. What do you see? What does it say about our concerns? Fears? Attention span? Tastes? Use your notes to write an essay that illustrates its points through multiple examples. If advertising doesn't seem to be a worthwhile subject, then choose another topic that you can use as a way to examine popular culture. Here are some suggestions:

   television shows
   films
   books
   styles
   fads
   franchises

2. What television ads do you remember and like? Make a short list (it only needs to make sense to you), and then select one to explain why you like it.

ADDITIONAL WRITING ASSIGNMENTS

Using Example

What does it mean to be a "good" employee, student, parent, friend, citizen, co-worker, or leader?

What is your idea of a "perfect" day, class, celebration, vacation, or meal?

What is your favorite television show, kind of music, fattening food, sport, or pastime? Offer examples to support your thesis.

What should an entering freshman know about registration, the faculty, courses, majors, or extracurricular activities? Use examples to support your thesis.

Evaluating the Essays

1. Though their subjects are different, Michael Barlow and Lena Williams both write about aspects of popular culture and both use humor. Reread both essays to determine which of the two you like better. Write an essay in which you make a case for your opinion, drawing examples from both of the essays.

2. The idea of persona, the person behind the *I* in an essay, comes through very clearly in the essays by Stacey Wilkins and Lena Williams. Reread the essays, noting as you read the various characteristics of each person. Of the two, which would you prefer to know and why? Use examples from the essays as evidence for your thesis.

3. Michiko Kakutani and Stacey Wilkins are both angry, Kakutani about advertising and Wilkins about tipping. Given that one essay is personal and the other general, which of the two writers makes the more logical argument? Quote both to prove your point.

4. The essays by Michiko Kakutani and Laura Lee use humor to support their theses, but the kind of humor is very different. Reread the essays, noting examples of humor and how they are used. How would you characterize the humor? Which brand of humor do you prefer and why? Again, use evidence from both to support your view.

On Using Division and Classification

5

The next time you shop in a supermarket or clean out a closet, think about how you are doing it and you will understand the workings of **division and classification.** "How often do I wear those shoes?" and "I never did like that sweater" imply that dividing items according to how frequently you wear them would be a good principle for sorting out your closet. Supermarkets, however, do the sorting for you. Goods are divided according to shared characteristics—all dairy products in one section, meat in another, and so on—and then items are placed in those categories. The process looks easy, but if you have ever tried to find reduced-salt soy sauce, you know the pitfalls: Is it with the spices? Sauces? Gourmet foods? Health foods? Ethnic products?

To divide a subject and then classify examples into the categories or classes that resulted from division you must be able to examine a subject from several angles:

How can it be divided?
How can you classify your examples by differences?
How can you classify them by similarities?

A huge topic such as animals invites a long list of ways they can be divided: wild animals, work animals, pets; ones that swim, run, crawl; ones you have owned, seen, or read about. These groups imply principles for division—by degree of domesticity, by manner of locomotion, by degree of familiarity. Division and classification often help define each other in that having divided your subjects, you may find that once you start classifying, you have to stop and redefine your principle of division. If your division of animals is based on locomotion, for instance, where do you put the flying squirrel?

Division and classification is often used at the paragraph level. If your essay argues that a particular television commercial for a toilet cleaner insults women, you might want to introduce the essay by enumerating other advertisements in that general category—household products—that you also find insulting to women.

From Julius Caesar's "Gaul is divided into three parts" to a 10-year-old's "animal, vegetable, or mineral," classification and division has had a long and useful history. And, of course, it has a useful present as well. In each of the essays in this chapter, you will see that the system of division and classification supports a thesis, though the essays use their theses for different purposes: to entertain, to explain, to argue.

Audience and Purpose

Knowing who your readers are and what effect you want to have on them will help you devise your system of classification and sharpen your thesis. Imagine that you are writing an essay for a newsletter put out by a health club or by students in a physical education program and that your subject is the positive effects of herbs. You've narrowed it further to the benefits of garlic. You know that your readers are interested in the positive effects of herbs but also that they may wrinkle their noses at the mere mention of garlic. Given the negative associations your audience may have, you would do well to begin with the unpleasant connotation, thus starting with what your readers already know, connecting your subject with their experience, and immediately addressing their first and probably negative ideas. After that, you might move quickly to the many good uses to which garlic can be put, classifying them according to the herb's different effects. Thus you would inform your readers and at the same time argue for garlic's positive qualities and the idea that it should do more than flavor a spaghetti sauce.

To explain, however, is the more obvious use of division and classification. You may well find that when you start off on a topic that lends itself to this pattern of organization, you need to define some of your terms. Writing about the ways in which a one-year-old can both annoy and delight you, for instance, you may want to define what you mean by your central terms. In so doing, you have a chance to link the definitions to your audience's experiences, so that even if some of your readers have never spent much time around a baby, they can still appreciate your points. For *annoy*, you might define your reaction as similar to hearing a car alarm going off in the middle of the night, and for *delight*, you might remind your readers of how they felt when opening an unexpected but perfect present. Both definitions help explain while at the same time drawing on common experiences.

Should you tackle that same topic with a humorous tone, you will not only be informing your audience but entertaining them as well. But humor comes in many forms, evoking everything from belly laughs to giggles to knowing smiles. To produce those responses, you may find yourself using exaggeration (also known as **hyperbole**), or **irony,** or **sarcasm,** or a combination of all three, and more. Your title can tip off your readers to your tone: "Baby Destructo" (exaggeration); "Little Baby, Big Problem" (irony); "The Joys of Parenthood" (sarcasm).

System of Classification

To work effectively, a system of classification must be complete and logical. The system that governs how goods are arranged in a supermarket needs to be broad enough to cover everything a supermarket might sell, and it needs to make sense. Can openers should be with kitchen implements, not with vegetables; cans of peas should be with other canned goods, not with milk.

So, too, when you are writing an essay all your examples should be in the correct category. If you were thinking of the subject of campaign spending in a recent presidential election and, in particular, who contributed what to which political party, you would first concentrate on the Republicans and the Democrats, ignoring the campaigns of the minor political groups (the money they raised being minor in comparison). Then you would sort out the kinds of contributions—small donations from private citizens, large ones from individuals, money from PACs, from corporations, and the like—made to each of those two political parties. At that point, you would find you had so much material that you would be better off narrowing your subject, but no matter what you did, you wouldn't mix in intangible gifts such as a volunteer's time or tangible ones such as the "free" donuts handed out to the campaign workers.

More likely, however, as you think about your topic and work on your draft, you will find your classifications are not watertight. Yet you can account for the occasional leak by explaining it or by adjusting your system of division. In the example of campaign contributions, for instance, it would be impossible to put an accurate price tag on the time spent by volunteers or on the goods and services donated to the two political parties, though it's reasonable to assume that the dollar figure would be high. And that's all you need to say. You've explained why you have omitted those kinds of contributions. Adjusting the system of division, the other alternative, so that it included every conceivable kind of donation isn't a reasonable solution as it would make an already large topic even larger, impossibly so.

Other Patterns of Organization

Earlier in this chapter, you read about what definition can add to classification and division, but description, narration, and example are useful as well. The essay on political contributions, for instance, might open with a brief narrative recounting your having been besieged by telephone callers trying to raise money for a particular candidate. And if that narrative described your listening to the callers' recorded message talking to your answering machine, then you could also underscore your point that raising money for campaigns has reached absurd heights (or depths).

Examples are also essential to classification, usually in the form of multiple illustrations. Your practice in using examples in other papers will help you here, for as you know, you can select examples from your own experience or that of others or both. Outside sources such as evidence drawn from books and magazines are also helpful, showing your reader that you have looked beyond your personal experience. When using examples, however, you need think through the most effective way to sequence them, which will often be according to dramatic effect—moving from least to most dramatic—or in chronological order.

Organization and Ideas

Some writers begin their essays by first dividing the subject into their system of classification, then moving on to focus on one of the classes. Say you chose as a topic the electronic objects we often take for granted. You might have found yourself making notes that include a huge list. Thinking through that list you might have noticed that you can divide it into machines that can be controlled with a remote device and those that cannot. In one category are items such as microwaves, answering machines, and computers, and in the other you've lumped together CD players, television sets, VCRs.

You sketch out notes that may look like this:

The more you think about it, the longer the list for remote-controlled objects becomes, so instead of writing about both categories, you stick to one, speculating on a world with the ultimate universal remote.

On the other hand, you may find your central question so intriguing that you want to get right to it, in which case you wouldn't need to discuss the division at all; instead, you can leap straight into presenting the category of remote-controlled objects, illustrating it with multiple examples.

Perhaps the greatest trap in writing an essay that uses division and classification is that what you have is a string of examples that don't lead anywhere. All your examples are well developed, yes, but they don't support an assertion. It's the cardinal sin—an essay without a thesis.

If you find yourself headed in that direction, one solution is to answer your own questions. In the course of thinking about your subject, you may well have come up with a solid, focused, central question, such as "What kind of life will the American consumer have in a remote-controlled world?" Your one-sentence answer to that question can be your thesis.

Often it helps to think of writing as a sort of silent dialogue with yourself. Reading a sentence in your draft and thinking about it, you find that thought leads to another sentence, and so on till you've filled up a number of pages. By the time you have stopped, you may realize that your first draft could more accurately be called a discovery draft, for in the course of writing it, you have found out what you want to say. Sum it up in one sentence that has a debatable point and you have your thesis.

If you are using division or classification to develop only one part of your paper, then where you place it depends on where you think it would be most effective. But if your essay, like most of those in this chapter, is structured primarily by division and classification, then you would do best to use a straightforward pattern of organization, devoting the body of the paper to developing the category or categories involved. Your reader can then follow your reasoning and understand how it supports your thesis. Because readers can get lost in a tangle of examples, you may opt for an explicit thesis in an obvious place, such as at the end of your introduction.

Useful Terms

Division and classification Methods of examining a subject. Division involves the process of separating, first dividing the subject into groups so that they can be sorted out—classified—into categories; classification focuses on shared characteristics, sorting items into categories that share a similar feature.

Hyperbole Obvious overstatement, exaggeration.

Irony A statement or action in which the intended meaning or occurrence is the opposite of the surface one.

Sarcasm A caustic or sneering remark or tone that is usually ironic as well.

POINTERS FOR USING DIVISION AND CLASSIFICATION

Exploring the Topic

1. **How can your topic be divided?** What divisions apply? Of those you list, which one is the best suited?
2. **What examples can you think of?** What characteristics do your examples have in common? Which do you have the most to say about?
3. **Are your categories for classification appropriate?** Are the categories parallel? Do they overlap? Do you need to make any adjustments?
4. **Do your examples fit your categories?** Are you sure the examples have enough in common? Are they obvious? Which are not?

(Continued)

POINTERS FOR USING DIVISION AND CLASSIFICATION (*Continued*)

5. **What is your principle for classification?** Have you applied it consistently to each category?
6. **Are your categories complete?** Do they cover the topic? Do they contain enough examples?
7. **How can your categories be sequenced?** From simple to complex? Least to most important? Least to most effective?
8. **What is your point?** What assertion are you making? Does your system of classification support it? Are your examples appropriate?
9. **What is your purpose?** Are you primarily making your point to express your feelings, to inform, to persuade, or to entertain?

Drafting the Paper

1. **Know your reader.** Where does your reader stand in relation to your system of classification? Is the reader part of it? If so, how? If the reader is not part of your system, is he or she on your side, say a fellow student looking at teachers? What does your audience know about your topic? About your system of classification? What does the reader not know? Your audience might be biased toward or against your subject and classification system. How can you best foster or combat the bias?

2. **Know your purpose.** If your primary purpose is to express your feelings, make sure that you are not just writing to yourself and that you are not treading on the toes of your audience. Similarly, if you are writing to persuade, make sure you are not convincing only yourself. Check to see that you are using material that may convince someone who disagrees with you or who, at the least, is either sitting on the fence or hasn't given the matter much thought. Writing to inform is probably the easiest here, for though your subject may be familiar, your system of classification is probably new. On the other hand, writing to entertain is difficult and requires a deft use of persona.

3. **Set up your system of classification early in the paper.** You may find that a definition is in order or that some background

information is necessary, but make your system clear and bring it out early.

4. **Explain the principle behind the system.** To give your system credibility, you need to provide an explanation for your means of selection. The explanation can be brief—a phrase or two—but it should be there.

5. **Select appropriate examples.** Perhaps you can best illustrate a class by one extended example, or maybe it would be better to pile on examples. If your examples are apt to be unfamiliar to your audience, make sure you give enough detail so that they are explained by their contexts.

6. **Make a point.** Remember that what you have to say about your subject is infinitely more interesting than the subject itself. So, too, your major assertion is more important than your system of classification: it is what your system of classification adds up to. It's easy, in writing this kind of paper, to mistake the means for the end, so make sure that you use classification to support an overall assertion.

A Good Word on Politics

Steven Doloff

Steven Doloff is a Professor of English at Pratt Institute in Brooklyn, New York. While much of his writing appears in scholarly journals, there's also a lot in more general publications such as the New York Times *and* Newsday. *His scholarly work focuses on Shakespeare and on various short story writers, but when it comes to a less academic audience, almost anything is fair game. The essay below examines politics and its verbal humbug and flimflam. It appeared in* Newsday *on March 1, 2004. As you read, you'll discover Doloff enjoys analyzing language and thinks it's fun.*

What to Look For   Doloff uses a wide range of diction and references, but he's always careful to define anything a reader may not know. As you read his essay, look for the places where he does just that—a technique you'll find useful in your own writing.

1   The 19th-century German philosopher Arthur Schopenhauer once suggested that "it would be a very good thing if each trick could receive some short and obviously appropriate name, so that when a man used this or that particular trick, he could at once be reproved for it."

2   Actually, long before Schopenhauer, classical Roman rhetoricians had done just that, coining names for devious political debating tactics such as argumentum and hominum ("arguing against the person"), attacking an opponent's character instead of addressing the issue at hand; and petitio principii ("begging the question"), posing a question that assumes an unproved point.

3   Unfortunately, these classical terms for oratorical flim-flam are familiar today only to academics and a few professional writers. And, even more unfortunately, modern public officials find new scams to add to their bag of traditional verbal tricks. Clearly, we could use

some simple and convenient Americanisms to quickly identify and denounce contemporary political humbug. Here are some:

4   Redlegging: When an incumbent (or his/her spokesperson) implies or outright declares political critics of his/her policies are unpatriotic.

5   Sitting on one's hat: When a public figure emphatically denies he/she intends to enter a particular political race (until it looks like there's a reasonable chance to win).

6   Pixelating: Staging media photo opportunities that frame politicians with emotionally evocative scenery (flags, aircraft carriers, Mt. Rushmore, etc.)

7   Chickenwinging: When a politician deliberately understates or waffles on his opposition to an incumbent's policy (because it would entail voicing a politically unpopular, if valid, criticism) until it is strategically safe (or advantageous) to be blunt.

8   Shroud waving: When a politician evokes the memory of a national tragedy as a means of eliciting emotional receptivity for an unrelated policy or proposal.

9   Calling a club a spade: When a politician sanctimoniously calls attention to his/her own moral backbone for voicing some unpopular truth while actually misrepresenting or distorting that truth.

10   Sheep shifting: When a politician retroactively revises the rationale for a policy (like, say, a popular military action) because ongoing events belie that rationale and suggest instead unstated, more controversial (or lupine) motives for the policy.

11   Barber polling: When a politician carefully shapes (shaves?) his positions on issues so as to smoothly wrap them around public opinion polls.

12   Gilding the lemon: When a politician redoubles the defense of a failing policy because the wonks can't figure out a way for him/her to withdraw gracefully from it.

13   Opening out of town: When a Hollywood celebrity starts a media circus by getting himself elected to public office in order to guarantee maximum box office for his next picture, or second term (whichever comes first).

14   What are the chances that the common use of such new terms will cast fear into the hearts of devious public officials and chasten the rhetoric of future political contests? Zip. Let's not flim-flam ourselves.

15   But it just might be worth our while to be able to call the good plays from the bad as we watch these contests, and know when to boo.

ORGANIZATION AND IDEAS

1. Think about the essay as using a problem–solution structure. What's the problem? The solution?
2. Doloff classifies the various types of political humbuggery. What pattern can you discern to the order in which he defines them?
3. Reread the essay's conclusion, paragraphs 14 and 15. How would you characterize Doloff's audience? To whom is he writing?
4. Take another look at paragraph 3 along with paragraphs 14 and 15 and also think about his examples. What exactly is his subject? His thesis?
5. Test out one of Doloff's terms. Perhaps a particular political commercial or photo op sticks in your mind. How well does Doloff's term fit?

TECHNIQUE AND STYLE

1. Use a handbook of grammar and usage to read up on the uses of parentheses. Then reread the essay marking every parenthetical statement. To what extent does Doloff's use conform to what the handbook describes? What effect does Doloff achieve?
2. Look up the term *word play* in a dictionary of literary terms or unabridged dictionary. What evidence of it can you find in the essay?
3. Try to pinpoint Doloff's tone. Do you find it mocking? Satirical? Arch? Condescending? Witty? Learned? What? What examples support your opinion?
4. Doloff uses an unusual pattern in the body of his essay, that of a term followed by a full colon and then an incomplete sentence. The format intentionally resembles a dictionary entry. To what extent do you find it noticeable? Effective?
5. For a full definition, look up *satire* in a dictionary of literary terms or an unabridged dictionary. How well does Doloff's essay fit the genre? What is he satirizing?

SUGGESTIONS FOR WRITING

Journal

1. Which of Doloff's new terms is your favorite and why?
2. Reread paragraph 15 and think about the metaphor embedded in "call the good plays from the bad" and "contests." What does the metaphor imply? How well does it fit the essay?

Essay

1. Doloff obviously had a lot of fun writing his essay, and you can do the same with your own subject. Once you've found a topic, think of ways in which it can be classified and make up a term for each category. Suggestions:

   sales people
   customers
   spam
   rock concert fans
   dog owners

   Like Doloff, you may want to write a satire, or maybe you just want to have fun with your subject, but don't forget that the classification has to support a thesis.

2. Use the Web or your library to track down an important political speech you can analyze by using Doloff's terms. You might start by choosing a candidate or elected official you don't like and then tracking down a speech that person made while running for office or on a special occasion. When you work on you draft, however, remember that your readers may not share your opinion, so aim your criticism at the words and logic, not the person.

Always, Always, Always

Bill Rohde

The essay that follows was written for a class required for students who intended to teach English. Focusing on both writing and the teaching of writing, the course asked students to analyze their own writing habits, including elements in the writing process that gave them problems. No matter what their stage of experience, most writers hit at least one question that sends them to the nearest handbook. The assignment here asked the class to choose one matter of grammar or usage that sent them in search of answers, then to research what the handbooks had to say, and to write an essay explaining both the question and the answers. Since the students were prospective English teachers, they were to use the Modern Language Association's (more familiarly known as the MLA) system of documentation and their audience was the class itself. Bill Rohde questioned the necessity of using a comma before the last item in a series.

What to Look For   Bill Rohde takes an inherently dry subject—the serial comma—and uses it to satirize composition teachers and classify students. As you read the essay, try to imagine the person behind the prose. Also keep in mind that Rohde creates a distinct personality for the narrator of the essay without ever using the first-person *I*.

1   A student inquiring about the "correctness" of the serial comma finds conflicting advice in her *Harbrace,* her teacher's *MLA Style Manual,* and the library's *Washington Post Deskbook on Style. Harbrace* tells her she may write either

>   *The air was raw, dank, and gray.*

or

>   *The air was raw, dank and gray.*

Ever accommodating, the tiny, red handbook considers the comma before the conjunction "optional" unless there is "danger of misreading" (132). *The MLA Style Manual,* with its Bible-black cover, neither acknowledges ambivalence nor allows for options. "Commas are required between items in a series," it clearly states in Section 2.2.4., after which it provides a typically lighthearted sample sentence:

>   *The experience demanded blood, sweat, and tears. (46)*

The paperback *Post Deskbook,* so user-friendly it suggests right in the title the handiest place to keep it, advises the student to "omit commas where possible," as before the conjunction in a series (126–27). Apparently written on deadline, the book offers sample sentence fragments:

>   *red, white, green and blue; 1, 2 or 3 (127)*

2   What should you, the composition teacher, tell this puzzled student when she approaches with her problem? Tell her she

must always use the serial comma—no ifs, ands, or buts about it. Regardless of whether you believe this to be true, you must sound convincing. If the student appears satisfied with your response and thanks you, you may go back to grading papers. If, however, she wrinkles her nose or bites her lip in a display of doubt, then you may safely label her a problem student and select one of the following tailor-made responses.

3   *The struggling student* appreciates any burden a teacher can remove. You should explain to her that out of sympathy for her plight—so much to keep track of when writing—you have just given her one of the few hard-and-fast rules in existence. Tell her to concern herself with apostrophes or sentence fragments, and not with whether the absence of a serial comma might lead to a misreading.

4   *The easily intimidated student* (often ESL) should have accepted your unequivocal answer, but perhaps you do not (yet) strike her as an authority figure. Go for the throat. Say, "Obey the MLA. It is the Bible (or Koran or Bhagavad-Gita) of the discourse community to which you seek entry. Expect blood, sweat, and tears if you do not use the serial comma."

5   *The skeptic* needs an overpowering, multifarious theory to be convinced, so pull out Jane Walpole's *A Writer's Guide* and read the following:

> [A]ll commas indicate an up-pause in the voice contour, and this up-pause occurs after *each* series item up to the final one. Listen to your voice as you read this sentence:
>
> *Medical science has overcome tuberculosis, typhoid, small pox, and polio in the last hundred years.*
>
> Only *polio,* the final series item, lacks an up-pause; and where there is an up-pause, there should be a comma. The "comma and" combination before the final item also tells your readers that the series is about to close, thus reducing any chance of their misreading your sentence. (95)

While that's still soaking in, drop the names of linguists who have stated that writing is silent speech and reading is listening. Then tell her that omitting the serial comma represents an arrogant, foolish, and futile attempt to sever the natural link between speech and text.

6   Show *the visually oriented student,* possibly an artist, how

       Chagall, Picasso, and Dali

   are nicely balanced, but

       Chagall, Picasso and Dali

   are not.

7   Tell *the metaphor-happy student* that commas are like dividers
   between ketchup, mustard, and mayonnaise; fences between dogs,
   cats, and chickens; or borders between Israel, Syria, and Lebanon.
   Without them, messes result. (Dodge the fact that messes may result
   even if they are present.)

8   If the student is *a journalism major* who cites the *Deskbook* as
   proof of the serial comma's obsolescence, point out that her entire
   profession is rapidly approaching obsolescence. Add that editors
   who attempt to speed up reading by eliminating commas in fact
   slow down comprehension by removing helpful visual cues.

9   One hopes that reading, seeing, and hearing so many strong
   arguments in favor of the serial comma has so utterly convinced you
   of its usefulness that every student from here on in will accept your
   rock-solid, airtight edict without question.

Works Cited

Achtert, Walter S., and Joseph Gibaldi. The MLA Style Manual. New York:
    MLA, 1985.
Hodges, John C., et al. Harbrace College Handbook. New York: Harcourt,
    1990.
Walpole, Jane. A Writer's Guide. Englewood Cliffs: Prentice, 1980.
Webb, Robert A. The Washington Post Deskbook on Style. New York:
    McGraw, 1978.

ORGANIZATION AND IDEAS

1. At what point in the essay does Rohde use division? What does he
   divide and into what groups?
2. Rohde begins his classification in paragraph 3 and ends it with paragraph 8. What reasons can you infer for the order in which he presents
   his categories?

3. Where in the essay do you find Rohde's thesis? How effective is that placement?
4. On the surface, Rohde's thesis is explicit, but what is his implied thesis?
5. In what ways is the essay a satire on education?

TECHNIQUE AND STYLE

1. How would you describe Rohde's tone? His persona? What does his research on the topic contribute to his persona?
2. Who is the *you* in the essay? How effective do you find the direct address?
3. Note the use of parentheses in paragraph 4. Check out what your handbook says about parentheses. To what extent does Rohde's use fit the handbook's explanation?
4. A writer's choice of pronoun has become an issue ever since the once generic *he* lost its general nature and gained a specific gender connotation. What is Rohde's solution? Explain why you do or do not find his choice of pronoun effective.
5. The point of documentation is to provide specific and relevant references in an unobtrusive manner. Evaluate how well Rohde uses his research and how well he documents it.

SUGGESTIONS FOR WRITING

Journal

1. Write out your response to Rohde's persona. Would you like to have him as your teacher? Would you like to have him in your class?
2. Commas give many writers fits. Thinking about your own writing, jot down the kinds of problems you have with commas. When you've finished, reread what you have written. Do you find a pattern?

Essay

1. Given that people's personalities range over a continuum with extremes at either end, the extremes can be good subjects for an essay that uses division and classification. Think about virtually any activity people are involved in and identify the behavior that represents the two extremes, thus dividing the subject. Then choose one of those groups and consider the categories your choice can be classified into. Here are some suggestions:

   drivers
   readers
   writers
   teachers
   professional athletes

2. Think about the various kinds of teachers you have had and have heard about. What categories can they be sorted into? Write an essay in which you explain those categories, giving examples for each.

The Search for Human Life in the Maze of Retail Stores

Michelle Higgins

Michelle Higgins is a staff reporter for the Wall Street Journal. *She joined the paper as an intern for the popular Friday* Weekend Journal *in 1999 and quickly moved up to reporter. At* Weekend Journal, *Ms. Higgins authored a weekly travel column, "Takeoffs & Landings" and wrote cover stories on everything from the online travel business to theme park vacations. In April 2002, Ms. Higgins began writing for the newspaper's new "Personal Journal" section. Featured as the "Cranky Consumer," her recent stories have included consumer issues concerning everything from online banking to 401(k) accounts to summer camp. The review that follows was published in the May 6, 2003, issue of the* Wall Street Journal.

What to Look For   A report on retail stores that critiques their ability to help shoppers find what they are looking for could be very dull indeed, but Michelle Higgins keeps it from being so. As you read, look for the ways she keeps her reader's interest.

1   When Jonathan Gordon went shopping at a Macy's in New Jersey for a vacuum cleaner recently, he couldn't find anyone to answer his questions. After a 10-minute search, he solved his problem by standing in the aisle and shouting, "Is there anybody here who can help me?"

2   Finally, a staffer appeared—who couldn't tell him anything he couldn't already read on the box.

3   Attention, shoppers: It is getting even tougher to get help in the aisles. The nation's third-largest discount retailer, **Kmart,** is expected to come out of bankruptcy Tuesday, and retailers overall are anticipating a postwar sales boost. But many are still in retrenching mode. In January, **Toys "R" Us** cut 700 positions in 400 stores. The next month, **Circuit City** eliminated 4.8% of its work force, including an average of three salespeople per store. Overall last year, the number of employees in retail fell for the first time in a decade, according to the Bureau of Labor Statistics.

4   All this comes on top of a major effort in recent years by retailers to build ever-more-colossal shops—while simultaneously redesigning them to encourage people to serve themselves instead of getting help from the staff.

5   To see just how tough it is out there, we recently went shopping at six retailers. They included two big discounters Kmart and **Wal-Mart Stores,** the home-improvement giants **Lowe's** and **Home Depot**—and what is often the lion's den of retail: sprawling, kid-packed toy stores.

6   We picked stores in six different cities and visited them all on a Saturday between the busy hours of one and five. At each place we tried to find an employee who would help us locate two items we knew the store stocked. To see how much staff knew about their merchandise, we also asked for help with a specific task; for example, we asked at the toy stores for gift suggestions for a smart 10-year-old boy—but nothing too nerdy.

7   Our experience varied widely. At **KB Toys,** we were out the door in eight minutes with our three purchases: A Furreal Friend robotic cat, Shrinky Dinks and a basketball-player action figure. But at Wal-Mart, it took us 30 minutes and conversations with 10 people—and still, we left without finding one of the three things we wanted (a fondue pot) because the staff didn't know where they were.

8   KB Toys stores, of course, are small in comparison to warehouse-style Wal-Marts. But the staff was among the most helpful: One person even offered to carry our purchases for us while we kept shopping.

9   The retail business, struggling through its worst slump in years, can ill afford to be alienating shoppers. The pace of annual sales growth has tumbled from a high of 6.7% four years ago to just 2.9% last year. The outlook continues to look grim. The month of March was the weakest for U.S. retailers since 1995, according to a survey by Bank of Tokyo-Mitsubishi Ltd.

10   "In the past year, customer service has absolutely become dreadful," says Judson Rees of Brand Marketing, a company that dispatches "mystery shoppers" to test service at stores and restaurants. In a survey of shoppers, he said, more than three-quarters reported that it's "common" to see salespeople ignoring customers this year, up from 39% last year.

11   It turns out there are a few ways to beat the system. Though we passed over it the first time, for example, Lowe's has buzzers in its stores to summon a staffer. Toys "R" Us has phones scattered around that you can pick up and ask for help.

12   We got off to a rocky start at a Toys "R" Us in Colma, California, when we asked where to find a Furreal Friend robotic cat. "It's right there," the staffer told us—pointing about 30 yards away and wagging his finger. "Right there! Right there!"

13   But later, the same guy warmed up and complimented us on our toys. While we had his attention, we asked where to find Shrinky Dinks. He consulted his walkie-talkie and announced: "The Imaginarium. Follow me." We were done shopping in 21 minutes.

14   A Toys "R" Us official said the first salesman should have been more polite.

15   The Lowe's we visited had a people-greeter at the front door, who deflected our question about a squirrel-proof birdfeeder to a customer-service desk that was already swarming with impatient shoppers. But after being directed to the right department, a staffer there told us Lowe's doesn't sell them—even though we later noticed that he was standing right in front of one. (Admittedly, it was on a very high shelf.)

16   After that, service picked up. Another employee got off a forklift and gave us detailed help after we asked for advice on closet organizers. He even drew us a sketch.

17   At a nearby Home Depot, we shopped for the same items and got efficient service. A cashier who was clocking out for the day even hung around to assist us.

18   Wal-Mart, Lowe's and Kmart said they are focusing on improving service.

19   Service was mixed at a Kmart in New York City. We asked the first employee we saw, a woman with an armful of clothes, for help finding a foot spa. She asked, "What is that?" before pointing us to the right department. There we asked another guy for help—who simply grunted and started walking away from us. We followed, on the chance that he intended us to, and he led us to the foot spas.

20   A third staffer helped us find cleaning products to take out a ketchup stain. "This one has a brush, so you can, shhh, shhh," he said, making a helpful brushing motion. We took it and said thanks. "You're welcome, sweetie," was the reply.

ORGANIZATION AND IDEAS

1. Outline the system of division and classification in an outline similar to the one on page 146.
2. In paragraph 6, Higgins outlines her methodology behind her system and examples. How trustworthy is it?
3. Higgins uses a framing device, beginning and ending the piece with narratives. In what ways are they similar? Different?
4. Higgins is careful to point out the stores' problems as well as those of the shopper. In what ways are the two sets of problems related?
5. How necessary and helpful is the chart that concludes the piece?

TECHNIQUE AND STYLE

1. What is Higgins' primary purpose: to entertain, inform, persuade? Some combination of the three?
2. Higgins writes under the title of the Cranky Consumer. How apt is the title?
3. What devices and techniques does Higgins use to keep the piece from being dry?
4. In what ways is the selection an appropriate article for the *Wall Street Journal?*
5. How appropriate is the article's title?

SUGGESTIONS FOR WRITING

Journal

1. Higgins uses a lot of examples in her article. Which do you find the most interesting and why?
2. In a way, the article seems to stop instead of end. Write a concluding paragraph for it.

Essay

1. Write your own division and classification essay, using retail stores as a general subject. One of two ways to divide the topic is to think about the people you would see in them, dividing the general "people in retail stores" into
   shoppers
   sales personnel
   cashiers

Or if you'd prefer a more abstract system, you can use the general "large retail stores" and divide it into

efficiency
convenience
variety of merchandise

Choose one of these divisions or your own and consider the possible classifications. While you do not need to begin with a thesis, one will probably evolve as you write about your topic.

2. One of the arguments against the megastores such as the ones Higgins writes about is that they undercut and in many cases destroy the smaller mom-and-pop stores. Think about the kinds of stores that fall into the mom-and-pop category and write an essay that describes them. Research will help you here, so you might do a Web search for the key terms. Depending on what you find and your analysis of it, your thesis can be linked to the smaller stores' value to the community or lack of it.

The Plot Against People
Russell Baker

Russell Baker is best known for his light tone, one that many readers have enjoyed during the 36 years he was a regular columnist for the New York Times. *Winner of two Pulitzer Prizes, one for biography and another for commentary, Baker is the author of several collections of essays and autobiographical books—*Growing Up *(1982),* The Good Times *(1989),* There's a Country in My Cellar *(1991)—and the editor of* The Norton Book of Light Verse *(1986) and* Russell Baker's Book of American Humor *(1993). The essay that follows typifies the humorous side of Baker's style, for he has discovered the principles behind the continuing battle between humans and inanimate objects. He discusses these principles as he neatly divides things into three categories and then places objects into his classifications.*

What to Look For   Transitions between paragraphs can be wooden, so obvious that they leap off the page to say "Look at me! I'm a transition." The more effective variety is subtle, and one way to bring that about is to pick up a key word from the previous sentence and repeat it in the first sentence of the paragraph that follows. After you've read Baker's essay, go back over it searching for his transitions between paragraphs.

1   $\mathbf{I}$nanimate objects are classified into three major categories—those that don't work, those that break down and those that get lost.

2   The goal of all inanimate objects is to resist man and ultimately to defeat him, and the three major classifications are based on the method each object uses to achieve its purpose. As a general rule, any object capable of breaking down at the moment when it is most needed will do so. The automobile is typical of the category.

3   With the cunning typical of its breed, the automobile never breaks down while entering a filling station with a large staff of idle mechanics. It waits until it reaches a downtown intersection in the middle of the rush hour, or until it is fully loaded with family and luggage on the Ohio Turnpike.

4   Thus it creates maximum misery, inconvenience, frustration and irritability among its human cargo, thereby reducing its owner's life span.

5   Washing machines, garbage disposals, lawn mowers, light bulbs, automatic laundry dryers, water pipes, furnaces, electrical fuses, television tubes, hose nozzles, tape recorders, slide projectors—all are in league with the automobile to take their turn at breaking down whenever life threatens to flow smoothly for their human enemies.

6   Many inanimate objects, of course, find it extremely difficult to break down. Pliers, for example, and gloves and keys are almost totally incapable of breaking down. Therefore, they have had to evolve a different technique for resisting man.

7   They get lost. Science has still not solved the mystery of how they do it, and no man has ever caught one of them in the act of getting lost. The most plausible theory is that they have developed a secret method of locomotion which they are able to conceal the instant a human eye falls upon them.

8   It is not uncommon for a pair of pliers to climb all the way from the cellar to the attic in its single-minded determination to raise its owner's blood pressure. Keys have been known to burrow three feet under mattresses. Women's purses, despite their great weight,

frequently travel through six or seven rooms to find a hiding space under a couch.

9   Scientists have been struck by the fact that things that break down virtually never get lost, while things that get lost hardly ever break down.

10   A furnace, for example, will invariably break down at the depth of the first winter cold wave, but it will never get lost. A woman's purse, which after all does have some inherent capacity for breaking down, hardly ever does; it almost invariably chooses to get lost.

11   Some persons believe this constitutes evidence that inanimate objects are not entirely hostile to man, and that a negotiated peace is possible. After all, they point out, a furnace could infuriate a man even more thoroughly by getting lost than by breaking down, just as a glove could upset him far more by breaking down than by getting lost.

12   Not everyone agrees, however, that this indicates a conciliatory attitude among inanimate objects. Many say it merely proves that furnaces, gloves and pliers are incredibly stupid.

13   The third class of objects—those that don't work—is the most curious of all. These include such objects as barometers, car clocks, cigarette lighters, flashlights, and toy train locomotives. It is inaccurate, of course, to say that they never work. They work once, usually for the first few hours after being brought home, and then quit. Thereafter, they never work again.

14   In fact, it is widely assumed that they are built for the purpose of not working. Some people have reached advanced ages without ever seeing some of these objects—barometers, for example—in working order.

15   Science is utterly baffled by the entire category. There are many theories about it. The most interesting holds that the things that don't work have attained the highest state possible for an inanimate object, the state to which things that break down and things that get lost can still only aspire.

16   They have truly defeated man by conditioning him never to expect anything of them, and in return they have given man the only peace he receives from inanimate society. He does not expect his barometer to work, his electric locomotive to run, his cigarette lighter to light or his flashlight to illuminate, and when they don't, it does not raise his blood pressure.

17   He cannot attain that peace with furnaces and keys and cars and women's purses as long as he demands that they work for their keep.

ORGANIZATION AND IDEAS

1. Paragraphs 3–6 explain the first category. What effects does the automobile achieve by breaking down? How do those effects support Baker's contention about "the goal of all inanimate objects"? What other examples does Baker put into his first category? What example does not fit?
2. Paragraphs 7–12 present the second classification. What causes, reasons, or motives are attributed to the examples in this group?
3. Paragraphs 13–16 describe the third group. What are its qualities? Why might Baker have chosen to list it last? What principle of organization can you discern beneath Baker's ordering of the three groups?
4. Consider how each group frustrates and defeats people together with the first sentence of paragraph 2. Combine this information into a sentence that states the author's thesis.
5. To what extent does Baker use the absurd in his essay? How is it appropriate?

TECHNIQUE AND STYLE

1. In part, the essay's humor arises from Baker's use of anthropomorphism, attributing human qualities to inanimate objects. How effectively does he use the technique?
2. Baker has a keen eye for the absurd, as illustrated by paragraph 10. What other examples can you find? What does this technique contribute to the essay?
3. Baker's stance, tone, and line of reasoning, while patently tongue-in-cheek, are also mock-scientific. Where can you find examples of Baker's explicit or implied "scientific" trappings?
4. The essay's transitions are carefully wrought. What links paragraph 3 to paragraph 2? Paragraph 7 to paragraph 6? Paragraph 10 to paragraph 9? Paragraph 12 to paragraph 11?
5. How an essay achieves unity is a more subtle thing. What links paragraph 8 to paragraph 6? Paragraph 9 to paragraphs 3–6? Paragraph 16 to paragraph 2? Paragraph 17 to paragraphs 10–12 and paragraphs 3–5?

SUGGESTIONS FOR WRITING

Journal

1. Describe a fight you have had with an inanimate object.
2. Of all the inanimate objects that can frustrate you, which one tops the list and why?

Essay

1. Write your own "plot" essay, imagining something else plotting against people. Like Baker, you can take a "scientific" stance or you may prefer your own humorous tone. Suggestions:

   clothes
   food
   pets
   the weather
   plants
   traffic

2. It's no news that we live in a highly technological society; it's also no news that at times that technology is frustrating. You may, for instance, have a number of objects that display the time—VCR, clock, stove, answering machine—but when the electricity goes off, getting them back in sync is a challenge. Choose a category and write an essay in which you explore whether or not that particular group of technological advances is good, bad, or somewhere in between.

Desert Religions

Richard Rodriguez

The son of Mexican immigrants, Richard Rodriguez did not learn English until he went to school but he learned it well. He earned a BA from Stanford University and a PhD in English literature from the University of California at Berkeley. He is best known, however, for his writing, particularly his memoirs: Hunger of Memory *(1982),* Days of Obligation: An Argument with My Mexican Father *(1992), and* Brown: The Last Discovery of America *(2002). A contributing editor at* Harper's *and the* Los Angeles Times, *Rodriguez has been called the "best American essayist" by the* Village Voice. *You might have heard his own voice on* The News Hour with Jim Lehrer *where he is a regular contributor. For his "outstanding achievement" there he won a Peabody Award, the most coveted honor in television. The essay reprinted here first was aired on that show on July 8, 2002.*

What to Look For When you think about placing items in categories, you are analyzing their shared characteristics, their similarities.

That's exactly what Rodriguez does, so as you read, look for the ways he tracks what the three "desert religions" have in common.

1   The Catholic priest is under arrest, accused of raping altar boys. The Muslim shouts out the name of Allah as the jetliner plows into the skyscraper. The Jewish settler's biblical claim to build on the West Bank is supported by fundamentalist Protestants who dream of the last days.

2   These have been months of shame and violence among the three great desert religions—Judaism, Christianity, and Islam—the religions to which most Americans adhere. These desert religions are sister religions in fact, but more commonly they have been brother religions, united and divided by a masculine sense of faith. Mullahs, priests, rabbis—the business of religion was traditionally the males. It was the male's task to understand how God exists in our lives.

3   Judaism gave Christianity and Islam a notion both astonishing and radical, the notion that God acts in history. The desert religions became, in response to this idea, activist religions, ennobled at times by a sense of holy purpose, but also filled with a violence fed by the assumption that God is on my side and not yours. The history of the desert religions oft repeated by old men to boys, got told through stories of battles and crusades, sultans and emperors.

4   But within the three great desert faiths there was a feminine impulse, less strong but ever present, the tradition of absorption rather than assertion, assertive rather than authority, of play rather than dogmatic servitude. Think of the delicate poetry of the song of songs or the delicacy of the celebration of the maternal represented by the Renaissance Madonna or the architectural lines of the medieval mosques of Spain, light as music. And yet the louder, more persistent tradition has been male, concerned with power and blood and dogmatic points.

5   Now on the evening news, diplomats come and go speaking of [everything from] truces and terrorists to the price of oil. In truth, we are watching a religious war, Muslim versus Jew—a war disguised by the language of diplomacy. In decades and centuries past there have been Holocausts and crusades and violence as fierce among the leaders of a single religion, for example, Catholics contending with Protestant and Eastern Orthodox over heresies and questions

of authority. Yahweh, God, Allah—the desert Deity rarely expressed a feminine aspect as in Hinduism.

6   The men who interpreted the Bible or Koran rarely allowed themselves a sense of unknowing or paradox as in Buddhism. And not coincidentally I know many Americans who are turning away from the desert religions or are seeking to moderate the mass unity of the desert religions by turning to the contemplative physics of yoga and the play of the Zen koan.

7   Meanwhile, in my own Catholic Church, there is the squalor of sexual scandal—men forcing themselves on boys. One hears conservative Catholics who speak of ridding the seminaries and the rectors of homosexuals. As one gay Catholic, a single man in this vast world, I tell you pedophilia is no more an expression of homosexuality than rape is an expression of heterosexuality. Pedophilia and rape are assertions of power. Polls indicate that a majority of American Catholics are more forgiving of the fallen priests than they are forgiving of the bishops and cardinals who have treated us like children, with their secret meetings and their clutch on power, apologizing but assuming no penance.

8   Polls indicate also that Catholics continue to go to church. We go to church because of the sacramental consolation our religion gives. All of us now in our churches and synagogues and mosques, what knowledge unites us now in this terrible season? Are we watching the male face of the desert religion merely reassert itself? Or are we watching the collapse of the tradition and the birth of—what?

9   I think of the women of America who have become priests and rabbis. I think of the women of Afghanistan who came to the school door the first morning after the Taliban had disappeared. I think of Mother Teresa whose name will be remembered long after we have forgotten the names of the cardinals in their silk robes. I think that we may be at the beginning of a feminine moment in the history of the desert religions, even while the tanks rumble and the priest is arrested and the girl, unblinking, straps explosives onto her body.

ORGANIZATION AND IDEAS

1. Rodriguez divides desert religions into three groups and then traces the masculine and feminine impulses within them. How valid is his view of the masculine principle?

2. Paragraph 4 examines the feminine principle in the three religions. What other examples can you think of?
3. Reread the first and last paragraphs. In what ways do they frame the essay?
4. In paragraph 8 Rodriguez speculates on why people still attend places of worship. What questions does he pose? What is his answer to those questions? How can you state it as a thesis?
5. The essay was aired in 2002, and many attitudes toward religion have changed since then. To what extent, if any, is it dated?

TECHNIQUE AND STYLE

1. In paragraph 4, Rodriguez defines what he means by the feminine impulse. How adequate is his definition?
2. The essay was written for television. What evidence can you find to show that Rodriguez shaped his prose to be heard instead of read?
3. Where in the essay does Rodriguez bring in his own experience? What does he achieve by doing so?
4. The details that Rodriguez uses, particularly those in paragraphs 1 and 9, are tied to the events of 2001 and 2002, times removed from that at which you are reading his essay. To what extent are those details still effective?
5. How would you describe the essay's overall tone: Pessimistic? Optimistic? Somewhere in between? What evidence supports your view?

SUGGESTIONS FOR WRITING

Journal

1. Think of your own religion or a religion you know well. Use your journal to write down examples of the masculine impulse.
2. Reread the essay, paying particular attention to Rodriguez's idea of the feminine impulse. To what extent does it apply to your religion or one that you know well?

Essay

1. Reread the essay, noting how Rodriguez defines the masculine and feminine impulses and the examples he uses to illustrate his definitions. Think about those impulses and consider how they operate in other areas or within other groups. If, for example, you were analyzing theme parks, you might think of all the kinds of rides, and then sort them into categories according to gender. Roller coasters would probably be masculine, ferris wheels feminine, and so on. Pick one of the

suggestions below or one of your own and write an essay in which you analyze how masculine and feminine characteristics operate:

musicians

writers

comics

sports

food

2. The terms *masculine* and *feminine* are very broad, encompassing a wide variety of behavior. Arnold Schwarzenegger and Jay Leno would both be called masculine, though they are very different. Choose one of the terms and write an essay in which you analyze the variations within the general category. You may find the Web a good source for researching the names that occur to you. Just tap the name into a search engine.

ADDITIONAL WRITING ASSIGNMENTS

Using Division and Classification

1. Consider the types of locomotion associated with sports: skateboard, Rollerblades, surfboard, skis, or snowshoes.
2. Consider what ads tell us about products and ourselves: cars, lingerie, liquor, beer, men's cologne, or men's underwear.
3. Consider the ideal house pet: dog, cat, gerbil, snake, exotic animal, or guinea pig.
4. Consider the ideal vehicle: SUV, pickup, sedan, convertible, or sports car.

Evaluating the Essays

1. "Always, Always, Always" and "A Good Word on Politics" both use division and classification but in very different ways. Rohde uses it to classify types of students mystified by the serial comma, and Doloff uses it to classify different types of political dodges. Rohde addresses the hapless composition teacher; Doloff aims at the observer of political games. Of the two, which is the more effective essay? Quote from both to support your stand.
2. The selections by Michelle Higgins and Russell Baker use very clear patterns of division and classification. Trace the organization of each essay to determine its structure. Granted that Baker's essay is humorous and Higgins' is serious, both rely on clear distinctions to maintain their tones and support their theses. Which does so more effectively?
3. Reread "A Good Word on Politics" and "The Plot Against People," considering the essays as satires. What is being satirized? How? Of the two writers, which is the more successful and why? Use quotations from both essays to back up your opinion.
4. Division and classification can be a predictable and dull kind of organization, but often is saved from that trap by the thesis it supports and the writer's style. Choose among the five essays in this chapter to argue for the one that makes the best use of the pattern. Draw on the other essays as evidence to prove your point.

On Using Comparison and Contrast

6

W hat's the difference?" gets at the heart of **comparison and contrast,** and it is a question that can fit into any context. In college, it often turns up in the form of essay questions; in day-to-day life, it implies the process behind most decisions: "What shall I wear?" "Which movie will I see?" "Should I change jobs?" All these questions involve choices that draw on comparison and contrast. Like description, narration, example, and classification, comparison and contrast forces you to observe, but here you are looking for similarities and differences. In a way, comparison and contrast is the simplest and most analytical form of division and classification in that you are examining only two categories, or perhaps only one example from each of the two categories. "Which sounds better, tapes or records?" compares two categories; "Which sounds better, compact discs or records?" compares two items in the same category.

No matter what you select, however, you need to be sure that the comparison is fair. Deciding where to go out to dinner often depends on how much you are willing to spend, so comparing a fast-food place to an elegant French restaurant doesn't have much of a point unless you want to treat the comparison humorously. If neither is worth the money, however, you have a serious assertion to work from, but you have to work carefully.

Sometimes the similarities will not be readily apparent. Imagine that Shaquille O'Neal decided to run for president of the United States and you decided to write a paper on his campaign; you might well wonder how he connected his basketball days with serving in public office. But as you think about what playing on a professional basketball team has in common with the presidency, similarities begin to emerge: both positions require teamwork and leadership; both depend on the ability to make quick decisions based on complex situations; both call for stamina and training, including what could be called homework. A cynic might add that both involve fancy footwork and the ability to dodge the opposition, but if you want to keep to a serious tone and carry the comparison further, you'd also realize that both jobs call for many public appearances and the ability to be at ease in front of cameras, to be a public figure, if not a celebrity.

There the similarity ends. One position is relatively short-lived and pays millions. The other is at least a four-year term and not nearly so well remunerated. And no matter how seriously you take basketball, it is essentially a game, a sport, whereas the other may well affect every citizen in the United States and potentially—as economic and foreign policies are involved—citizens elsewhere as well.

Essays that depend primarily on other modes, such as description, narration, and definition, often use comparison and contrast to heighten a difference or clarify a point, but the pieces in this section rely on comparison and contrast as their main principle of organization, even though their purposes differ.

Audience and Purpose

Often you may want only to inform your reader; that gives you at least three possible theses:

x is better or worse than *y*.
x has a lot in common with *y*, though not obviously so.
x is quite different from *y*, though superficially similar.

If, for instance, your college is primarily residential, you might be interested in how it differs from a nonresidential institution. Assuming that your classmates are your audience, they might be surprised to find that on the average, students at nonresidential campuses are quite different. Compared to those at residential institutions, they are older, work more hours at jobs, miss more classes, carry fewer hours, attend fewer sports events, participate in fewer on-campus activities, and take longer to earn a degree.

You could easily turn what started out as an informative essay into an argumentative one if, in the course of writing, you decide that living on a campus that is primarily residential has some drawbacks that may not be apparent at first. A dorm room may not be half as pleasant as an apartment off campus, and eating in the cafeteria can be monotonous. On the other hand, living on campus makes it easier to form solid friendships, and classes don't have to be over at the bell—the discussion can continue without the pressure of having to race off for a job downtown. As you come up with more and more information, you are able to assess the pros and cons and, therefore, to construct a strong argument in favor of the side you believe is best.

Comparison can also be used to entertain your readers. A seemingly simple job such as washing the dog can be as much of a challenge as performing major surgery. At least at hospitals, you don't have to catch the patient first.

Analogy

One useful form of comparison is **analogy,** for it can emphasize a point or illuminate an idea. If you are writing about an abstraction, for example, you can make it more familiar by using an analogy to make it concrete and, therefore, more understandable. An intangible word such as *rumor* becomes more distinct, more memorable, if you write of it as cancer. Or, if you are explaining a process, analogy can often make the unfamiliar familiar; many a tennis instructor has said, "Hold your racquet as though you are shaking hands with a person."

An analogy is an extended **metaphor,** in which a primary term is equated with another, quite dissimilar term. The process of writing, for example, is a far cry from making music, but if you think of all the elements of the writing process—coming up with a topic and ideas about it, planning how to organize what you want to say, working on drafts, editing as you go along—then you can see how you can extend the description into a metaphor. You, the writer, are the leader of the orchestra. Organizing your ideas for an essay is rather like getting all the members of the orchestra to play the same tune. Can't find quite the right word? That's similar to having a musician missing from the string section. Wonder if that comma is in the right place? One of the horns skipped a note. Tone not quite what you want it to be? Some of the musicians are flat. Once you have a solid draft, however, it's as though rehearsal is over and the piece is ready for an audience.

So in exposition, analogy clarifies—because by making x analogous to y, you bring all the associations of y to bear on x. If you were to compare the differences in the style of two television newscasters, you might find that one delivers the news in a rush, like a machine gun firing, whereas the other is more like a single-shot target rifle. The machine gun person fires rapid lines and barely pauses for breath, a sharp contrast to the target rifle person, who hesitates between sentences as though to reload an idea before aiming it at the viewers.

To use analogy well, however, you have to use it cautiously. Work one into a sentence or paragraph instead of using it for an entire essay. Five pages of the ship of state can make your readers seasick.

Method of Comparison

Comparison and contrast essays group information so that the comparison is made by **blocks** or **point by point** or by a combination of the two. If you were to write an essay explaining the differences between an American feast, such as Thanksgiving, and a Chinese one, here is what the two major types of organization would look like in outline form:

Type	**Structure**	**Content**
Block	Paragraph 1	Introduction
	Block A, paragraphs 2–4	American culture
	Point 1	Preparation
	Point 2	Courses and types of food
	Point 3	Manners
	Block B, paragraphs 5–7	Chinese culture
	Point 1	Preparation
	Point 2	Courses and types of food
	Point 3	Manners
	Paragraph 8	Conclusion
Point by point	Paragraph 1	Introduction
	Point 1, paragraph 2	Preparation
		Chinese
		American
	Point 2, paragraph 3	Courses and types of food
		Chinese
		American

And so on. As you can see, sticking rigorously to one type of organization can become boring or predictable, so writers often mix the two.

In this chapter you'll find essays organized by block, point by point, and by a combination of the two. Outlining an essay readily reveals which type of organization the writer uses. In your own writing, you might first try what comes easiest; then, in a later draft, you might mix the organization a bit and see what you find most effective. Fortunately word processing makes such changes easy, but if you don't have a word processor, try writing each paragraph on a separate piece of paper. Shuffling them around is then a simple task, though you'll have to supply some transitions after you decide on the best sequence for your paragraphs.

Other Modes

A close look at any of the essays that follow will show how you can use other modes, such as description, narration, and cause and effect, to help flesh out the comparison and contrast. A brief narrative or anecdote is often a good way to begin an essay as it usually sets a conversational tone and establishes a link between writer and reader. Examples can clarify your points and description can make them memorable, while exploring why the differences or similarities exist or what effect they may have will lead you into pondering cause-and-effect relationships.

Organization and Ideas

The one-sentence thesis placed at the end of an introductory paragraph certainly informs your readers of your subject and stance, but you might find your paper more effective if you treat your thesis more subtly, trying it out in different forms and positions. While some of the essays in this chapter save their major assertion until last, others combine ideas from various points in the essay to form a thesis. And, of course, not all theses are explicit, but if you want to imply yours, you have to be sure your implication is clear or the reader may miss the point.

Although some writers begin the writing process with a thesis clearly set out, many find that it is easier to write their way into one. As a result, you may find that the last paragraph in your draft will make a very good introductory one, for by the time you write it, you have refined your thesis. At that point, you'll find writing a new introduction isn't the task it was to begin with; you already know where you ended up and how you got there.

Useful Terms

Analogy An analogy examines a subject by comparing it point by point to something seemingly unlike but more commonplace and less complex. An analogy is also an extended metaphor.

Block comparison A comparison of *x* to *y* by grouping all that is to be compared under *x* and then following with the same information under *y*.

Comparison and contrast An examination of two or more subjects by exploring their similarities and differences. Similarities and differences are usually developed through literal and logical comparisons within like categories.

Metaphor An implied but direct comparison in which the primary term is made more vivid by associating it with a quite dissimilar term. "Life is a bed of roses" is a familiar metaphor.

Point by point A comparison that examines one or more points by stating the point, then comparing subject *x* to subject *y,* and then continuing to the next point.

POINTERS FOR COMPARISON AND CONTRAST

Exploring the Topic

1. **What are the similarities?** What characteristics do your two subjects share? Are the two so similar that you have little to distinguish them? If so, try another subject; if not, pare down your list of similarities to the most important ones.

2. **What are the differences?** In what ways are your two subjects different? Are they so different that they have little in common? If so, make sure you can handle a humorous tone or try another subject; if not, pare down your list of differences to the most important ones.

3. **Should you emphasize similarities or differences?** Which pattern of organization best fits your material? Block? Point by point? A combination of the two?

(Continued)

POINTERS FOR COMPARISON AND CONTRAST *(Continued)*

4. **What examples will work best?** If your reader isn't familiar with your topic, what examples might be familiar? What examples will make clear what may be unfamiliar?

5. **What metaphor does your subject suggest?** Given the metaphor and your subject, what characteristics match? How can the metaphor be extended into an analogy? How can you outline the analogy as an equation? What equals what?

6. **What other modes are appropriate?** What modes can you draw on to help support your comparison and the organization of the essay? Do you need to define? Where can you use description? narration? example? Do any of your comparisons involve cause and effect?

7. **What is your point? Your purpose?** Do you want to entertain, inform, persuade? Given your point as a tentative thesis, should you spell it out in the essay or imply it? If you are writing to inform, what information do you want to present? If you are writing to persuade, what do you want your reader to believe or do?

8. **What persona do you want to create?** Is it best for you to be a part of the comparison and contrast or to be an observer? Do you have a strongly held conviction about your subject? Do you want it to show? Does your persona fit your audience, purpose, and material?

Drafting the Paper

1. **Know your reader.** Use your first paragraph to set out your major terms and your general focus and to prepare the reader for the pattern of organization and tone that will follow. Reexamine your list of similarities and differences to see which ones may be unfamiliar to your reader. Jot down an illustration or brief description by each characteristic that the reader may not be familiar with. If your reader is part of the group you are examining, tread carefully, and if your teacher may have a bias about your topic, try to figure out what the bias is so you can counter it. Reread your paper from the perspective of the reader who is biased so that you can check your diction as well as your choice of examples and assertions.

2. **Know your purpose.** If you are writing to persuade, keep in mind the reader's possible bias or neutral view and see how you can use your persona as well as logical and emotional appeals to get the reader on your side. Informative papers run the risk of telling readers something they already know, so use description, detail, example, and diction to present your information in a new light. If your paper's main purpose is to entertain, these techniques become even more crucial. Try adding alliteration, allusions, paradox, and puns to the other techniques you draw on.

3. **If you use an analogy, double-check it.** Make sure your analogy is an extended metaphor, not a statement of fact. See what you want to emphasize. Also make sure the placement is effective by trying out the analogy in different positions. Perhaps it works best as a framing device or standing alone in a sentence or paragraph.

4. **Use other modes to support your comparison.** Description and example are probably the most obvious modes to use, but consider narration, cause and effect, definition, and analogy as well. Perhaps a short narrative would add interest to your paper, or perhaps cause and effect enters into your comparisons. Definition may be vital to your thesis, and analogy may help clarify or expand a point.

5. **Check your pattern of organization.** If you are using block comparison, make sure you have introduced your two subjects and that your conclusion brings them back together. In the body of the paper, make sure that what you cover for one, you also cover for the other. In point-by-point comparison, check to see that your points are clearly set out. You may want to use both types of organization, though one will probably predominate.

6. **Make a point.** Perhaps you want to use your comparison to make a comment on the way we live, perhaps to clarify two items that people easily confuse, perhaps to argue that one thing is better than the other. Whatever your point, check it to make sure it is an assertion, not a mere fact. Whether your purpose is to inform or to persuade, take a stand and make sure that your thesis clearly implies or states it.

Living on Tokyo Time

Lynnika Butler

During the five years Lynnika Butler spent in Japan, she taught English, worked as a coordinator for international relations, and volunteered as an interpreter—experience that made her an astute observer of how the Japanese treat time. That experience, together with her BA in English and Spanish, may have also contributed to her decision to pursue a graduate degree in linguistics, and she is now enrolled at the University of Arizona. Her goal is "to use what I am learning about the science of language to help communities who are trying to preserve or revitalize their native languages." Butler's essay was first published in the Salt Journal, *Fall 2001, and then reprinted in* Utne's *January–February 2003 issue.*

What to Look For   The concept of time is a slippery one, but Butler explains it clearly. As you read her essay, be aware of how she leads into it and then explains how the two cultures view it.

1   It's fair to say that Japanese people are unbelievably busy. Working 10 hours a day, and often coming in on days off, they rarely take a vacation of more than three or four days. A straight week is a hedonistic luxury. Students have less than a month for summer vacation, and even then they have all kinds of assignments to do.

2   Watching people live like this, with almost no time for themselves, makes an American like me wonder why more of them don't throw themselves under subway trains. But I seem to have far more anxiety about free time than my Japanese friends do—even though, compared to them, I have much more of it. Why doesn't this cradle-to-grave, manic scheduling bother them?

3   A lot of Westerners make the glib assumption that Japanese people are simply submissive, unoriginal, or masochistic enough to put up with such a punishing system. I don't think that's it. In Japan, time is measured in the same hours and minutes and days as anywhere else, but it is experienced as a fundamentally different phenomenon. In the West, we save time, spend time, invest time, even kill time—all of

which implies that it belongs to us in the first place. We might find ourselves obliged to trade huge chunks of our time for a steady salary, but most of us resent this as something stolen from us, and we take it for granted that our spare hours are none of our teachers' or bosses' business.

4   The Japanese grow up with a sense of time as a communal resource, like the company motor pool. If you get permission, you can borrow a little for your own use, but the main priority is to serve the institution—in this case, society as a whole. Club activities, overtime, drinks with the boss, and invitations to the boring weddings of people you hardly know are not seen as intruding on your free time—they are the *shikata ga nai* (nothing you can do about it) duties that turn the wheels of society. "Free" time (*hima*) is something that only comes into existence when these obligations have all been fulfilled. This is nicely borne out by an expression my boss uses whenever he leaves work a little early: *chotto hima morau* ("I'm going to receive a little free time").

5   Though I can't pretend I like living on a Japanese schedule, I try hard not to make judgments. *Oku ga fukai*—things are more complicated than they appear. The Japanese sacrifice their private time to society, but in return they get national health insurance, a wonderful train system, sushi, the two thousand temples of Kyoto, and traditional culture so rich that every back-water village seems to have its own unique festivals, seasonal dishes, legends, and even dialect. All of which are invaluable social goods that I would not trade for a lifetime of free hours.

ORGANIZATION AND IDEAS

1. Butler opens by stating that the Japanese are "busy." How effective are the examples that support her statement?
2. In paragraph 2, Butler poses a question. What is the answer?
3. Sum up the Japanese attitude toward time. What is the American one?
4. Of the two views of time, which does Butler prefer and why?
5. Butler says that Americans treat time as though "it belongs to us" (paragraph 3). How accurate do you find that statement?

TECHNIQUE AND STYLE

1. Butler states a paradox in paragraph 2. How effective is it?
2. The essay opens with a description of Japanese "busyness" and follows it with a paragraph that gives Butler's reaction to it. To what extent is her response similar to the reader's?

3. Think about the simile Butler uses in paragraph 4. How effective is it?

4. Butler occasionally uses a Japanese term that she then translates. What does her use of the Japanese add to the essay?

5. Reread the last paragraph. Given your sense of what a conclusion should do, how effective is it?

SUGGESTIONS FOR WRITING

Journal

1. To what extent do you share the American sense of time being a personal possession?

2. How difficult would it be for you to adapt to the Japanese sense of time? Explain.

Essay

1. You can use Butler's essay as a model for your own, one in which you compare and contrast two groups' attitudes toward something. Think, for instance, of the difference between how you and your parents view vacations. For your own topic, consider first two different groups and then think your way into their attitudes toward *x*, with *x* standing for what they differ about. Suggestions for different categories:

generations
regions, for example, North and South
city and country residents
males and females
teachers and students

2. Butler contrasts the various intrusions on what Americans would think of as their free time to what Japanese see as "duties that turn the wheels of society" (paragraph 4). Think about your own sense of obligation and those things you do and do not feel a sense of duty toward. Write an essay in which you define your sense of duty by contrasting examples of where it does and does not apply.

Who's Watching? Reality TV and Sports

Frank Deford

It's hard to find something Frank Deford doesn't do and do well: if you read Sports Illustrated, *you've probably seen his byline; if you listen to National Public Radio's "Morning Edition," you've heard his commentary; if you watch Bryant Gumbel's "RealSports" on HBO, you've even seen him. Deford taught at Princeton University before he took up journalism as his career, and he has won almost every prize for sports writing there is to win: the National Magazine Award, the U.S. Sportswriter of the Year, the Christopher Award, and the Peabody Award. The author of several screenplays and fourteen books, his latest is* The Old Ball Game *(2005), focusing on baseball and its players at the turn of the twentieth century. The piece that follows was broadcast on NPR on June 2, 2004.*

What to Look For   Though Deford depends on comparison and contrast to examine his subject, be on the lookout for how he also uses examples and explains causal relationships—why x happened and the results. Note how these other modes support the main one.

1   It would seem to me that reality TV is nothing more than a form of sport. It's a competition, a game, but on a coast-to-coast basis it's more emotionally appealing than many of our sports. So I have to believe that as many people get more interested in the reality shows, they lose some interest in the old-fashioned sports.

2   The constant problem that sports in this country suffers from is that there are just too many teams playing too many games. People, especially local fans, can follow their teams, but only the hard-core zealots monitor a whole sport. As a consequence, especially in the team sports with myriad games—baseball, basketball and hockey—home attendance may remain high, while at the same time ratings for national games decrease. That may sound contradictory, but it makes sense.

3   Let's just take one city as example. The good people in Dallas may have cared passionately about their basketball and hockey teams, but as soon as the Stars and the Mavericks were eliminated in the playoffs, I would suspect that a goodly number of the Dallas fans dropped their interest altogether in the NBA and NHL playoffs and started devoting their attention to the local baseball team, the Texas Rangers.

4   Reality TV focuses. There are only a small number of competitors and we get to meet them and know them well, a whole lot better than our friends in Dallas ever got to know the Calgary Flames or the Milwaukee Bucks during the regular season. In many respects, in fact, reality TV shows essentially start with the elimination play-offs, which concentrate the mind without having to bother us with the long, boring regular season. Reality television shows also are scheduled for just once a week. Every competition becomes important, in TV language, "appointment viewing."

5   Football has become the one traditional team sport that continues to have a growing national audience, and a large reason for that is that there are only a limited number of games, with the vast majority taking place on the weekends. It's no coincidence, I think, that the one sport which has shown great ratings gains in the last few years is NASCAR, which follows the once-a-week NFL model. NASCAR is like an all-star reality show every week. Everybody who follows the sport knows all the major drivers. Contrast NASCAR, say, to the PGA, where each week there are different contenders. The casual fan can't keep them all straight, so he only stays tuned when Tiger Woods has a chance.

6   Familiarity is so important when we are watching any kind of game. If we know the contestants, we can decide whether we want to root for them or against them. That's why the NFL and the NBA drafts are more interesting to more people than most actual games. We become familiar with the prospects before the draft and get involved.

7   Anyway, with all the competition from the new once-a-week television competitions, maybe major-league baseball, the NBA and the NHL are just going to have to settle for having intense local followings with declining national impact, and the hero that a nation turns its lonely eyes to is not going to be a great star who hits home runs or scores baskets, but some guy who sings songs or picks a bride or gets a job with Donald Trump. Yes, indeed, your new American idol, but that's reality.

ORGANIZATION AND IDEAS

1. What paragraph or paragraphs function as the introduction? How much information does it give you?
2. Deford cites examples in paragraphs 3 and 4. How apt are they?
3. In what ways are reality shows and sports similar? Different? What kind of organizational pattern does Deford use?
4. Reread the essay to see how many examples of sports Deford provides and how many of reality shows. How fair is his comparison?
5. Think about what Deford says about NASCAR (paragraph 5). Is that also true of the World Series? The Super Bowl? Why or why not?

TECHNIQUE AND STYLE

1. How important is Deford's use of cause and effect in supporting his points? Explain what it adds to or detracts from the essay.
2. What is Deford's purpose? Is he writing to argue, explain, speculate, lament, complain, what?
3. Consider the examples Deford draws from sports. What definition can you deduce for his concept of what is covered by the word *sports?*
4. Deford's essay was written to be heard on radio. What can you spot that shows he was aware of how his essay would sound?
5. How would you describe Deford's persona? What examples can you cite to support your view?

SUGGESTIONS FOR WRITING

Journal

1. What are your least and most favorite sports and why?
2. What are your least and most favorite television shows and why?

Essay

1. "Reality show" is a broad label, but Deford does bring out some of the shows' characteristics. Think about them and think also of the various kinds of shows that appear on television:

   quiz shows
   major sports events (Indy 500, Kentucky Derby)
   survival shows
   talent shows
   talk shows (such as Oprah, Jerry Springer, Jay Leno, David Letterman)

   Select two programs within a category and compare them, analyzing the kind of "reality" that is being presented. What conclusion can you draw? State it as an assertion and you have your thesis.

2. If you think about the word *sports*, you'll find it covers a large group of activities. Aside from the obvious ones, the term can also be applied to many that are less obvious, such as fencing, synchronized swimming, logrolling, and fox hunting. Take your own favorite sport and compare it to one that you don't think deserves the name. The essay that results will use comparison and contrast to explain what you mean by *sport*.

Playing House

Denise Leight

As a student at Middlesex County College in Edison, New Jersey, Denise Leight wrote "Playing House" in response to Daniel Zimmerman's research assignment for his English class. The essay was then published in the Spring 2001 issue of "Becoming Writers," one of the English Department's three journals. The collection, according to its editors, "celebrates the achievements of our students, who worked hard over the past semester to translate the insights and responses of full and busy lives into the well-crafted and thoughtfully imagined essays reprinted here. As writers we know it is never easy to find the words and form that most accurately communicate what we know, and the finished piece almost never emerges in the shape we originally imagined it. But it is in the struggle to express ourselves that our thoughts become fully ours, and the battle is always a richly rewarding process." "Becoming Writers" is an appropriate title for such a collection.

What to Look For   As you read Denise Leight's essay, figure out if she is explaining her subject or arguing for a specific position or something in between.

1   More and more couples today live together or "play house" before taking the matrimonial plunge. Living together before marriage has become so popular that approximately half the couples in

America participate in this activity (Gorrell 16). Some couples choose to live together to test their compatibility and possibly avoid an unsuccessful marriage. With the number of marriages ending in divorce these days, it sounds reasonable that many couples want to give marriage a trial run before making any formal commitment. But do the chances of a successful marriage actually improve by cohabiting?

2   "Cohabitation isn't marriage," says sociology professor Linda Waite of the University of Chicago (qtd. in Jabusch 14). Married and cohabiting couples do not have the same characteristics. According to Professor Waite, cohabiting couples lack both specialization and commitment in their relationships (Jabusch 14). Unwed cohabitants generally live more financially and emotionally independent of one another to allow themselves the freedom to leave. This often results in less monogamous, short-term relationships.

3   Married couples specialize—while one partner might take over the cooking, the other might specialize in cleaning. They pool their money, time, and other resources, creating a higher quality lifestyle. Unmarried couples find it much harder to trust each other financially without the legal bond and, therefore, do not move quickly to pool those resources. While marriage does not ensure monogamy, married couples have more invested in their relationship and think longer before acting on their impulses and stepping outside of the relationship. Unmarried couples do not operate as a partnership, says Waite: "they are being two separate people—it is trading off freedom and low levels of commitment for fewer benefits than you get from commitment" (qtd. in Jabusch 15).

4   Many singles believe that by practicing marriage they will receive the commitment they desire. With this in mind, they move in together intending to tie the knot eventually. Time passes and the couple rarely talks seriously about finalizing the commitment. And so, they often end up cohabiting for a few years until eventually someone gets tired of waiting and leaves. Cohabitation can suppress the development of a higher level of commitment.

5   Sometimes, one or both of the people involved become complacent in the relationship, and without any pressure to move forward, they won't. As social psychologist Dr. Julia Hare puts it, "Why would you go to the store to buy some milk with the cow standing in the living room?" (qtd. in "Why . . . Marriage?" 53). Certainly, to call a marriage successful, it must actually take place.

6   A study conducted by an assistant professor of human development and family studies at Pennsylvania State University, Catherine
Cohan, Ph.D., found that those who had lived together before
marriage "displayed more negative and fewer positive problem
solving and support behaviors than couples that had not cohabi-
tated prior to marriage" (Gorrell 16). For example, if one partner of
a cohabiting couple diagnosed a particular topic as a problem, the
other would express more negative behaviors such as forcefulness
and attempts to control. Women who had lived with their partners
before marriage generally exhibited more verbal aggressiveness
than those in the couples without premarital cohabitation.

7   One cannot ignore the possibility that cohabitants as a group
may have certain distinguishable characteristics that make them
more likely to divorce. The type of people who would choose to
cohabit before marriage may simply be less willing to put the full
amount of effort required into a relationship. However, a recent
study determined that "the cohabitor selectivity reflected in four
sociodemographic variables—parental divorce, marital status
homogamy, age homogamy, and stepchildren—is unable to mate-
rially account for the cohabitation effect" (Hall and Zhao 424). In
other words, the study did not show that these predisposing factors contributed greatly to the marriage dissolution of cohabiting
couples.

8   Cohabiting does not necessarily equal the tragic end of a relationship, but couples who do marry after living together have higher
rates of separation and divorce (Gorrell 16). The lack of commitment
in such a relationship plays a large role in this scenario. If a couple
wishes to have a successful marriage, they should show their commitment to each other from the beginning. If they trust each other
enough not to cohabit before marriage, their marriage already has a
higher probability of success.

Works Cited

"Why Are So Many Couples Living Together Before Marriage?" *Jet* 3 Aug.
    1998: 52–55.

Gorrell, Carin. "Live-in and Learn." *Psychology Today.* Nov. 2000: 16.

Hall, David R., and John Z. Zhao. "Cohabitation and Divorce in Canada:
    Testing the Selectivity Hypothesis." *Journal of Marriage & the Family*
    57.2 (1995): 421–27.

Jabusch, Willard F. "The Myth of Cohabitation." *America* 7 Oct. 2000: 14–16.

ORGANIZATION AND IDEAS

1. Leight poses a question in paragraph 1. What is it and what is her answer?
2. What are the characteristics of a cohabiting couple? A married couple?
3. What is Leight's view of cohabitation versus marriage? What evidence supports your opinion?
4. As expected in a research paper, you find Leight cites evidence throughout. Is it sufficient? Why or why not?
5. What arguments or loopholes can you think of that Leight does not mention?

TECHNIQUE AND STYLE

1. In what ways is the title a pun?
2. What is the function of paragraph 7 and how necessary is it?
3. How would you describe Leight's level of diction? How appropriate is it for the assignment?
4. Think about what Leight lists as works cited. What conclusions can you draw from her list?
5. What is the essay's aim—to explain, argue, both? What evidence can you find to back up your view?

SUGGESTIONS FOR WRITING

Journal

1. Set a timer for 15 minutes and then use your journal to explore the extent to which you are convinced by Leight's essay.
2. How would you describe Leight's persona, the person behind the writing? Quote from the essay to illustrate your impressions.

Essay

1. Leight's essay focuses on an important decision that many people face. Think about the decisions you have made between two choices, choose one, and write an essay in which you explain the choice and analyze whether it was the correct one. Suggestions:

   to go to college
   to take a particular job
   to pick a major
   to stand up for a friend
   to take a risk

2. Write your own version of "Playing House," using your library or the Web to research the subject, then selecting your own sources, using Leight's essay as an additional source. Argue for your own point of view.

World and America Watching Different Wars

Danna Harman

Any newspaper would be hard-pressed to find someone as qualified to cover the war in Iraq as Danna Harman. After earning a BA in history from Harvard, she studied economics and Arabic at the University of California, Berkeley, and received an MPhil from Cambridge University in Islamic Studies. Now based in Washington DC as a feature writer for the Christian Science Monitor, *Harman has served as the paper's Africa correspondent with special assignments in Egypt, Israel, Yemen, Jordan, and Iraq. Her work has also been published in the* New Republic, *the* London Times, *the* Sunday Times, *the* Chicago Sun Times, *and* Elle. *Sent to cover the war for the* Monitor, *she was stationed in Egypt. There, she says, "I spent the whole month with the TV tuned to the local channels and went out to talk to people in the street as much as possible about what they believed was going on—and found the gap between the perceptions here and in the U.S. of what was happening pretty amazing." You'll see what she means. Her piece was published in the* Monitor *on March 25, 2003, where she also acknowledges the assistance of special correspondent Dan Murphy in Jakarta, Indonesia, and Alexandra Marks in New York.*

What to Look For   As you read Harman's piece, keep in mind that it was written for a newspaper. The paragraphs are set to fit a news column, and the subheadings guide the reader through the story. Look to see how they help.

1   CAIRO, EGYPT—The Hamouda family is gathered around the TV, sipping sugary tea and glued to the pictures of captured U.S. soldiers being interrogated by Iraqis on the popular Qatar-based satellite station Al Jazeera.

2   "What's your name?" A terrified young female POW is asked. "How old are you?" The camera moves to her feet, which are bloody and bare.

3   "Yieee!" cheers eldest son Ahmed, knocking over a fake geranium plant as he shoots up from the couch in excitement. "Show it how it is!"

4   It is not that they are happy to see suffering, says Hellmy, the father, somewhat apologetically, as the camera weaves between several bodies. "But the other side of the story needs to be told."

5   The gruesome video shown Sunday on Al Jazeera—reaching 35 million Arab-speakers worldwide, including about 20 percent of the Egyptian population—will probably never be seen by the average American TV viewer.

6   In fact, American audiences are seeing and reading about a different war than the rest of the world. The news coverage in Europe, the Middle East, and Asia, reflects and defines the widening perception gap about the motives for this war. Surveys show that an increasing number of Americans believe this is a just war, while most of the world's Arabs and Muslims see it as a war of aggression. Media coverage does not necessarily create these leanings, say analysts, but it works to cement them.

7   "The difference in coverage between the United States and the rest of the world helped contribute to the situation that we're in now," says Kim Spencer, president of WorldLink TV, a U.S. satellite channel devoted to airing foreign news. "Americans have been unable to see how they're perceived."

8   For example, most Americans, watching CNN, Fox, or the U.S. television networks, are not seeing as much coverage of injured Iraqi citizens, or being given more than a glimpse of the antiwar protests now raging in the Muslim world and beyond.

9   In the Middle East, Europe, and parts of Asia, by comparison, the rapid progress made by U.S.-led troops has been played down. And many aspects of the conflict being highlighted in the U.S.—such as the large number of Iraqi troops surrendering, the cooperation between U.S.-led forces and various Gulf states, commentary on America's superior weapons technology, and the human interest angles on soldier life in the desert—are almost totally absent from coverage outside the U.S.

10   "Sure, the news we get in the Arab world is slanted," admits Hussein Amin, chair of the department of journalism and mass communication at Cairo's American University. "In the same way the news received in the U.S. is biased."

The View from Europe

11   Some analysts note that European press ownership is less concentrated than its counterparts in the U.S. and is seen as providing more

perspectives than either the Arab or American outlets. In Frankfurt, for example, readers have access to 16 different German-language newspapers—many of which present different vantage points, which makes for a more lively and varied debate.

12   European journalists also seem to ask different, more skeptical, questions of this war, often being the ones at White House and Pentagon press conferences to ask whether the invasion of Iraq has turned up any of the weapons of mass destruction that used to justify the invasion—even as their American counterparts repeatedly focus on such questions as whether Saddam Hussein is alive or dead.

13   Media watchers say the European press has tended to be more balanced than the U.S. media in dealing with the war, in part because Europe is so much closer to the Muslim world. John Schmidt, a former reporter for the *International Herald Tribune,* who has just returned from Europe, notes that in Marseille, France, 30 percent of the population is Muslim. In Berlin, the biggest minority population is the Turks.

14   "These are countries in Europe that live cheek by jowl with Islamic people, they know how deep the dislike for the West can be, they know how sensitively some of these issues have to be transmitted," says Mr. Schmidt, who is now an economics writer for the *Milwaukee Journal Sentinel.*

15   "There are really two stories unfolding here, one is the war and its progress and the second one is the progress of world opinion," says Tom Patterson, a media expert at Harvard University's Kennedy School of Government. "That second dimension is there in the American press, but it's clearly way underreported."

16   For instance, American media outlets may report on the demonstrations in other countries, particularly if there are violent clashes. But they don't devote as many resources to covering in depth the growing anti-American sentiment—even among American allies—or its implications for the future, says Professor Patterson.

Reporter or Soldier?

17   Back in his Cairo living room, the elder Mr. Hamouda flips to CNN for a moment, over cries of protest from the rest of the family. It is vaguely possible to make out U.S. troop maneuvers on a grainy green screen. In the corner there is a small photo of a middle-aged man in an Army jacket.

18   Nadia, the great-grandmother in the family, wonders aloud who CNN correspondent Walter Rogers is and what he is doing with the troops. "He is in bed with them," says an English speaking nephew, laughing at the well-worn joke, a pun on "embedding," in which the Pentagon allows journalists to report from within military units. Nadia has no idea what the boy is talking about. "Turn it back to Al Jazeera," she demands, adjusting her false teeth, "let's see those bodies again."

19   Across the globe, in Indonesia, student leader and antiwar activist Muhammad Hermawan has seen these same pictures on his local channel, which pirates Al Jazeera's signal and adds simultaneous Indonesian translation. "The more these pictures are shown, the more people will understand America's brutal aggression," he says. "People will learn, and we'll see bigger and bigger protests."

20   Interest in the war has been so high that Indonesia's TV7 began pirating Al Jazeera's signal shortly before the start of the war. The new station carries the Arab-language broadcast with simultaneous Indonesian translation. Though Al Jazeera is only shown from 10 in the evening until 11 in the morning an official at TV7 says the news department is receiving about 100 calls a day from viewers, up from "almost zero" before the U.S. invasion began.

21   The news broadcasts in Indonesia, the world's most populous Muslim nation, have been tamer than the news in the Middle East, focusing on protests against the war at home, with official statements against the war from abroad.

22   But they have also carried some stories sympathetic to U.S. soldiers, including an interview with Anecita Hudson of Alamogordo, Texas. Mrs. Hudson says her son, 23 year-old Army Specialist Joseph Hudson, was one of the prisoners of war shown on Al Jazeera. She said seeing her son captured was "like a bad dream."

23   Mrs. Hudson didn't see her son on American news outlets. She spotted him on a Filipino cable channel she subscribes to. She is originally from the Philippines.

24   The pictures of U.S. troops drew condemnation from U.S. Defense Secretary Donald Rumsfeld and other officials. "It seems to me that showing a few pictures on the screen, not knowing who they are and being communicated by Al Jazeera, which is not a perfect instrument of communication, obviously is part of Iraqi propaganda," Mr. Rumsfeld told CBS.

25   "War is ugly by nature and we did not create these pictures—we are only there to reflect reality on the ground," says Jihad Ali Ballout, Al Jazeera's media relations head. "Truth is sometimes unpleasant and gruesome, and I feel distressed when people ask me to dress it up."

Washington Watches Al Jazeera

26   The Bush administration sees Al Jazeera—the cable news channel made famous for its airing of Osama Bin Laden tapes—as having an anti-American bias. But, since the seven-year-old Al Jazeera has grown from six to 24 hours of daily programming and reaches more than 35 million Arab speakers around the world, including 150,000 in the United States, Washington seems to be attempting to work more closely with the network.

27   The Pentagon offered Al Jazeera four choice spots for its reporters to be embedded with U.S. military units and assigned it a special media liaison officer, and both National Security Adviser Condoleezza Rice and Defense Secretary Donald Rumsfeld have given extensive interviews to Al Jazeera in recent days. Al-Arabiya and Abu Dhabi, two other 24-hour Arab-language stations, have received similar attention from the administration.

28   Al Jazeera says that it has two of its correspondents "embedded" with U.S. units—but the units in question are in Kuwait. It has no reporters with U.S. troops directly participating in the invasion.

Variety Breeds Objectivity?

29   Professor Amin in Cairo argues that while watching this war unfold in the various media outlets is a good example of how bias clearly exists on all sides, there are nonetheless positive signs that international media are collectively moving toward becoming more objective, by force of necessity.

30   "The fact that the common man has access to different sources today means that it's harder for one source to get away with showing only one side of the story. You can piece together a broader, more accurate story yourself," he says.

31   There is some awareness in the Hamouda living room that Arab broadcasters may also spread propaganda.

32   In 1967, four days after Israel had won the war against Egypt, Egyptian radio was still declaring victory, recalls Hellmy Hamouda.

"I was in the Suez Canal at the time and I had seen some of the war with my own eyes," he says, "I had a hunch that radio was not telling the truth."

33   "Today, we can find the better truth by simply changing channels or going on the Internet," says Hamouda. He then flips back to Al Jazeera at the demand of grandma Nadia, "If we want to."

ORGANIZATION AND IDEAS

1. Harman covers a lot of topics in her essay—the media, bias, anti-American sentiment, the war in Iraq, pro-Muslim sentiment. What is her primary subject and what evidence supports your view?
2. In what ways does the American media differ from that in the Middle East, Europe, and much of Asia?
3. When published, the piece was subtitled "CNN vs. Al Jazeera: Seeing is Often Believing." What evidence can you find to support that idea?
4. To what extent is Harman explaining the situation? Arguing for a particular point of view?
5. In one sentence, state Harman's thesis. How valid is it now?

TECHNIQUE AND STYLE

1. Throughout the piece, Harman makes extensive use of sources with both quotations and summaries. What do they contribute to the essay?
2. The Hamouda family appears in paragraphs 1–4, 17 and 18, and again in 31–33. What do they add to the piece?
3. Look again at the subheadings. To what extent do they work to guide you through the essay?
4. In what ways is Harman's essay appropriate for the *Christian Science Monitor*?
5. The story opens and closes with a narrative. What does it add?

SUGGESTIONS FOR WRITING

Journal

1. Would you call Harman optimistic, pessimistic, something in between? Explain.
2. How do you obtain world news? To what extent do you find the source credible and why?

Essay

1. The media is often accused of bias or sensationalism, but other considerations are also at work—time constraints, availability of sources, concerns

of the readership, and so on. Use a recent major event to analyze the accuracy and depth of its reporting. You might compare the same story as covered in two

national daily newspapers
national evening television news shows
weekly news magazines
national Sunday newspapers
daily Web news reports

2. Choose a political news story of some importance and read about it—start to finish—in a major American newspaper and one from Great Britain, using print versions from the library or available on the Web. What differences do you note? What, if any, biases can you find? Where does the truth lie?

The Raven

Barry Lopez

Although Barry Lopez was born in Port Chester, New York, he spent much of his early life in southern California. It was there where he first fell in love with landscapes in general and deserts in particular, the Mojave Desert to be precise. After returning to New York and then graduating from Notre Dame with a major in English, he became a professional photographer specializing in nature and landscape scenes. Finding that his lens didn't get close enough to nature, he turned to writing, traveling the world to write about its wonders. His work is published regularly in journals such as Harper's Magazine *and the* Paris Review, *and his list of books is a long and distinguished one. Of* Wolves and Men *(1982) received the John Burroughs Medal for distinguished natural history writing, and* Arctic Dreams: Imagination and Desire in a Northern Landscape *(1986) won the National Book Award for Best Book of Nonfiction. His most recent book is a collection of his writings,* Vintage Lopez *(2004). Lopez's writing has often been compared to that of Henry David Thoreau. According to one interviewer, Lopez "brings an acute sense of obligation to detail and integrity with his every observance, and something that can only be described as a spiritually driven, almost Zen-like regard for non-fiction." The essay that follows appeared in* Desert Notes: Reflections in the Eye of a Raven *(1976).*

What to Look For   You'll find that Lopez's essay rides a fine line between fantasy and reality, although his point is a serious one. In that sense, you can read the piece as a sort of fable, much like those of Aesop, the sixth century Greek who wrote the still familiar tale of the tortoise and the hare, among many others. The idea of depicting animals with human traits is still much with us, though the creatures have changed into the likes of the Roadrunner and Mickey Mouse.

1   I am going to have to start at the other end by telling you this: there are no crows in the desert. What appear to be crows are ravens. You must examine the crow, however, before you can understand the raven. To forget the crow completely, as some have tried to do, would be like trying to understand the one who stayed without talking to the one who left. It is important to make note of who has left the desert.

2   To begin with, the crow does nothing alone. He cannot abide silence and he is prone to stealing things, twigs and bits of straw, from the nests of his neighbors. It is a game with him. He enjoys tricks. If he cannot make up his mind the crow will take two or three wives, but this is not a game. The crow is very accommodating and he admires compulsiveness.

3   Crows will live in street trees in the residential areas of great cities. They will walk at night on the roofs of parked cars and peck at the grit; they will scrape the pinpoints of their talons across the steel and, with their necks outthrust, watch for frightened children listening in their beds.

4   Put all this to the raven: he will open his mouth as if to say something. Then he will look the other way and say nothing. Later, when you have forgotten, he will tell you he admires the crow.

5   The raven is larger than the crow and has a beard of black feathers at his throat. He is careful to kill only what he needs. Crows, on the other hand, will search out the great horned owl, kick and punch him awake, and then, for roosting too close to their nests, they will kill him. They will come out of the sky on a fat, hot afternoon and slam into the head of a dozing rabbit and go away laughing. They will tear out a whole row of planted corn and eat only a few kernels. They will defecate on scarecrows and go home and sleep with 200,000 of their friends in an atmosphere

of congratulation. Again, it is only a game; this should not be taken to mean that they are evil.

6   There is however this: when too many crows come together on a roost there is a lot of shoving and noise and a white film begins to descend over the crows' eyes and they go blind. They fall from their perches and lie on the ground and starve to death. When confronted with this information, crows will look past you and warn you vacantly that it is easy to be misled.

7   The crow flies like a pigeon. The raven flies like a hawk. He is seen only at a great distance and then not very clearly. This is true of the crow too, but if you are very clever you can trap the crow. The only way to be sure what you have seen is a raven is to follow him until he dies of old age, and then examine the body.

8   Once there were many crows in the desert. I am told it was like this: you could sit back in the rocks and watch a pack of crows working over the carcass of a coyote. Some would eat, the others would try to squeeze out the vultures. The raven would never be seen. He would be at a distance, alone, perhaps eating a scorpion.

9   There was, at this time, a small alkaline water hole at the desert's edge. Its waters were bitter. No one but crows would drink there, although they drank sparingly, just one or two sips at a time. One day a raven warned someone about the dangers of drinking the bitter water and was overheard by a crow. When word of this passed among the crows they felt insulted. They jeered and raised insulting gestures to the ravens. They bullied each other into drinking the alkaline water until they had drunk the hole dry and gone blind.

10   The crows flew into canyon walls and dove straight into the ground at forty miles an hour and broke their necks. The worst of it was their cartwheeling across the desert floor, stiff wings outstretched, beaks agape, white eyes ballooning, surprising rattlesnakes hidden under sage bushes out of the noonday sun. The snakes awoke, struck and held. The wheeling birds strew them across the desert like sprung traps.

11   When all the crows were finally dead, the desert bacteria and fungi bored into them, burrowed through bone and muscle, through aqueous humor and feathers until they had reduced the stiff limbs of soft black to blue dust.

12   After that, there were no more crows in the desert. The few who watched from a distance took it as a sign and moved away.

13   Finally there is this: one morning four ravens sat at the edge of the desert waiting for the sun to rise. They had been there all night

and the dew was like beads of quicksilver on their wings. Their eyes were closed and they were as still as the cracks in the desert floor.

14   The wind came off the snow-capped peaks to the north and ruffled their breath feathers. Their talons arched in the white earth and they smoothed their wings with sleek, dark bills. At first light their bodies swelled and their eyes flashed purple. When the dew dried on their wings they lifted off from the desert floor and flew away in four directions. Crows would never have had the patience for this.

15   If you want to know more about the raven: bury yourself in the desert so that you have a commanding view of the high basalt cliffs where he lives. Let only your eyes protrude. Do not blink—the movement will alert the raven to your continued presence. Wait until a generation of ravens has passed away. Of the new generation there will be at least one bird who will find you. He will see your eyes staring up out of the desert floor. The raven is cautious, but he is thorough. He will sense your peaceful intentions. Let him have the first word. Be careful: he will tell you he knows nothing.

16   If you do not have the time for this, scour the weathered desert shacks for some sign of the raven's body. Look under old mattresses and beneath loose floorboards. Look behind the walls. Sooner or later you will find a severed foot. It will be his and it will be well preserved.

17   Take it out in the sunlight and examine it closely. Notice that there are three fingers that face forward, and a fourth, the longest and like a thumb, that faces to the rear. The instrument will be black but no longer shiny, the back of it sheathed in armor plate and the underside padded like a wolf's foot.

18   At the end of each digit you will find a black, curved talon. You will see that the talons are not as sharp as you might have suspected. They are made to grasp and hold fast, not to puncture. They are more like the jaws of a trap than a fistful of ice picks. The subtle difference serves the raven well in the desert. He can weather a storm on a barren juniper limb; he can pick up and examine the crow's eye without breaking it.

ORGANIZATION AND IDEAS

1. Reread paragraph 1. What does it imply about the rest of the essay? How does it set up the focus of paragraphs 2–4?

2. What does Lopez tell you about the crow? About the raven? Write down the details and the paragraphs they come from.

3. What do paragraphs 15–18 convey about the relationship between humans and ravens?

4. To come up with a thesis for the essay, first think about the crow versus the raven: which one does Lopez prefer and why? Take your answer to that question and add to it your answer to question 3. Then reduce your responses to a one-sentence assertion and that will be the thesis.

5. How successfully does Lopez mix fantasy and reality?

TECHNIQUE AND STYLE

1. To what extent does Lopez's essay fit the genre of the fable? Does it have a moral? If so, what is it?

2. How would you describe the tone of the essay?

3. To what extent does Lopez use the first person pronoun *I*? What reasons can you discover for the degree to which he uses it?

4. If you are familiar with the desert, to what extent does Lopez portray it realistically? If you are not familiar with the desert, to what extent does he make you understand what it is like?

5. Reread the essay, marking every time Lopez mentions *patience*, either directly or indirectly. What is he saying about patience? How does that point reinforce the tone of the essay?

SUGGESTIONS FOR WRITING

Journal

1. Take a few minutes to write up your response to Lopez's essay. Do you have questions about it? To what extent did you like or dislike it and why?

2. We often discover human characteristics in animals we know well, pets in particular. Describe an animal you know well, attributing human traits to it.

Essay

1. Write your own version of a fable or semifable. Like Lopez, you may want to mix fantasy and reality, or you may want to shape your tone to the one or the other. To start off with, consider a possible subject such as two similar

animals
clothing styles
foods
game shows
textbooks

Once you have a topic to work with, decide on the kind of tone you want for the essay and then start to play with characteristics that you can attribute to your choices. If it's a fable that you're writing, you can be an observer, like Lopez, or remove yourself from the narrative and have the characters speak for themselves.

2. Reread Lopez's essay, noting what is fantasy and what is reality. Does he treat the two equally or is one predominant? What effect is he trying to achieve? Write an essay in which you compare his use of the two and analyze its effect.

ADDITIONAL WRITING ASSIGNMENTS

●●

Using Comparison and Contrast

1. Compare two dissimilar subjects to make a satirical point: partying vs. studying, pets vs. children, poker vs. football, bicycle vs. car, or junk food vs. a home-cooked meal.
2. Compare two ways to the same goal: studying or cramming, using logic or emotion, knee-jerk or thoughtful reaction, planning fun or being spontaneous.
3. Compare yourself to someone else: parent, celebrity, political figure, friend, or sibling.
4. Compare two people who had a distinct influence on their fields: sports, music, film, medical research, history, or politics.

Evaluating the Essays

1. "Living on Tokyo Time" and "World and America Watching Different Wars" examine different cultures: the Japanese attitude toward time, and an Egyptian family's view of the war in Iraq. Which essay do you find the more interesting and why? Use quotations from both to make your point.
2. "The Raven" and "World and America Watching Different Wars" both deal with reality, but in very different ways. Lopez writes a fable that demands the reader interpret the reality it represents, whereas Harman reports the reality she observes. Which do you find more effective and why?
3. Although the essays by Lopez and Deford don't seem to have much in common, they share a similar purpose: Deford explains why reality shows are eating into the audience for sports, and Lopez explains why there are no crows in the desert. Reread the essays and think about which side each author is on: reality TV or sports; crow or raven. Of the two writers, which is better at disguising his bias? Use quotations from the essays to support your thesis.
4. Reread "Living on Tokyo Time" and "Playing House." Butler analyzes how the Japanese view time, and Leight explains how couples view marriage. List the qualities each group values or represents. Write an essay in which you explain what you discover and analyze the values involved.

On Using
Process

7

I f you have ever been frustrated in your attempts to put together a barbecue grill or hook up a stereo system, you know the value of clear and complete directions. And if you have tried to explain how to get to a particular house or store, you also know that being able to give clear directions is not as easy as it seems. We deal with this practical, how-to kind of **process analysis** every day in recipes, user's manuals, instruction booklets, and essays. Process analysis calls for:

- dividing the topic into the necessary steps
- describing each step in sufficient detail
- sequencing the steps so they are easy to follow
- anticipating trouble spots

While explaining directions is one kind of process analysis, questions such as "How does it work?" and "How did it happen?" get at other kinds—the scientific and the historical. Lab reports exemplify scientific process analysis, as do the kinds of papers published in *Scientific American* or the *New England Journal of Medicine*. Like the practical, how-to process paper, the report of an experiment or explanation of a physical process clearly marks the steps in a sequence. The same is true of essays that rely on historical process, though sometimes it's harder to discern the steps. A paper that analyzes how the United States became involved in the Vietnam War, for instance, identifies the major stages of involvement and their chronology, the steps that led up to open warfare. Essays that focus on a historical process often condense time in a way that practical or scientific process analysis does not, but the chronology itself is still important.

0

Although process analysis is usually associated with specialized subjects—how to do *x*, how *y* works, or how *z* came about—it also finds its way into less formal prose. If you were to write about how you got interested in a hobby, you would be using process analysis, as you would if you were writing an explanatory research paper on the history of Coca-Cola. Process analysis can also be a means of discovery. If you were to analyze the process you go through to revise a draft, you might find out that you overemphasize a particular stage or leave out a step. Because process analysis is often equated with the simpler forms of how-to writing, it's easy to underrate it as a way of thinking and expressing ideas. It can even be used to have fun with a subject, as several of the essays in this chapter show. Process analysis need not be dull.

Audience and Purpose

The concept of audience is crucial to process essays, for you must know just how familiar the reader is with the topic so you know what you need to explain and how to explain it. Familiar topics present you with a challenge, for how can you interest your readers in a subject they already know something about? The answer lies in what you have to say about that subject and how you say it. A seemingly dull topic such as making bread can be turned into an interesting paper if you start with the negative associations many readers have about the topic—air bread, that tasteless, white, compactible substance better suited to bread ball fights than human consumption—and then go on to describe how to make the kind of bread that is chewy, substantive, tasty, and worth $4.50 a loaf in a specialty food store.

Your purpose in such an essay is informative, but if you want your essay to be read by people who don't have to read it, then you need to make your approach to your subject interesting as well. If you relate the bread-baking process, for example, so that your reader enjoys the essay, then even the person who would never willingly enter a kitchen will probably keep reading.

If what you have to say involves a personal subject, you need to present the information in a believable way, and at the same time, adjust it to the audience. The process involved in friends growing apart, for instance, can be explained in terms so personal that only the writer could appreciate it. If that were your topic, you would need to gear your description to the general reader who may have experienced something similar. That way, you would place your personal narrative into a larger, more general context. On the other hand, if you know not only more but also more specialized information than the reader, you must be careful your audience follows every step.

Sometimes a writer explores a process to inform the reader and other times to persuade, but always the writer has an assertion in mind and is trying to affect the reader. If, for example, you enjoy scuba diving and you're trying to describe the physiological effects the body is subject to when diving, you might first describe the necessary equipment and then take the reader on a dive, emphasizing the different levels of atmospheric pressure—the instant and constant need to equalize the air pressure in your ears, the initial tightness of your mask as you sink to 10 feet, the gradual "shrinking" of your wet suit as the pressure increases with the depth of the dive. Then after a quick tour of the kinds of fish, sea creatures, and coral formations you see during the dive, you would return your reader to the surface, stopping at 15 feet to release the buildup of nitrogen in the blood. The whole process may strike your reader as not worth the risk, so you would want to make sure not only that your thesis counters that opinion, but also that you describe what you see, so the attractions outweigh the hazards and momentary discomfort.

Sequence

Chronology is as crucial to process as it is to narration. In fact, it is inflexible. A quick safety check of the necessary equipment has to come before the dive. And then you must account for all the important steps. If time is crucial, then you have to account for it, although in a historical process essay, time is apt to be compressed or deemphasized to underscore a turning point. An essay on the Civil Rights movement, for instance, might well begin with a brief account of the slave trade, even though the body of the paper focuses on the 1950s and 1960s, culminating with the assassination of Martin Luther King in 1968.

Undergirding the concept of sequence, of course, is the pattern of cause and effect—in the example above, you might want to explore the effect of King's death on the Civil Rights movement. What's most important to process analysis, however, is neither cause nor effect, but the stages or steps, the chronology of events. Without a set sequence or chronology, neither cause nor effect would be clear.

Other Modes

In writing a process analysis, you will draw on the same skills you use for description, narration, definition, and example papers, for without supporting details and examples, a process essay can be tedious indeed. An essay on the Civil Rights movement would probably need to draw on statistics—such as the percentage of the population held in slavery in 1860—as well as examples of protests and boycotts, and quotations from those involved, both for and against equal rights for African Americans. An essay on scuba diving may need to define some terms and bring in examples from mathematics and physiology, as well as from scientific articles on the relative health of coral reefs in the Caribbean. Incorporating references to well-known people—a Mohammed Ali or a Jacques Cousteau—or to current events or adding a narrative example or even an amusing aside can make what might otherwise be little more than a list into an interesting paper.

Transitions

To make the stages of the process clear, you will need to rely on logically placed transitions that lead the reader from one stage to the next. Most writers try to avoid depending only on obvious links, such as *first, next, next,* and instead use chronology, shifts in tense, and other indicators to spell out the sequence. The process itself may have markers that you can use as transitions. An essay explaining a historical event, for instance, will have specific dates or actions that you can use to indicate the next stage in the sequence.

Organization and Ideas

The body of a process essay almost organizes itself because it is made up of the steps you have identified, and they must occur in a given sequence. Introductions and conclusions are trickier, as is the thesis, for you must not only set out a process but also make an assertion about it. Your thesis should confront the reader with a point, implicit or explicit, about the process involved, and in so doing, head off the lethal response, "So what?"

Useful Terms

Chronology The time sequence involved in events; what occurred when.

Process analysis A type of analysis that examines a topic to discover the series of steps or acts that brought or will bring about a particular result. Whereas cause and effect analysis emphasizes *why*, process emphasizes *how*.

POINTERS FOR USING PROCESS

Exploring the Topic

1. **What kind of process are you presenting?** Is it a practical, "how-to" process? A historical one? A scientific one? Some mixture of types?
2. **What steps are involved?** Which are crucial? Can some be grouped together? Under what headings can they be grouped?
3. **What is the sequence of the steps?** Are you sure that each step logically follows the one before it?
4. **How familiar is your reader with your subject?** Within each step (or group of steps), what information does the reader need to know? What details can you use to make that information come alive? What examples? What connections can you make to what the reader already knows? Do you use any terms that need to be defined?
5. **Is setting or context important?** If so, what details of the setting or context do you want to emphasize?
6. **What is the point you want to make about the process?** Is your point an assertion? Will it interest the reader?

Drafting the Paper

1. **Know your reader.** Using two columns, list what your reader may know about your topic in one and what your reader may not know in the other. If you are writing about a practical process, figure out what pitfalls your reader may be subject to. If you are writing about a historical or scientific process, make sure your diction

(Continued)

POINTERS FOR USING PROCESS *(Continued)*

suits your audience. Be on the lookout for events or actions that need further explanation to be understood by a general audience. If your reader is apt to have a bias against your topic, know what that bias is. If your topic is familiar, shape your first paragraph to enlist the reader's interest; if the topic is unfamiliar, use familiar images to explain it.

2. **Know your purpose.** If you are writing to inform, make sure you are presenting new information and that you are making an assertion about your topic. Don't dwell on information that the reader already knows if you can possibly avoid it. If you are writing to persuade, remember that you do not know whether your audience agrees with you. Use your persona to lend credibility to what you say, and use detail to arouse your reader's sympathies.

3. **Define your terms.** Think through the process you have chosen for your topic to make sure that your reader is familiar with all the terms associated with it. If any of those terms are technical or unusual ones, be sure you define them clearly.

4. **Present the steps in their correct sequence.** Make sure that you have accounted for all the important steps or stages in the process and that they are set out in order. If two or more steps occur at the same time, make sure you have made that clear. If time is crucial to your process, see that you have emphasized that point. If, on the other hand, the exact time at which an event occurred is less important than the event itself, make sure you have stressed the event and have subordinated the idea of time.

5. **Use details and examples.** Whether you are writing an informative or a persuasive essay, use details and examples that support your purpose. If you are explaining how to make your own ice cream, for example, draw on what the reader knows about various commercial brands and flavors to bolster the case for making your own. After all, your reader may not want to take the time and trouble to complete that process and may have to be enticed into trying it. Choose details and examples that combat your reader's negative associations.

6. **Double-check your transitions.** First mark your stages with obvious transitions or with numbers. After you have turned your

notes into a working draft, review and revise the transitions you have used, checking to see that they exist, that they are clear, and that they are not overly repetitious or obvious. Make sure each important stage (or group of stages) is set off by a transition. See if you can indicate shifts by using verb tense or words and phrases that don't call attention to themselves as transitions.

7. **Make a point.** What you say about a subject is far more interesting than the subject itself, so even if you are writing a practical process essay, make sure you have a point. A paper on a topic such as "how to change a tire" becomes unbearable without a thesis. Given an assertion about changing a tire—"Changing my first flat was as horrible as I had expected it to be"—the paper at least has a chance.

Accessorizing the Scoops of Summer

Kay Rentschler

You may have seen Kay Rentschler's recipes or articles in Cook's Illustrated, the *New York* Times, *or various Web sites associated with cooking. Her careers as a chef and journalist insure that her recipes are easy to follow, and her work as a test cook for the* Ladies Home Journal *further backs up her practical experience. She once started a minor furor by writing an article defending okra, but she is perhaps best known for creative uses of whole grains and making vegetarian dishes delicious. Delicious is also a good word for what she describes in the essay that follows. It was published on June 30, 2004, in the* New York Times.

What to Look For   While it's tempting to use numbers to mark the steps and sequences in an essay that uses process, it's so obvious that it's rarely effective. As you read Rentschler's essay, look for how she begins by describing ingredients and then shifts to process analysis.

1   The French may have given refinement to ice cream with their coupes and parfaits, but it took American excess and ingenuity to create the sundae—as messy and irresistible as democracy itself.

2   Irresistibility aside, for most adults, the sundae occupies a world where a fleeting tryst with several hundred calories is considered a bad idea. This is why ice cream sundaes, like summer loves, bloom best when the real world backs off—at a dinner party's end, when surfeit is indulged (not midafternoon with the children).

3   Any proper sundae begins with a couple of scoops of deeply chilled ice cream dropped into a tall, footed dish. The ice cream is easy: with premium brands everywhere, why toil? It is the jarred sauces and commercial knickknacks that must go. These can be made, much improved and availed of a certain sophistication, at home.

4   Classic ice cream flavors like chocolate, vanilla and coffee— stately, resonant or richly neutral—make the best foundations. Skip

flavors that scream with high notes or stutter with chunks. They need to go off in a cone.

5   In practical terms, the temperature of the ice cream is crucial. Optimally, the full surface of each scoop has a flowing, liquid sheen, while the inside stays elastic enough to cleave to a spoon. Perfection (oh so ephemeral) is typically wrested from frigid ice cream with a hot scoop. But do not be afraid to prescoop: arrange similar flavors on a plastic-lined tray and freeze them in advance of serving. A firm start is essential, because it is all history when freeze comes to thaw in a warm, flowing sauce.

6   Ice cream sundaes, of course, find expression in their sauces, which provide layers of flavor and seismic contrasts in temperature and tone. Typically, sundae sauces inhabit two spheres: the soft, rich and unctuous and the vivid and bright. One lulls the ice cream, while the other jolts it a bit.

7   The chief members of the lulling category are hot fudge, marshmallow, caramel and butterscotch. Commercial versions are prepared with lavish amounts of corn syrup and an army of stabilizers to give them presence and flow. But we are not going there.

8   A well-constructed homemade hot fudge sauce moves forward with dark smoky accents and arrives with plenty of chew. High-fat cocoa and a couple of chunks of bittersweet chocolate cooked in sugar and cream make all that possible, without a double boiler.

9   Caramel and butterscotch sauces give fits of excess to ice cream: caramel begins with granulated sugar seared to aromatic molten amber, while butterscotch takes its character from brown sugar. Both contain cream and, yes, butter, and both strike round, rich, pleasingly burnished notes. Either will embrace a foundation ice cream flavor with abandon.

10   Lush and glamorous, real marshmallow sauce does exist outside the jar and will make itself comfortable in any sundae setting, particularly as an opposites-attract foil for dark chocolate ice cream.

11   To the category of vivid and bright belong fruit sauces, particularly those with a touch of acidity and a shake of vibrant color. Strawberries, raspberries, blueberries, sour cherries or pineapples—sweet, just-ripe fruits cooked briefly with sugar—will brighten vanilla's pallor (high-pectin fruits can often go it alone without cornstarch for body).

12   Ice cream sundaes need proper sequencing, too. Start with chilled glasses if the weather is steamy. Bottommost, a ribbon of the dominant sauce, then one large or two small scoops of ice cream

and a blast of sauce. (For a two-sauce sundae, the tonal transition, or secondary sauce, flows here.)

13   Elaborate in softness, a sundae wants interruption in the form of crunch. Sugar-toasted nuts or crisp flake coconut, meringue buttons, macaroons, paper-thin cookie bits, even crushed peppermints or skinny pretzels look festive, taste good and get stuck in your teeth.

14   Toss one or more of these embellishments into the fray (leaving more for the finish), and keep going. Build the sundae's crown with additional scoops, followed by sauce. Reckon half a cup total sauce to a sundae and remember, it is the size of the glass that dictates a sundae's dimensions, not your conscience.

15   The collective excess would diminish, of course, without whipped cream drifting like a cloud overhead. It is more, yes, but whipped cream actually lightens the interplay between elements in a sundae and ultimately defines its look.

16   The effect, however, must be virginal, so toss the can, ditch the Cool Whip and head for pure heavy cream. Put a dead chill on it and whip it lightly with a touch of sugar and a thimble of vanilla. It should nearly faint from languor.

17   Arrange additional toppings (accessories, after all, are everything) and rush forth from the kitchen, creation in hand.

18   An ice cream sundae is summer's Cinderella. Enjoy her, if possible, before midnight.

ORGANIZATION AND IDEAS

1. What paragraph or paragraphs provide the introduction? Conclusion?

2. How does Rentschler avoid numbering steps in the sequence she presents in paragraphs 12–17?

3. Where does Rentschler use division and classification? What does it achieve?

4. Rentschler points out some pitfalls. What are they? How necessary are the warnings?

5. The essay exemplifies an implied thesis. Think about the essay as a whole and state the thesis as fully as you can.

TECHNIQUE AND STYLE

1. Where does Rentschler use metaphor and simile? How effective are they?

2. What verbs strike you as unusual? What substitutes can you think of? Which is preferable and why?

3. The paragraphing conforms to the short newspaper style. Which ones can be combined? What is gained? Lost?
4. In paragraph 1, Rentschler specifies her audience. To what extent is it important to the rest of the essay?
5. Which sense does Rentschler appeal to the most? What reasons can you think of for her choice?

SUGGESTIONS FOR WRITING

Journal

1. How apt is the title? Explain.
2. Rentschler obviously has little use for store-bought sauces, "knick-knacks," or Cool Whip. To what extent is her opinion justified?

Essay

1. Rentschler's essay deals with a common experience, and you can find your subject in the same general area. Think, for example, of various common actions, how you

   wash dishes
   study
   make a sandwich
   wait in line
   deal with boring people

   Once you have a subject, then consider the steps involved and write them down. Review the list to make sure you have them in an order that makes sense.
2. Like most Americans, you've probably tried to lose a pound or two. Think about the various popular diet programs: Mayo, South Beach, Atkins, Sugar Busters, Jenny Craig, to name a few. If you've tried one, write an essay in which you explain the process you went through. If you've tried to gain weight or muscle, explain that process. Supplement your own experience with some research on the program itself and its scientific basis.

Runner

Laura Carlson

*Running has been a sport Laura Carlson has enjoyed for more than
10 years, both on her own and for her school. As a junior at Valley
City State University in Valley City, North Dakota, she wrote the essay
that follows in a class taught by Noreen Braun, who reprinted the
essay on a Web page devoted to what she titled "Some Fine Student
Writing from Composition I, Fall Semester, 1997." Thinking about the
essay and reading it over, Carlson comments: "I am really taken
aback. I remember writing it and thinking that this is my favorite type
of writing, descriptive, and that I could really do a good job on it—if I
wanted to. It was really hard for me to sit down and write something
with a due date. One thing I did was to basically forget that I had to
do it for class, but that I had to write the essay for myself."*

*Stumped for a subject, Carlson thought about what she enjoyed and
came up with the topic that is the title of the essay. She notes that the
idea for the essay "came naturally to me. I actually went out that day
to run." Thinking about that experience, she "tried to remember what
it had been like; the feelings that I felt, the cold and the pictures in my
mind, and I tried to incorporate them back into my writing. I think it
really worked. I really just wrote about what I knew and how I really
felt. Visualization was the key to my success with this essay." What
worked for Laura may well work for you.*

What to Look For   Not everyone knows what it feels like to run for a
fairly long distance, and even those who do may not know what it's like
to do that on a cold North Dakota morning. To make her experience
come alive and to make it immediate, Carlson, therefore, chooses the
present tense and descriptive details. The result is an essay that explains
the process she goes through when she runs and makes the reader feel
what Carlson feels.

1   When I wake up this morning, I can feel the chill of the air in
my joints. I am almost reluctant to give up the warmth of my bed,
but I know I need to. Slowly, I step out of my bed and quickly
throw on a sweatshirt and pants. Leaving my room, still tired, but
slowly awakening, I yawn.

2   I stretch my tired limbs, first my arms, then my legs. Noticing a tightness in my right hip, I take a little extra time to stretch it. I am still moving slowly as if in a drugged stupor. Maybe I should just go back to bed. Before I change my mind, I hurry outside into the brisk early morning air. I take three or four breaths to acclimate myself to the cold, cold air. I can see my breath on the air in little white puffs. I want to reach out as if I could float away with the rising mist. It is still dark outside. The sun hasn't quite poked his head out to greet the day. The blue black sky is waiting to engulf me as his arms extend as far as I can see.

3   Running on an October morning is so exhilarating! I think it is only about 20 degrees this morning. I am so cold!

4   My steps are slow to start. I feel my legs tighten and restrain me, not wanting to exert the effort to propel me forward, yet I know that it is mind over matter and I am going to win this battle! I tell myself that I need to get ready for the big meet that is coming up at the end of the month. My adrenaline is pumping and my mind is whirling at a mile a minute taking in the frosty scenery that is surrounding me. The trees are covered in a fine layer of crystals forming together to make a wintry scene unlike any other I have seen yet this season. My breathing is accelerating and my pulse is beating in my ears. The biting cold is gnawing at my skin. I refuse to give into the cold of the air and the gripping of my lungs.

5   As I slowly retreat into a solid pace, my body is more aware of my feet steadily pounding on the pavement and of the crunching of the leaves and twigs as they collapse under the weight of my body. The burning in my lungs is lessening as my pace is increasing. The steady flow of traffic helps keep my mind from wandering and keeps me focused. I only have a couple of miles to go. My nose is running just as fast as my feet. I feel the slight burning as if the air were actually freezing the breath entering and exiting my nostrils.

6   I can tell by the landmarks of the city that I am closing in on my destination: home. I pass the fenced-in yard with the barking dog who chooses to torment me each time I pass. I keep running, my pace not faltering. As I come within three blocks of my house, I pick up my pace as if in a race. I am feeling winded as my stride lengthens and my breathing becomes much more shallow. I am almost home. The scenery is changing as the sun has finally approached the horizon. The hues of the sky are changing rapidly with the approaching daylight.

7   My house is in sight. I slow my pace to a fast walk and slowly make my way to my driveway. I take deep breaths to get used to

the different pace. I am done for another day. I feel refreshed and awakened. I am now ready to continue with another day.

Organization and Ideas

1. Which paragraph or paragraphs make up the essay's introduction? What does it tell you?
2. Trace the process of the run itself. What paragraphs describe it?
3. One technique Carlson uses to avoid the stilted *first-next-then* marking of the essay's chronology is to use the progress of the sunlight. Where in the essay does she note that progress?
4. Is Carlson's thesis stated or implied? What evidence can you find to support your idea?
5. If you're a runner, how well does Carlson describe the experience? If you're not, to what extent does she convince you that running is a pleasure?

Technique and Style

1. Carlson gives the essay unity by frequently referring to the weather. What descriptive details does she use?
2. Throughout the essay, Carlson uses the first person *I*. Does she avoid overusing it or not? How can you back up your opinion?
3. In paragraph 2, Carlson personifies the sun and the sky by referring to them with the pronoun *he*. What would be lost without that personification? What is gained?
4. The first sentence of paragraph 6 uses a colon. What other punctuation could be used? Which is the most effective and why?
5. Reread the last paragraph. How else might the essay have ended that would fit in with what has come before? Which is the more effective ending and why?

Suggestions for Writing

Journal

1. Write your own last paragraph for the essay and then, briefly, explain why you think it is better or not as good as Carlson's.
2. Briefly describe the feelings you have when you are involved in a sport, either as a spectator or a participant.

Essay

1. Like Carlson, you might start by thinking about what you enjoy. Perhaps it's a sport or a hobby, but no matter what the subject you

can use Carlson's essay as a model to write your own description of the process involved. You may find it easiest to start with the process, jotting down the steps or stages. Then once you have a rough draft, you can decide on the kind of introduction and conclusion that would be most effective for the essay, and, of course, where best to put the thesis, if you want to state rather than imply it. Suggestions for a topic:

  playing a sport
  being involved with your hobby
  playing a card game
  cooking a favorite dish
  enjoying a "do nothing" day

2. Even though many people participate in sports, even more watch games on television. During play-offs and championships, watching television has almost turned into a ritual. Choose a sport you like or a television show you are addicted to and describe the process you go through to watch it.

Independence Day

Dave Barry

It's a rare columnist who can claim both a Pulitzer Prize and a television sitcom, but few things aren't unusual about Dave Barry. Barry was the focus of the show "Dave's World," which ran from 1993 to 1997 and was based on two of his 32 books, and in 1988, he won a Pulitzer for Commentary "for his consistently effective use of humor as a device for presenting fresh insights into serious concerns." A humor writer for the Miami Herald, *his columns are carried by over 500 newspapers. A number of those columns have been collected in his most recent book* Dave Barry's Money Secrets: Like: Why Is There a Giant Eyeball on the Dollar? *(2006), but Barry has also written two novels:* Big Trouble *(1999) and* Tricky Business *(2002). His Web site (<davebarry.com>) notes that he "lives in Miami, Florida, with his wife, Michelle, a sportswriter. He has a son, Rob, and a daughter, Sophie, neither of whom thinks he's funny." "Independence Day" first appeared in* Tropic *magazine and was reprinted in* Mirth of a Nation, *Michael J. Rosen, editor.*

What to Look For   As you read Barry's essay, look for the ways he avoids using obvious markers as he takes his readers through a typical Fourth of July celebration.

1   This year, why not hold an old-fashioned Fourth of July picnic?

2   Food poisoning is one good reason. After a few hours in the sun, ordinary potato salad can develop bacteria the size of raccoons. But don't let the threat of agonizingly painful death prevent you from celebrating the birth of our nation, just as Americans have been doing ever since that historic first July Fourth when our Founding Fathers—George Washington, Benjamin Franklin, Thomas Jefferson, Bob Dole and Tony Bennett—landed on Plymouth Rock.

3   Step one in planning your picnic is to decide on a menu. Martha Stewart has loads of innovative suggestions for unique, imaginative and tasty summer meals. So you can forget about her. "If Martha Stewart comes anywhere near my picnic, she's risking a barbecue fork to the eyeball" should be your patriotic motto. Because you're having a *traditional* Fourth of July picnic, and that means a menu of hot dogs charred into cylinders of industrial-grade carbon, and hamburgers so undercooked that when people try to eat them, they leap off the plate and frolic on the lawn like otters.

4   Dad should be in charge of the cooking, because only Dad, being a male of the masculine gender, has the mechanical "know-how" to operate a piece of technology as complex as a barbecue grill. To be truly traditional, the grill should be constructed of the following materials:

- 4 percent "rust-resistant" steel;
- 58 percent rust;
- 23 percent hardened black grill scunge from food cooked as far back as 1987 (the scunge should never be scraped off, because it is what is actually holding the grill together);
- 15 percent spiders.

5   If the grill uses charcoal as a fuel, Dad should remember to start lighting the fire early (no later than April 10) because charcoal, in accordance with federal safety regulations, is a mineral that does not burn. The spiders get a huge kick out of watching Dad attempt

to ignite it; they emit hearty spider chuckles and slap themselves on all eight knees. This is why many dads prefer the modern gas grill, which ignites at the press of a button and burns with a steady, even flame until you put food on it, at which time it runs out of gas.

6   While Dad is saying traditional bad words to the barbecue grill, Mom can organize the kids for a fun activity: making old-fashioned ice cream by hand, the way our grandparents' generation did. You'll need a hand-cranked ice-cream maker, which you can pick up at any antique store for $1,875. All you do is put in the ingredients, and start cranking! It makes no difference what specific ingredients you put in, because—I speak from bitter experience here—no matter how long you crank them, they will never, ever turn into ice cream. Scientists laugh at the very concept. "Ice cream is not formed by cranking," they point out. "Ice cream is formed by freezers." Our grandparents' generation wasted millions of man-hours trying to produce ice cream by hand; this is what caused the Great Depression.

7   When the kids get tired of trying to make ice cream (allow about twenty-five seconds for this) it's time to play some traditional July Fourth games. One of the most popular is the "sack race." All you need is a bunch of old-fashioned burlap sacks, which you can obtain from the J. Peterman catalog for $227.50 apiece. Call the kids outside, have them line up on the lawn and give each one a sack to climb into; then shout "GO!" and watch the hilarious antics begin as, one by one, the kids sneak back indoors and resume trying to locate pornography on the Internet.

8   Come nightfall, though, everybody will be drawn back outside by the sound of loud, traditional Fourth of July explosions coming from all around the neighborhood. These are caused by the fact that various dads, after consuming a number of traditionally fermented beverages, have given up on conventional charcoal-lighting products and escalated to gasoline. As the spectacular pyrotechnic show lights up the night sky, you begin to truly appreciate the patriotic meaning of the words to *The Star-Spangled Banner,* written by Francis Scott Key to commemorate the fledgling nation's first barbecue:

And the grill parts' red glare;
Flaming spiders in air;
Someone call 911;
There's burning scunge in Dad's hair.

9   After the traditional visit to the hospital emergency room, it's time to gather 'round and watch Uncle Bill set off the fireworks that he purchased from a roadside stand operated by people who spend way more on tattoos than dental hygiene. As Uncle Bill lights the firework fuse and scurries away, everybody is on pins and needles until, suddenly and dramatically, the fuse goes out. So Uncle Bill relights the fuse and scurries away again, and the fuse goes out again, and so on, with Uncle Bill scurrying back and forth with his Bic lighter like a deranged Olympic torchbearer until, finally, the fuse burns all the way down, and the firework, emitting a smoke puff the size of a grapefruit, makes a noise—"phut"—like a squirrel passing gas. Wow! What a fitting climax for your traditional old-fashioned July Fourth picnic!

10   Next year you'll go out for Chinese food.

ORGANIZATION AND IDEAS

1. You could describe Barry's essay as a "how-to" guide for a traditional celebration on the Fourth of July, but his breaking down the event into steps is subtle. How does he do it?
2. It's possible to argue that the essay is organized by process (steps), chronology (time), drama (least to most effective), or some combination. Make a case for the way you read the organization.
3. How effective is Barry's last paragraph?
4. Barry's essay is obviously a satire, but of what: the Fourth of July, family gatherings, American values, the consumer culture, American sense of history, tradition, or some combination? What in the essay supports your view?
5. Take a look at the biographical information and note the reason Barry was awarded a Pulitzer Prize. In what ways does that statement apply to this essay?

TECHNIQUE AND STYLE

1. Look up *hyperbole* (pp. 144, 147). To what extent does Barry use the device? How effective is it?
2. Barry includes contemporary figures (paragraphs 2 and 3). Why might he have done that and what effect does he achieve?
3. What is the point of the fractured "facts" in paragraph 2?
4. Granted that the essay is humorous, but what kind of humor? How would you describe Barry's tone?
5. Reread the essay marking every use of *traditional*. To what extent is the repetition effective? What is Barry's point in using it?

SUGGESTIONS FOR WRITING

Journal

1. In what ways is the title a pun?
2. What description do you find the most amusing and why? Quote from the essay to back up your view.

Essay

1. Write your own "how-to" essay on the preparations for a typical, traditional, or important time. Like Barry, you may want to remove yourself from the scene and generalize, or you may want to be part of it. Suggestions:
   Thanksgiving
   first date
   first day of classes
   looking cool
   dealing with a computer problem
2. Barry does an amusing job depicting the "typical" American family at play on a celebratory occasion. Think about the family gatherings you have attended, those of either your own family or someone else's, and write your own survivor's guide.

Halloween and the Eulogy: Death, Be Not Ponderous

Cyrus M. Copeland

Cyrus M. Copeland abandoned his career as a copywriter and, later, executive in advertising to devote himself to more memorable words— the art of the eulogy. His first book, Farewell, Godspeed: The Greatest Eulogies of Our Time, *published in 2003, is a collection that celebrates both the speakers and the spoken of. The title of his second book—* A Wonderful Life: 50 Eulogies to Lift the Spirit *—published in 2006, sets out the kind of attitude toward his subject that is also apparent in the essay that follows. When not speaking before groups of funeral directors, he lives in New York City, home of the* New York

Times, *where this essay was published on October 31, 2004, which, appropriately enough, was the day of Halloween.*

What to Look For As you read Copeland's essay, be aware of how he uses multiple examples to illustrate each section of his advice, a technique you can use as well.

1 **M**y father loved Halloween. Finally, an excuse to don ghoulish attire, erect a haunted house and scare my friends. When he died a decade ago, I delivered his eulogy—a bittersweet but cathartic experience that left me drunk on the power of final words.

2 This Halloween, I'm happy to raise the dead once again. Not just because Hollywood, with ineffable timing, has just released a comedy called "Eulogy," but rather because the holiday began as a way to honor the dead with offerings. Today, we honor the dead with words.

3 The eulogy has a strange reputation. Maligned as ponderous and weepy, it is also a vibrant and adaptable form whose best examples shine down the ages. From Pericles' funeral oration to Lincoln's Gettysbury address, from Ronald Reagan's remembrance of the Challenger astronauts to Earl Spencer's inflammatory tribute to his sister, Diana, eulogies transcend the intimate farewell to offer a blueprint for dealing with loss. And they aren't all sad.

4 Or religious. As recently as 1990, the great majority of American eulogies were delivered by members of the clergy, but now the proportion is about half and falling. One reason is generational. Baby boomers tend to be less hesitant about grabbing a microphone than their parents were. We may have an uneasy relationship with death, but we are a little less frightened of reverb.

5 Throw in the more transient nature of American life, the general trend away from formality and the proliferation of celebrity memorial services (Christopher Reeve's was Friday), and it is clear how the eulogy has evolved away from sermons and toward something more intimate, vernacular, even irreverent. Without recourse to the divine, then, how best to inspire the dearly beloved? Here are five hallmarks of great goodbyes.

6 START STRONG. Great eulogies do not begin with "We are gathered here today to remember." The gathered know why they are there.

7 When Madonna eulogized Gianni Versace, her first words were "I slept in Versace's bed." She went on to explain that he wasn't in it at

the time, and then told some intimate stories about visiting him at his villa and how he was riveted by her daughter's blue toenail polish.

8   The writer Alan Zweibel on his colleague, Gilda Radner: "About 14 years ago, I was hiding behind a potted plant, and this girl asked me if I could help her be a parakeet—and I've been smitten with Gilda ever since."

9   Diane Sawyer on Lucille Ball: "There is a debate that is one of the longest running theological arguments in Christianity. The issue is this: Is there laughter in heaven?"

10   With openings like those, the eulogizer has you spellbound.

11   PERSONAL IS PREFERABLE. We all want to think our presence in this world has made a difference, opened a heart, changed a life. Speaking personally about the dead is not egotistical, it is a recognition of this truth. Great eulogies tell stories, often in the first person and often quite irreverent.

12   When Bob Fosse died, Neil Simon recounted 10 personal memories of him. No one accused Mr. Simon of self-promotion. Mourners are not appraisers or critics; we want something real, and if it elicits a laugh in a dark moment, we are grateful for the balm.

13   TELL THE TRUTH. People generally do not expect to see the departed canonized, and they can smell insincerity a mile away.

14   There are ways to be truthful without being disrespectful. Witness Bob Hope on Jack Benny: "He was eternally stingy. He gave us only 80 years, and it wasn't enough." William Styron did not flinch from remembering Lillian Hellman's temper. Together, he said, they had "carved up a few mutually detested writers and mediocre politicians" over the years—but in the end we learn that anger was a front for "some sort of transcendent idea, which is love." There is no judgment in Styron's words, only respect, and the intimacy that comes of seeing someone truthfully.

15   BE SPECIFIC. If Aunt Mary's eulogy could as easily be about Aunt Louise, the eulogizer has not accomplished anything; one might as well have the mailman read a generic eulogy downloaded from the Internet like a term paper ("Mary, we hardly knew ye.")

16   FINISH MEMORABLY. A great eulogy launches the dearly departed into the afterlife on a powerful updraft. James Woods delivered my favorite closing line, at Bette Davis's memorial service, the first held on a Hollywood sound stage: "Fasten your seatbelts, it's going to be a bumpy eternity."

17   Ossie Davis on Malcolm X: "What we place in the ground is no more now a man, but a seed, which, after the winter of our discontent,

will come forth again to meet us. And we will know him then for what he was and is: a prince, our own black shining prince, who didn't hesitate to die because he loved us so."

18   President Reagan on the Challenger crew: "A nation, too, will feel the loss of her seven sons and daughters, her seven good friends. We can find consolation only in faith, for we know in our hearts that you who flew so high and so proud now make your home beyond the stars, safe in God's promise of eternal life."

19   RONALD REAGAN and Ossie Davis in the same breath? There is the point of great eulogies. When the final curtain falls, our differences fade away, and we concentrate on what really matters: not the prosaic stuff of an obituary—jobs held, awards won, races run—but the essence of a life.

20   When I set out to compose my father's eulogy, I could hear his voice in my head—quite audibly, and for the first time, because I'm not especially schizophrenic—telling me that it was not as sad an occasion as I imagined. It was a kind of bridge across the chasm of his absence in my life.

21   A good eulogy can be that, too: A bridge between the living and the dead, between us and them, memory and eternity. The more specific and real the remembrances spoken, the stronger the bridge.

22   "There may be little or much beyond the grave," Robert Frost wrote, "but the strong are saying nothing until they see." Frost was wrong. Suited and miked and taking the floor, the strong are saying plenty.

Organization and Ideas

1. What are the "five hallmarks"?
2. Of the five, which receives the most attention from Copeland? The least? What reasons can you find for that choice?
3. What paragraph or paragraphs provide the introduction? What case can you make for your choice?
4. How does Copeland define an effective eulogy? To what extent is his definition his thesis?
5. To what extent does Copeland's idea of an effective eulogy match your own?

Technique and Style

1. Take another look at Copeland's examples. What variety do you find? What effect does it achieve?
2. How would you define Copeland's audience? How aware of it is he?

3. Copeland uses allusions: John Donne's sonnet "Death Be Not Proud" in his title; the Irish folk song, "Johnny, we hardly knew ye" in paragraph 15; and Robert Frost's poem "The Strong are Saying Nothing" in paragraph 22. What effects does he achieve with the allusions?
4. In paragraphs 6 and 15, Copeland uses negative examples. To what extent do they add or detract from his explanations?
5. Paragraph 20 introduces a metaphor that Copeland turns into an analogy in paragraph 21. How effective is it?

SUGGESTIONS FOR WRITING

Journal

1. Take 10 or 15 minutes to write down what you associate with the word *eulogy*. When you've finished, summarize what you have said in one sentence. If the result is an assertion, you have a thesis for an essay.
2. Which of Copeland's examples do you find the most effective and why?

Essay

1. Using Copeland's advice, write your own eulogy or that of a good and living friend.
2. Use your library or the Web to do enough research to write an effective eulogy for someone. Suggestions:
   historical figure
   movie star
   athlete
   politician
   musician

A Woman's Place

Naomi Wolf

Naomi Wolf was working on her PhD at Princeton University when she adapted her dissertation into The Beauty Myth: How Images of Beauty Are Used Against Women, *a best seller published in 1991. As the title implies, Wolf is concerned with issues that affect women, an interest that runs through all of her work as she tries to redefine feminism. She has explored the relation between women and politics in* Fire with Fire: The

New Female Power *(1993); girls, women, and sexuality in* Promiscuities: The Secret Struggle for Womanhood *(1997); women, childbirth, and the medical industry in* Misconceptions: Truth, Lies and the Unexpected on the Journey to Motherhood *(2001); and father/daughter relationships in* The Treehouse: Eccentric Wisdom from My Father on How to Live, Love, and See *(2005). Her essays have been published in print media as diverse as* Ms., Glamour, *the* Wall Street Journal, *and the* New Republic. *The essay below was published in the* New York Times *on May 31, 1992, and is adapted from a commencement address she gave at Scripps College, a women's college in California.*

What to Look For   Many writers steer away from beginning a sentence with the word *and* because they are afraid of creating a sentence fragment. But as long as the sentence has a subject and main verb, it can begin with *and* (or, like this one, *but* or any other conjunction) and still be an independent clause, a complete sentence, with the conjunction serving as an informal transition. To see how effective that kind of sentence can be, notice Wolf's last paragraph.

1   Even the best of revolutions can go awry when we internalize the attitudes we are fighting. The class of 1992 is graduating into a violent backlash against the advances women have made over the last 20 years. This backlash ranges from a senator using "The Exorcist" against Anita Hill, to beer commercials with the "Swedish bikini team." Today I want to give you a backlash survival kit, a four-step manual to keep the dragons from taking up residence inside your own heads.

2   My own commencement, at Yale eight years ago, was the Graduation from Hell. The speaker was Dick Cavett, rumored to have been our president's "brother" in an all-male secret society.

3   Mr. Cavett took the microphone and paled at the sight of hundreds of female about-to-be Yale graduates. "When I was an undergraduate," I recall he said, "there were no women. The women went to Vassar. At Vassar, they had nude photographs taken of the women in gym class to check their posture. One year the photos were stolen, and turned up for sale in New Haven's redlight district." His punchline? "The photos found no buyers."

4   I'll never forget that moment. There we were, silent in our black gowns, our tassels, our brand new shoes. We dared not break the

silence with hisses or boos, out of respect for our families, who'd come so far; and they kept still out of concern for us. Consciously or not, Mr. Cavett was using the beauty myth aspect of the backlash: when women come too close to masculine power, someone will draw critical attention to their bodies. We might be Elis, but we still wouldn't make pornography worth buying.

5   That afternoon, several hundred men were confirmed in the power of a powerful institution. But many of the women felt the shame of the powerless: the choking on silence, the complicity, the helplessness. We were orphaned from our institution.

6   I want to give you the commencement talk that was denied to me.

7   Message No. 1 in your survival kit: redefine "becoming a woman." Today you have "become women." But that sounds odd in ordinary usage. What is usually meant by "You're a real woman now"? You "become a woman" when you menstruate for the first time, or when you lose your virginity, or when you have a child.

8   These biological definitions are very different from how we say boys become men. One "becomes a man" when he undertakes responsibility, or completes a quest. But you, too, in some ways more than your male friends graduating today, have moved into maturity through a solitary quest for the adult self.

9   We lack archetypes for the questing young woman, her trials by fire; for how one "becomes a woman" through the chrysalis of education, the difficult passage from one book, one idea to the next. Let's refuse to have our scholarship and our gender pitted against each other. In our definition, the scholar learns womanhood and the woman learns scholarship; Plato and Djuna Barnes, mediated to their own enrichment through the eyes of the female body with its wisdoms and its gifts.

10   I say that you have already shown courage: Many of you graduate today in spite of the post-traumatic stress syndrome of acquaintance rape, which one-fourth of female students undergo. Many of you were so weakened by anorexia and bulimia that it took every ounce of your will to get your work in. You negotiated private lives through a mine field of new strains of VD and the ascending shadow of AIDS. Triumphant survivors, you have already "become women."

11   Message No. 2 breaks the ultimate taboo for women: *Ask for money in your lives.* Expect it. Own it. Learn to use it. Little girls learn a debilitating fear of money—that it's not feminine to insure we are fairly paid for honest work. Meanwhile, women make 68 cents

for every male dollar and half of marriages end in divorce, after which women's income drops precipitously.

12   Never choose a profession for material reasons. But whatever field your heart decides on, for god's sake get the most specialized training in it you can and hold out hard for just compensation, parental leave and child care. Resist your assignment to the class of highly competent, grossly underpaid women who run the show while others get the cash—and the credit.

13   Claim money not out of greed, but so you can tithe to women's political organizations, shelters and educational institutions. Sexist institutions won't yield power if we are just patient long enough. The only language the status quo understands is money, votes and public embarrassment.

14   When you have equity, you have influence—as sponsors, shareholders and alumnae. Use it to open opportunities to women who deserve the chances you've had. Your B.A. does not belong to you alone, just as the earth does not belong to its present tenants alone. Your education was lent to you by women of the past, and you will give some back to living women, and to your daughters seven generations from now.

15   Message No. 3: Never cook for or sleep with anyone who routinely puts you down.

16   Message No. 4: Become goddesses of disobedience. Virginia Woolf wrote that we must slay the Angel in the House, the censor within. Young women tell me of injustices, from campus rape coverups to classroom sexism. But at the thought of confrontation, they freeze into niceness. We are told that the worst thing we can do is cause conflict, even in the service of doing right. Antigone is imprisoned. Joan of Arc burns at the stake. And someone might call us unfeminine!

17   When I wrote a book that caused controversy, I saw how big a dragon was this paralysis by niceness. "The Beauty Myth" argues that newly rigid ideals of beauty are instruments of a backlash against feminism, designed to lower women's self-esteem for a political purpose. Many positive changes followed the debate. But all that would dwindle away when someone yelled at me—as, for instance, cosmetic surgeons did on TV, when I raised questions about silicone implants. Oh, no, I'd quail, people are mad at me!

18   Then I read something by the poet Audre Lorde. She'd been diagnosed with breast cancer. "I was going to die," she wrote, "sooner or

later, whether or not I had ever spoken myself. My silences had not protected me. Your silences will not protect you. . . . What are the words you do not yet have? What are the tyrannies you swallow day by day and attempt to make your own, until you will sicken and die of them, still in silence? We have been socialized to respect fear more than our own need for language."

19   I began to ask each time: "What's the worst that could happen to me if I tell this truth?" Unlike women in other countries, our breaking silence is unlikely to have us jailed, "disappeared" or run off the road at night. Our speaking out will irritate some people, get us called bitchy or hypersensitive and disrupt some dinner parties. And then our speaking out will permit other women to speak, until laws are changed and lives are saved and the world is altered forever.

20   Next time, ask: What's the worst that will happen? Then push your-self a little further than you dare. Once you start to speak, people *will* yell at you. They *will* interrupt, put you down and suggest it's per-sonal. And the world won't end.

21   And the speaking will get easier and easier. And you will find you have fallen in love with your own vision, which you may never have realized you had. And you will lose some friends and lovers, and realize you don't miss them. And new ones will find you and cherish you. And you will still flirt and paint your nails, dress up and party, because as I think Emma Goldman said, "If I can't dance, I don't want to be part of your revolution." And at last you'll know with surpassing certainty that only one thing is more frightening than speaking your truth. And that is not speaking.

ORGANIZATION AND IDEAS

1. Wolf's essay could easily be retitled "How to Survive the Backlash." What is the backlash?
2. Why does Wolf include the anecdote about Dick Cavett? How is it related to the backlash?
3. What are the four steps for survival?
4. Wolf's essay gives advice and explains how to survive, but it also com-ments on women's place in society today. Combine those comments with her advice and the result will be the thesis.
5. The original audience for the essay was women, but it was republished for an audience that also includes men. Explain whether men would find the essay offensive. To what extent is it antimale? Dated?

TECHNIQUE AND STYLE

1. What saying does Wolf's title refer to? How does her title set up her essay?
2. Throughout the essay, Wolf uses allusion—Anita Hill (paragraph 1), Plato and Djuna Barnes (paragraph 9), Virginia Woolf (paragraph 16), Audre Lorde (paragraph 18), and Emma Goldman (paragraph 21). Use an encyclopedia to look up one of these allusions so that you can explain to the class how it is (or is not) appropriate.
3. To explore the effect of Wolf's repeated use of *and* in her last paragraph, try rewriting it. What is gained? Lost?
4. What can you find in the prose that suggests that "A Woman's Place" was written to be heard, not read?
5. Wolf is obviously a feminist, but think of feminism as a continuum ranging from conservative to radical. Based on this essay, what kind of feminist is Wolf? What evidence can you find for your opinion?

SUGGESTIONS FOR WRITING

Journal

1. Choose one of Wolf's "messages" and test it out against your own experience. Do you find the advice helpful? Necessary?
2. Relate an experience in which you ran into sexism, either antimale or antifemale. You could use this entry later as the basis for an essay in which you explain how to cope with sexism.

Essay

1. All of us at one time or another have played a role we didn't believe in or didn't like. Those roles vary greatly. Think about the roles you have had to play and how you broke out of them. Choose one and draft a paper explaining "How to Survive" or "How to Break Out." Some roles to think about:
   dutiful daughter
   responsible sibling
   perfect husband (or wife)
   brave man
   happy homemaker
2. Write your own version of the essay but title it "A Student's Place" and create the advice and explanation to fit the title.

ADDITIONAL WRITING ASSIGNMENTS

Using Process

1. Explain a familiar chore so that you make it less boring: washing the car, mowing the lawn, painting a room, cleaning out a closet, preparing for an exam, or vacuuming.
2. Give a positive spin to a negative action: how to procrastinate, tell a white lie, stay awake in class, or hide dislike.
3. Explain how to survive a difficult or unpleasant job: filing, reviving a computer crash, recycling, changing diapers, or weeding.
4. Argue for the best way to party, study, enjoy a sport, or find a parking space.

Evaluating the Essays

1. The essays by Cyrus Copeland and Kay Rentschler bolster their process analysis with other modes. Copeland depends heavily on example, Rentschler on description. Which is more effective and why? Back up your opinion with quotations from both essays.
2. To be effective, the steps or stages in an essay organized by process need to be subtle. Reread the essays by Laura Carlson and Dave Barry, paying particular attention to how they mark the various stages in their processes. Which is the more subtle and how? Quote from both essays to support your point.
3. Copeland and Rentschler face different hurdles: Rentschler's subject is quite familiar; Copeland's far less so. Rentschler has to make the reader see the familiar anew, while Copeland has to make the reader appreciate what can often be wrenching or maudlin. Which of the two is the more successful and why? Use evidence from the essays to support your thesis.
4. Review the concept of *persona* (pp. 81, 82, 274–277) to have a clear understanding of how it operates and then think about how it functions in the five selections in this chapter. Of those five, which writer uses it most effectively? Write an essay in which you analyze how that writer uses persona. Use examples from several of them to bolster your argument.

On Using
Cause and
Effect

8

Process analysis focuses on *how;* causal analysis emphasizes *why.* Though writers examine both **cause and effect,** most will stress one or the other. Causal analysis looks below the surface of the steps in a process and examines why they occur; it analyzes their causes and effects, why *x* happens and what results from *x*. As a way of thinking, causal analysis is a natural one.

Let's say you've followed the directions that came with your new audio system and have finally reached the moment of truth when it's ready. You load your favorite CD, push the switch marked "power"; it clicks, nothing happens. The receiver is on, as is the CD player, but no sound comes out of the speakers. Probably you first check for the most immediate possible cause of the problem—the hookups. Are all the jacks plugged into the correct sources? Are they secure? Are the speaker wires attached correctly? If everything checks out, you start to search for less immediate causes, only to discover that the wrong switch was depressed on the receiver so that it's tuned to a nonexistent tape deck. You push "CD," and music fills the room. The problem is solved.

Essays that analyze cause and effect usually focus on one or the other. If you are writing about your hobby, which, let's say, happens to be tropical fish, you could emphasize the causes. You might have wanted a pet but were allergic to fur; you might have been fascinated with the aquarium in your doctor's office, and your aunt gave you two goldfish and a bowl. These reasons are causes that you would then have to sort out in terms of their importance. But if you wished to focus on effect, you might be writing on how your interest in tropical fish led to your majoring in marine biology.

You can see how causal analysis can be confusing in that a cause leads to an effect, which can then become another cause. This kind of causal chain undergirds Benjamin Franklin's point that "a little neglect may breed great mischief . . . for want of a nail the shoe was lost; for want of a shoe the horse was lost; and for want of a horse the rider was lost."

You can avoid the traps set by causal analysis if you apply some of the skills you use in division and classification and in process analysis:

1. Divide your subject into two categories—causes and effects.
2. Think about the steps or stages that are involved and identify them as possible causes or effects.
3. List an example or two for each possible cause or effect.
4. Sort out each list by dividing the items into primary or secondary causes and effects, that is, those that are relatively important and those that are relatively unimportant.

When you reach this final point, you may discover that an item you have listed is only related to your subject by time, in which case you should cross it out.

If you were writing a paper on cheating in college, for instance, your notes might resemble these:

	Possibilities	**Examples**	**Importance**
Causes	Academic pressure	Student who needs an A	Primary
	Peer pressure	Everybody does it	Primary
	System	Teachers tolerate it No real penalty	Secondary
	Moral climate	Cheating on income taxes	Secondary
		False insurance claims	
		Infidelity	
		Breakup of family unit	
Effects	Academic	Grades meaningless	Primary
	Peers	Degree meaningless	Primary
	System	Erodes system	Secondary
	Moral climate	Weakens moral climate	Secondary

The train of thought behind these notes chugs along nicely. Looking at them, you can see how thinking about the moral climate might lead to speculation about the cheating that goes undetected on tax and insurance forms, and for that matter, the cheating that occurs in a different context, that of marriage. The idea of infidelity then sets off a causal chain: infidelity causes divorce, which causes the breakup of families. Pause there. If recent statistics show that a majority of students have cheated, and if recent statistics also reveal a large number of single-parent households, is it safe to conclude that one caused the other? No. The relationship is one of time, not cause. Mistaking a **temporal relationship** for a causal one is a **logical fallacy** technically called **post hoc reasoning.**

It is also easy to mistake a **primary cause** or effect for a **secondary** one. If the notes above are for an essay that uses a narrative framework, and if the essay begins by relating an example of a student who was worried about having high enough grades to get into law school, the principle behind how the items are listed according to importance makes sense. To bring up his average, the student cheats on a math exam, justifying the action by thinking, "Everybody does it." The essay might then go on to speculate about the less apparent reasons behind the action—the system and the moral climate. For the student who cheated, the grade and peer pressure are the more immediate or primary causes; the system and climate are the more remote or secondary causes.

Audience and Purpose

What you know or can fairly safely assume about the intended audience determines both what to say and how to say it. If you went straight from high school into a full-time job, for example, and wanted to write an essay about deciding five years later to enroll in college, you know your reader is familiar with both high school and college but knows nothing about you—your job and what led to your decision. The reality of your work— perhaps you found it wasn't sufficiently demanding and that your lack of a higher education stood in the way of promotion—and your expectations of what college will do to enrich your life are the reasons, the causes, behind your change in direction.

Perhaps your subject is less personal but still one that your reader knows something about, say the high school dropout rate. Like your reader, you know that it's high in your city because you remember a story in the local newspaper pointing that out. What you didn't know your reader probably doesn't know either: How high is high? Why do students drop out? What happens to them after that? You'll have to do some research to find out some answers (the news story is a good place to start), but you'll find plenty to say. And as you amass information on your topic, you'll start to sense a purpose. Perhaps you simply want to inform your reader about the magnitude of the problem, or perhaps you will want to argue that more needs to be done about it.

An awareness of the reader and that person's possible preconceptions can also guide your approach to the topic. If, for example, your topic is the single-parent family, and you want to dispel some ideas about it that you think are misconceptions, you might safely assume that your audience regards single-parent families as at best incomplete and at worst irresponsible. It's obvious that you won't win your argument by suggesting that anyone with such ideas is a fool and possibly a bigot as well; it's also obvious that making your point while not offending some readers requires a subtle approach. One way to avoid offense is to put yourself in the shoes of the reader who has the negative associations. Then just as you learned more about the topic and became enlightened, so, with any luck, may your reader.

Valid Causal Relationships

As noted earlier, it is easy to mistake a temporal relationship for a causal relationship and to assign significance to something relatively unimportant. That's another way of saying that evidence and logical reasoning are essential to cause-and-effect essays. If, for instance, you find yourself drawn to one example, you need to think about how to avoid resting your entire argument on that one example.

Writing about collegiate sports, for instance, you might have been struck by the story of a high school basketball star who wanted to play pro ball but wasn't good enough to go straight to the pros; yet he couldn't meet the admission requirements for an NCAA Division I basketball school. After playing at several junior colleges, he finally transferred to an NCAA I institution. There, he was tutored and received a lot of individual attention, so he was able to maintain his academic eligibility. Then one year short of graduation, all that support vanished because he had used up his time limit and was no longer eligible to play. The effect—no degree, little education, and few chances for review by pro scouts—was devastating. You want to write about it. You want to argue that college sports take advantage of high school athletes, but you have only one example. What to do?

You can use your one example as a narrative framework, one that is sure to interest your reader. But to make that example more than an attention-getting device that enlists the reader's emotions, you have a number of alternatives. If your research shows that a fair number of athletes have a similar story, then you have multiple examples to support your point. If only a few share the experience, you'll need to modify your thesis to argue even a few is too many. And if you can't find any other examples, then you must narrow your focus to fit what you have, arguing that this particular individual was victimized. While you can ask how many more like him there may be, you cannot state that they exist.

Organization and Ideas

Although a cause can lead to an effect that then becomes a cause leading to another effect and so on, most essays are organized around either one or the other: why high school students drop out, why a person returns to college, what happens if a college takes advantage of an athlete, what effect does a one-parent household have on children. That's not to say that if your essay focuses on cause, you have to avoid effect and vice versa. Whichever one you don't emphasize can make a good conclusion. Your introduction, however, is a good place for your thesis; the reader can then follow the logical relationships between ideas as you develop your main point.

Useful Terms

Cause and effect An examination of a topic to discover, explain, or argue why a particular action, event, situation, or condition occurred.

Logical fallacy An error in reasoning. Assigning a causal relationship to a temporal one and reaching a general conclusion based on one example are both logical fallacies.

Post hoc reasoning A logical fallacy in which a temporal relationship is mistaken for a causal one. The fact that one event preceded another only establishes a temporal not a causal relationship.

Primary cause The most important cause or causes.

Secondary cause The less important cause or causes.

Temporal relationship Two or more events related by time rather than anything else.

Pointers for Using Cause and Effect

Exploring the Topic

1. **Have you stated the topic as a question that asks why *x* happened?** What are the possible causes? The probable causes? Rank the causes in order of priority.

2. **Have you stated the topic as a question that asks what results from *x?*** What are the possible effects? The probable effects? Rank the effects in order of priority.

3. **Is a temporal relationship involved?** Review your lists of causes and effects, and rule out any that have only a temporal relationship to your subject.

4. **Which do you want to emphasize, cause or effect?** Check to make sure your focus is clear.

5. **What is your point?** Are you trying to show that something is so or to explore your topic? Are you making an argument?

6. **What evidence can you use to support your point?** Do you need to cite authorities or quote statistics? If you depend on personal experience, are you sure your experience is valid, that is, representative of general experience?

7. **What does your reader think?** Does your audience have any preconceived ideas about your topic that you need to account for? What are they? How can you deal with them?

8. **Do you need to define any terms?** What words are crucial to your point? Are any of them abstract and, therefore, need to be defined? Have you used any technical terms that need definition?

9. **What role do you want to play in the essay?** Are you an observer or a participant? Do you intend to inform, persuade, or entertain? What point of view best serves your purpose?

Drafting the Paper

1. **Know your reader.** Figure out what attitudes your reader may have about your topic. If the causal relationship you are discussing is unusual, you might want to shape your initial attitude so that it is as skeptical as your reader's. On the other hand, you may want to start with a short narrative that immediately puts the reader on your side. How much does your reader know about

(Continued)

POINTERS FOR USING CAUSE
AND EFFECT *(Continued)*

your topic? If you are the expert, make sure you explain everything that needs to be explained without being condescending.

2. **Know your purpose.** Adjust your tone and persona to your
   purpose. If you are writing a persuasive paper, make sure your
   persona is credible and that you focus your ideas to change
   the mind of a reader or at least rethink a position. If you are
   writing an informative paper, choose a persona and tone that
   will interest the reader. Tone and persona are even more
   crucial to essays written to entertain, in which the tone can
   range from ironic to lighthearted.

3. **Emphasize a cause or effect.** Essays that focus on cause will
   probably cover a variety of reasons that explain the result.
   Though there may be only one effect or result, you may want to
   predict other possible effects in your conclusion. For instance,
   an essay that explores the causes of violence may examine a
   number of reasons or causes for it but may then conclude by
   speculating on the possible effects of a rising crime rate. On the
   other hand, essays that focus on effect will more than likely
   cover a number of possible effects that are produced by a single
   cause, though again you may want to speculate on other causes.
   If you are writing about the effects of smoking, at some point in
   the essay you may want to include other harmful substances in
   the air such as dust, hydrocarbons, and carbon monoxide.

4. **Check for validity.** Don't hesitate to include quotations, allusions, statistics, and studies. Choose your examples carefully to
   buttress the relationship you are trying to establish, and be sure
   you don't mistake a temporal relationship for a causal one.

5. **Make a point.** The cause-and-effect relationship you examine
   should support an assertion: video games not only entertain,
   they also stimulate the mind and improve coordination; video
   games are not only habit-forming, they are also addictive.

6. **Proofread.** Check to make sure you are using *affect* and *effect*
   correctly. While a handbook will provide a longer explanation,
   the short one is to think of *affect* as a verb and *effect* as a noun.
   That's not always true, but it is most of the time.

Tiffany Stephenson—An Apology

Bjorn Skogquist

Bjorn Skogquist came to Concordia College in Moorhead, Minnesota, with a firm interest in drama (having been in productions at Anoka High School that were recognized for excellence by the Kennedy Center for the Performing Arts) but a distinct aversion to writing. His freshman year, however, when his instructor, James Postema, encouraged him to "include anything I wanted, anything that I felt to be important," Skogquist "began to find it rather easy, and in a way, almost entertaining." He comments, "About halfway through, after I had written about various mishaps and comical incidents in my life, I decided to write about the things that a person would rather forget." The result is the essay that follows, although the name of the subject has been changed to Tiffany Stephenson. Skogquist relates "one of those things that I would rather forget, but instead of forgetting it, I apologized. It was something that I began and couldn't put down until I had finished."

What to Look For   If you find yourself thinking about an incident that occurred to you and mulling over its effect, you may well be on the way to an essay that takes a personal narrative and reexamines it through the lens of cause and effect. That is what Bjorn Skogquist does with what happened to him in the fourth grade. As you read the essay, look for the ways he handles different time periods—what had been happening before he entered his new school, his first day there, the incident that occurred, and the present.

1   When I was in the fourth grade, I moved from a small Lutheran school of 100 to a larger publicly funded elementary school. Lincoln Elementary. Wow. Lincoln was a big school, full of a thousand different attitudes about everything from eating lunch to how to treat a new kid. It was a tough time for me, my first year, and more than anything, I wanted to belong.

239

2   Many things were difficult; the move my family had just made, trying to make new friends, settling into a new home, accepting a new stepfather. I remember crying a lot. I remember my parents fighting. They were having a difficult time with their marriage, and whether it was my stepfather's drinking, or my mother's stubbornness, it took an emotional toll on both me and my siblings. Despite all this, the thing that I remember most about the fourth grade is Tiffany Stephenson.

3   The first day of fourth grade at Lincoln Elementary School was an emptiness, and it felt enormous. I wasn't the only one who felt this way, but I was too absorbed in my own problems to notice anyone else's. I was upset that my father, my blood father, was in the hospital for abusing alcohol. Among other things, he was a schizophrenic. I was too young to understand these diseases, but I understood all too well that my daddy was very sick, and that I couldn't see him any more.

4   My first day at Lincoln was a very real moment in my life. The weather was both cloudy and intolerably sunny at the same time. Maybe it wasn't that the sun was so bright, maybe it was just that our eyes were still adjusted to morning shadows. It was one of those sequences that somehow stand out in my memory as unforgettable. I remember feeling gray inside. I think that all of us felt a little gray, and I would guess that most of us remember that first day as you might remember your grandmother's funeral, whether you liked it or not.

5   I walked in and sat near the back of the class, along with a few others. If you were different or weird or new, from another planet, you sat in the back because those were the only desks left. I sat at the far left of the room, in the back near the windows. For a while I just stared out into the playground, waiting for recess to come. Our teacher, Mrs. Bebow, came into the room and started talking to us. I don't remember exactly what she said that day, because I wasn't listening. I was numb to the world, concentrating solely on that playground. She seemed distant, far away, and I think that my whole day might have stayed numb if it weren't for a boy named Aaron Anderson.

6   Aaron, who sat to my right, leaned over and whispered, "My name's Aaron. And that's Tiffany Stephenson. Stay away from her. She's fat and ugly and she stinks." At that, a few others laughed, and I felt the numbness leaving me. Mrs. Bebow remarked that if

we had something so terribly amusing to say, everyone had a right to know just what it was. Of course, we all quieted down. Then I asked which one was Tiffany, and Aaron pointed. There she was, coloring contentedly, sitting alone in the corner, in the very back, just like me. She was not fat or ugly, and as far as I knew, she didn't stink either. I even remember thinking that she was cute, but I quickly dismissed the thought because I already had a new friendship, even though it was in the common disgust of Tiffany Stephenson.

7   While all this was happening, our teacher Mrs. Bebow managed to take roll, after which she proceeded to lecture the boys on good behavior and then the girls on being young ladies. Every time she turned her back, airplanes and garbage flew across the room at Tiffany, along with a giggle. I don't think Tiffany Stephenson thought too much of us, that day or ever.

8   A few days later, one of the girls passed Tiffany a note. It ended up making her cry, and it got the girl a half an hour of detention. I was too busy trying to fit in to notice though, or didn't notice, or was afraid to notice, or simply didn't care.

9   That fall, both the boys and girls would go up to Tiffany on the playground and taunt her. They made absurd accusations, accusations about eating boogers at lunch, or about neglecting to wear underwear that day. Interestingly, this was the only activity that we participated in where a teacher didn't command, "OK, boys and girls need to partner up!" What we did to Tiffany Stephenson was mean, but in using her we all became common allies. I wonder if the teachers knew what we were up to when we made our next move, or if they thought that we were actually getting along. I think they knew at first, but we got craftier as time passed. And Tiffany had quit telling the teacher what happened. She knew that when we were ratted on, her taunts got worse. And they did get worse. We were mean, but we kept on because there was no one to stand out and say, "Enough."

10   When I think about that year, and about Tiffany, I remember that she was almost always alone. Toward the second half of the year, a retarded girl named Sharon Olsen befriended her. Sharon and Tiffany were a lot alike. They spent most of their time together coloring and drawing pictures, and those pictures always found their way to the prize board at the end of the week. The teacher knew that they needed a little encouragement, but mostly that "encouragement"

ended up making us hate them more. We picked on Sharon a lot too, but not as much as we targeted Tiffany.

11   Through the long winter, our taunts became hateful jeers, and our threats of pushing and shoving became real acts. We carried our threats out against Tiffany, but with no real reason to hate her. A couple of times when we walked down to lunch, we even pushed her around the corner to an area under the stairs. We knew that if no other classes followed us, we could get away with our plan, which was to tease her until tears flowed. We always asked her if she was scared. She never gave us the right answer. In a quiet voice she would reply, "No. Now leave me alone." Sometimes we left her alone, and sometimes we just laughed. Tiffany must have felt so very scared and alone, but she had more than us, she had courage. We didn't care. The more we could scare her, the better, the closer, the stronger knit we somehow felt.

12   One afternoon, heading for lunch, a few of us stayed behind and blocked the doorway. Tiffany was there, alone again, and cornered by three boys. Looking back, I realized why we began pushing her around. We felt unbelievably close, so close to each other through our hatred. It was a feeling that I have experienced only a few times since. And not only was the experience ours to cherish, it was a delight for Mrs. Bebow's entire fourth grade class. We were a purpose that afternoon, and we knew it. Looking back to that moment, I feel more remorse for my coldness than I have felt for any other passing wrong. But then, there, I felt alive, unafraid, and strangely whole.

13   That afternoon changed me forever.

14   By the time we sent Tiffany Stephenson to the green linoleum, she was no longer a person. Her full name, given to her at birth as a loving gesture, was now a fat, smelly, ugly title. There, on the green linoleum of Mrs. Bebow's fourth grade classroom, amidst the decorations and smell of crayfish aquariums, Tiffany Stephenson received many kicks, punches and unkind words. We didn't kick or punch her very hard, and the things we said weren't especially foul, but they were inhuman. This event was the culmination of the inhumane hate and vengeance that had been growing inside of us all year long. And yet, if any one of us stopped for a second to look, to really take a good look at who it was lying there on the ground, curled up in a ball crying, we would have realized that she was one of us.

15   At the beginning of the year, all of us had felt like we were in the back of the room. We were all unknowns. But somehow during that year we had put ourselves above her by force, and I admit that for a long time I couldn't see my wrong. But I had wronged. I had caused someone pain for my own personal ambitions. I was now popular, and it was at Tiffany Stephenson's expense. I was a coward, stepping on her courage for one moment in the warm sunlight, above my own pale clouds.

16   Only recently do I realize my error. I wish I could have been the one to say, on that first fall afternoon, "Tiffany's not ugly, fat or stinky. She's just like you and me, and we're all here together." Really, I wish anyone would have said it. I know now that people need each other, and I wish I could tell the fourth grade that we could all be friends, that we could help each other with our problems. I wish that I could go back. But all I can do is apologize. So Tiffany, for all my shortcomings, and for sacrificing you for the sake of belonging, please forgive me.

ORGANIZATION AND IDEAS

1. What paragraph or paragraphs introduce the narrative?
2. Trace the causal relationships in paragraphs 1–5 and 6–14. What does the author feel and why?
3. Paragraphs 15 and 16 sum up the incident that occurred "that afternoon." What did the author realize then? Now?
4. Consider all the cause-and-effect relationships in the narrative and state the thesis of the essay.
5. What is the emotional effect of the essay? How does Skogquist achieve it?

TECHNIQUE AND STYLE

1. Tiffany Stephenson's name first appears in paragraph 2 but not again until paragraph 6. Explain what is gained by the delay.
2. How does the author try to connect his experience with that of the reader? Why might he have chosen to do that?
3. In paragraph 15 Skogquist says "I was a coward, stepping on her courage for one moment in the warm sunlight, above my own pale clouds." What does he mean by "the warm sunlight, above my own pale clouds"?
4. Paragraph 13 consists of one sentence. Explain its function and effect.
5. Skogquist gives his audience a lot of information about his family. Explain why he may have chosen to do that and what it contributes to the essay.

Journal

1. Do you identify with the author or with Tiffany Stephenson?

2. If you were Tiffany Stephenson, would you forgive Skogquist? Why or why not?

Essay

1. Write your own personal narrative about an experience in which you explore the effect it had on you. Like Skogquist, you will probably want to have a dual perspective: the effects then and now. For a subject, consider your first

day at a new school

attempt at a sport

acquaintance with death

friendship

visit to the dentist or doctor or hospital

2. Place yourself in Tiffany Stephenson's position and write the essay from her point of view, looking back on the fourth grade from a time much later.

When Music Heals Body and Soul

Oliver Sacks

For Oliver Sacks, medicine is a family tradition. Born in England to parents who were both physicians, he is one of three sons who became doctors. Armed with a medical degree from Oxford University, Sacks moved to the United States for his internship and residency and is now Clinical Professor of Neurology at the Albert Einstein College of Medicine in New York. Sacks is probably best known for his book Awakenings *(1974), an account of his work with "frozen" patients that was made into a film in 1990, starring Robin Williams and Robert De Niro. His other medical works include* The Man Who Mistook His Wife for a Hat *(1985),* An Anthropologist on Mars *(1995), and* Island of the Colorblind *(1998). Sacks' autobiographical books are* A Leg to Stand On *(1989), where he recounts the accident he refers to in his essay below,* Uncle Tungsten: Memories of a Chemical Boyhood *(2001), and* Oaxaca Journal *(2002). Though Sacks calls himself a "lonely person, not at ease socially," it's obvious that he cares deeply about people in general and the link between "body and soul" in particular. The essay reprinted here was published in* Parade Magazine, *on March 31, 2002.*

What to Look For   It's often difficult for someone in a highly technical field to write in a way that is understood by ordinary readers. That's the problem Sacks faces when he describes a number of medical cases and neurological symptoms. As you read his essay, check to see if his prose is clear and comprehensible.

1   All of us have all sorts of personal experiences with music. We find ourselves calmed by it, excited by it, comforted by it, mystified by it and often haunted by it. It can lift us out of depression or move us to tears. I am no different. I need music to start the day and as company when I drive. I need it, propulsively, when I go for swims and runs. I need it, finally, to still my thoughts when I retire, to usher me into the world of dreams.

2   But it was only when I became a patient myself that I experienced a *physical* need for music. A bad fall while climbing a mountain in Norway had left me incapacitated by damage to the nerves and muscles of one leg. After surgery to repair the torn tendons in my leg, I settled down to await some return of function in the torn nerves.

3   With the leg effectively paralyzed, I lost all sense of its existence—indeed, I seemed to lose the very *idea* of moving it. The leg stayed nonfunctional for the longest 15 days of my life. These days were made longer and grimmer because there was no music in the hospital. Radio reception was bad. Finally, a friend brought me a tape recorder along with a tape of one of my favorite pieces: the Mendelssohn *Violin Concerto.*

4   Playing this over and over gave me great pleasure and a general sense of being alive and well. But the nerves in my damaged leg were still healing. Two weeks later, I began to get small twitches

in the previously flaccid muscle and larger sudden, involuntary movements.

5   Strangely, however, I had no impulse to walk. I could barely remember how one would go about walking—until, unexpectedly, a day or two later, the *Violin Concerto* played itself in my mind. It seemed, suddenly, to lend me its own energy, and I recovered the lost rhythm of walking—like remembering a once-familiar but long-forgotten time. Only then did walking regain its natural, unconscious, kinetic melody and grace.

6   Music can have the same effect on the neurologically impaired. It may have a power beyond anything else to restore them to themselves—at least in the precious few minutes that it lasts.

7   For reasons we do not yet understand, musical abilities often are among the last to be lost, even in cases of widespread brain damage. Thus, someone who is disabled by a stroke or by Alzheimer's or another form of dementia may still be able to respond to music in ways that can seem almost miraculous.

8   After a stroke, patients may suffer from *aphasia*, the inability to use or comprehend words. But the ability to sing words is rarely affected, even if an aphasic cannot speak them. Some patients can even be "reminded" in this way of words and grammatical constructions they have "forgotten." This, in turn, may help them start to regain old neural pathways for accessing language or to build new pathways in their place. Music becomes a crucial first step in a sequence followed by spontaneous improvement and speech therapy.

9   Some of my patients with strokes or Alzheimer's are unable to carry out a complex chain of actions: to dress, for example. Here, music can work as a mnemonic—a series of promptings in the form of verse or song, as in the childhood rhyme "One, two, buckle my shoe."

10   My patient Dr. P. had lost the ability to recognize or identify even common objects, though he could see perfectly well. He was unable to recognize a glove or a flower when I handed it to him, and he once mistook his own wife for a hat. This condition was almost totally disabling—but he discovered that he could perform the needs and tasks of the day if they were organized in song. And so he had songs for dressing, songs for eating, songs for bathing, songs for everything.

11   As a result of a brain tumor, my patient Greg has not been able to retain any new memories since the 1970s. But if we talk about or play

his favorite Grateful Dead songs, his amnesia is bypassed. He becomes vividly animated and can reminisce about their early concerts.

12   I first saw the immense therapeutic powers of music 30 years ago, in the postencephalitic patients I later wrote about in *Awakenings*. These 80 individuals all were victims of *encephalitis lethargica*, the viral sleeping sickness that swept the globe just after World War I. When I came to Beth Abraham Hospital in the Bronx in 1966, most of them had been "frozen," absolutely motionless, for decades.

13   Their voices, if they could speak, lacked tone and force; they were almost spectral. Yet these patients were able to *sing* loudly and clearly, with a normal range of expressiveness and tone. Among those who could walk and talk—though only in a jerky, broken way—music gave their movement or speech the steadiness and control it usually lacked.

14   We could observe this effect on the patients' electroencephalograms. If we found music that worked, their EEGs—often exceedingly slow, reflecting their frozen states—would become faster and more regular. We noted this when patients listened to music or sang it or played it—even when they imagined it.

15   Take Rosalie B., a patient who had a severe form of parkinsonism. She tended to remain transfixed for hours a day, completely motionless, stuck, usually with one finger on her spectacles. But she knew all of Chopin's works by heart, and we had only to say "Opus 49" to see her whole body, posture and expression change. Her parkinsonism would vanish as soon as she even imagined Chopin's *Fantaisie in F minor*. Her EEG would become normal at the same instant the Chopin played itself in her mind.

16   Clearly, human brains are able to tenaciously hold and replay musical stimuli. This is why tunes may repeat themselves endlessly, sometimes maddeningly, in the mind. Musical hallucinations are far more common than visual hallucinations. There even seems to be a sort of normal "reminiscence" or "recycling" of early musical memories, especially in the aging brain.

17   To help, however, the music must be the right kind for each patient—music that has meaning and evokes feeling for that individual. Music therapists who work with a geriatric population often find that only old popular songs can bring such patients to life. While singing them, these patients are able to find a brief but intense sense of community and connectedness with their past lives—and perhaps a deep emotional catharsis.

18   This almost universal responsiveness to music is an essential part of our neural nature. Though analogies often are made to birdsong or animal cries, music in its full sense—including complexities of rhythm and harmony, of pace, timbre and tonality no less than of melody—seems to be confined to our own species, like language. Why this should be so is still a mystery. Our research is only now beginning to unlock those secrets.

ORGANIZATION AND IDEAS

1. What kind of music do you enjoy? How does it affect you?
2. To what extent are your responses similar to those Sacks describes in paragraph 1?
3. Trace the pattern of general and particular through the essay. How would you describe it?
4. How does music affect Sacks' recovery? Those who are neurologically damaged?
5. Consider all the effects Sacks shows that music can have on people and in one sentence state what you find to be his thesis.

TECHNIQUE AND STYLE

1. Paragraphs 10–15 set out a number of examples. What do they add to the essay?
2. You may be familiar with *Parade Magazine,* for it accompanies many a Sunday newspaper. Its readership is about as general as one can be, yet Sacks is very much a specialist. How well does he tailor his knowledge to his audience?
3. Sacks blends personal narrative with examples from his medical practice. How effective is his use of the subjective and the objective?
4. Sacks focuses on the effects of music. To what extent does he bring in causal analysis?
5. Paragraphs 16–18 provide the essay's conclusion. How satisfactory is it? Explain.

SUGGESTIONS FOR WRITING

Journal

1. In what ways is the title of the essay appropriate? What others can you think of?
2. What surprises you most in Sacks' essay? Explain why.

Essay

1. Almost everyone uses leisure time to relax by pursuing some form of pleasure. Think about what you do for day-to-day fun and make a list of what you come up with. Choose one subject and consider why you do it as well as its effects on you. Then draft an essay in which you explain what you do and why. You may want to emphasize cause rather than effect or vice versa. Suggestions:

   talking to friends
   playing a sport
   watching television
   pursuing a hobby
   exercising

2. Think about the ways in which music affects you and explore that subject in an essay. You might begin by defining the kind of music you like and then go on to analyze its effect.

Wrestling with Myself

George Felton

Author of the textbook Advertising: Concept and Copy *and teacher of writing and copywriting at the Columbus College of Art and Design, George Felton is also a freelance writer whose topics cover the hot spots of popular culture—Richard Simmons, the "healthism" craze, not understanding how things work, and the like. Here, he investigates his (and our) fascination with pro wrestling. The essay was originally published in* Sun Magazine, *the supplement to the Baltimore* Sun, *on November 11, 1990. Felton has also published his work in the* New York Times, Newsweek, *and* Advertising Age *and has been a contributor to the Bread Loaf Writers' Conference.*

What to Look For   Felton's audience is composed of readers who share his enthusiasm for pro wrestling, those who regard it as silly or worse, and those who know little if anything about it. At times, you may find yourself faced with a similar variety of readers, which is when you can employ some of the techniques Felton uses. As you read his essay, look for the ways he addresses the attitudes of these various readers.

1   It's Saturday morning, 11 a.m., right after the cartoons: time for "The NWA Main Event." As I watch the ringside announcer set up today's card, a huge wrestler—topless and sweating, wearing leather chaps and a cowboy hat, carrying a lariat with a cowbell on it—bursts into the frame, grabs the announcer by his lapels, and, chunks of tobacco spraying out of his mouth, begins to emote: "Well lookee here, this is just what eats in my craw. . . . I don't care if you're the president or the chief of police, it don't matter, I'm gonna do what I wanna do," and what he mostly wants to do is wrassle somebody good for once—enough nobodies in the ring, enough wimps running the schedule. As quickly as he spills into camera, he veers out, having delivered exactly the 20-second sound bite required. Our announcer blithely sends us to a commercial, and another Saturday's wrestling hour has begun. I feel better already.

2   I soon find out this cowboy's name is Stan Hanson, he's from Border, Texas, and lately he's been getting disqualified in all his matches for trying to kill his opponents and then "hogtying" them with his lariat. We get to watch a recent match in which he kicks some poor guy's stomach furiously with his pointed-toe cowboy boots and drop-slams his elbow into his neck and, after getting him down, hits him over the head with the cowbell, and first whips, then strangles him with his lariat. It's great stuff, with the bell ringing madly and the referee waving his arms, but Stan's already yanked the guy outside the ring onto the apron and he's still on top, trying to kill him.

3   Why do I love this? Why am I crazy about Stan Hanson, who's old and fat and a man the announcer warns us "ought to be in a straitjacket and chains"? Because he personifies the great redemption of pro wrestling, the way it delivers me from civilization and its discontents. Not only is Stan Hanson mad as hell and not taking it anymore, but he's doing it all for me—getting himself disqualified so that I won't run the risk myself, but inviting me to grab one end of the rope and pull. He is my own id—the hairy beast itself—given a Texas identity and a push from behind, propelled out there into the "squared circle" where I can get a good look at it: sweat-soaked, mean, kicking at the slats, looking for an exposed neck. My heart leaps up, my cup runneth over.

4   Obviously I can't tell my friends about too much of this. If I even mention pro wrestling, they just stare at me and change the subject. They think I'm kidding. I am not supposed to like pro wrestling—its

demographics are too downscale, its Dumb Show too transparent. They complain that it's fake and silly, which to me are two of its great charms. If it were real, like boxing, it'd be too painful to watch, too sad. I like knowing it's choreographed: the staged mayhem lets me know someone has studied me and will toss out just the meat the dark, reptilian centers of my brain require to stay fed and stay put. Sadomasochism? Homoeroticism? I am treated to the spectacle of Ric "The Nature Boy" Flair, astride the corner ropes and his opponent. His fist may be in the air, triumphant, but his groin is in the other guy's face, and he keeps it there. For once the ringside announcers are speechless as we all stare, transfixed, at this clearest of symbolic postures. Consciously I am squirming, but my reptilian center feels the sun on its back.

5   Racism? Ethnocentrism? Am I unsettled about Japanese hegemony? No problem. There is, in the World Wrestling Federation, a tag team of scowling, unnervingly business-oriented Japanese toughs—the Orient Express, managed by Mr. Fuji—who invite me to hate them, and of course I do. Their failure is my success, and I don't even have to leave the living room. Two oversized, red-trunked Boris types used to parade around the ring under a red flag and insist, to our booing, on singing the Russian national anthem before wrestling. Since the Cold War has become passé, however, I've noticed matches pitting Russians *against each other,* and that, as my newspaper tells me, is not passé. I hear groans of delight from below, as this reprise of Cain and Abel croons its libidinal tune.

6   I mean where else can I take my id out for a walk, how else to let it smell the sweaty air, root its nose through the wet leaves? Cartoons? No amount of Wile E. Coyote spring-loaded bounces, no pancakings of Roger Rabbit, none of the whimsical annihilations of Cartoonville can approximate the satisfactions of a real boot in a real belly, a man's head twisted up in the ropes, the merry surfeit of flying drop kicks, suplexes, sleeper holds, and heart punches, all landed somewhere near real bodies. Pro sports? I get more, not less, neurotic rooting for my teams—my neck muscles ache, my stomach burns with coffee, after enduring another four-hour Cleveland Browns loss on TV. The Indians? Don't even get me started. The violence of movies like *The Last Action Hero* and *Cliffhanger?* Needlessly complicated by storyline.

7   No, give it to me straight. Wrestling may be a hybrid genre—the epic poem meets Marvel Comics via the soap opera—but its themes,

with their medieval tone, could hardly be simpler: warrior kings doing battle after battle to see who is worthy, women pushed almost to the very edges of the landscape, *Beowulf*'s heroic ideal expressed in the language of an after-school brawl: "I wanna do what I wanna do. You gonna try to stop me?"

8   I also appreciate the pop-culture novelty of pro wrestling, its endearing way of creating, a little smudged and thick-fingered, but with a great earnest smile ("Here, look at this!") new *bêtes noires* for our consumption. One of the newest is something called Big Van Vader, a guy in a total upper torso headgear that looks like Star Wars Meets a Mayan Temple. He carries a stake topped with a skull and can shoot steam out of ventricles on his shoulders, but it looks like all he can do to keep from toppling over. He's horrifying and silly all at once, an atavistic nightdream wearing a "Kick Me" sign.

9   Such low rent Show Biz, this admixture of the asylum and the circus, is central to wrestling's double-tracked pleasure. Its emotional *reductio ad absurdum* taps my anger like a release valve, but its silliness allows me to feel superior to it as I watch. I can be dumb and intelligent, angry and amused, on all fours yet ironically detached, all at the same moment.

10   It's a very satsifying mix, especially since my life between Saturdays is such an exercise in self-control, modesty, and late twentieth-century angst. To my students I am the helpful Mr. Felton. To my chairman I am the responsible Mr. Felton. To virtually everybody and everything else I'm the confused and conflicted Mr. F. My violence amounts to giving people the finger, usually in traffic. When I swear I mutter. To insults I quickly add the disclaimer, "just kidding," a move I learned from watching David Letterman temper his nastiness. I never yell at people, threaten them, twist my heel into their ears, batter their heads into ring posts, or catch them flush with folding chairs. I don't wear robes and crowns and have bosomy women carry them around for me, either. In short, I never reduce my life to the satisfying oversimplification I think it deserves.

11   I'm a wimp. Just the sort of guy Cactus Jack or old Stan himself would love to sink his elbows into, a sentiment with which I couldn't agree more. And that brings us to the deepest appeal of pro wrestling: It invites me to imagine the annihilation of my own civilized self. When Ric Flair jabs his finger into the camera and menaces his next opponent with, "I guarantee you one thing— Junkyard Dog or no Junkyard Dog, you're going to the hospital," when another of the Four Horsemen growls, "I'm gonna take you

apart on national television," the real thrill is that they're coming for me. And when Stan offers me one end of the rope, we both know just whose neck we're pulling on. Ah, redemption.

ORGANIZATION AND IDEAS

1. What paragraph or paragraphs make up Felton's introduction? What are the reasons for your choice?
2. Paragraphs 4 and 5 rely heavily on examples. What ideas do Felton's examples illustrate?
3. Comparisons take up much of paragraphs 6 and 10. What are the comparisons? What are Felton's points in using them?
4. Where in the essay does Felton discuss the effect pro wrestling has on him? Felton saves his most important reason till his last paragraph. Putting that reason together with the others in the essay, state Felton's thesis in your own words.
5. If you watch professional wrestling, how accurate do you find Felton's view? If you do not watch it, to what extent does Felton persuade you to give it a try?

TECHNIQUE AND STYLE

1. Felton uses dashes in paragraphs 1, 3, and 7. After examining those examples, what conclusions can you draw about the proper function of dashes?
2. What impression do you have of Felton's persona? Explain whether it fits his self-description in paragraphs 10 and 11.
3. Both the first and last paragraphs use dialogue. What does it add?
4. Paragraph 3 is riddled with allusions: to Freud's *Civilization and Its Discontents*, to the film *Network*, to a poem by Wordsworth, to the *Bible*. What do these allusions contribute to Felton's persona? To the essay as a whole?
5. Although the essay is written in first person, Felton uses *we* in paragraphs 2 and 11. Who does *we* refer to? What is gained or lost by switching pronouns?

SUGGESTIONS FOR WRITING

Journal

1. Which category of readers do you belong to—wrestling fan, wrestling debunker, wrestling innocent, or some other? Evaluate the effectiveness of the essay from your perspective.
2. Felton maintains that pro wrestling appeals to the id, to "the hairy beast itself." What other sports can you think of that appeal to the id? Select one and detail its appeal.

Essay

1. Whether or not you are a fan, there's no arguing with the popularity of watching sports events. Select a sport that you enjoy or one of which you cannot understand the appeal, and use it as the subject for an essay in which you explain or speculate on its popularity. Suggestions:

   football or baseball
   tennis or golf
   racing (cars, horses, dogs)
   roller derby, amazon contests, demolition derby
   motocross

2. Assuming you actively participate in a sport, think about why you do it and how it affects you. Write an essay in which you explain what you discover.

Black Men and Public Space

Brent Staples

Any woman who walks along city streets at night knows the fear Brent Staples speaks of, but in this essay we learn how that fear can also affect the innocent. We see and feel what it is like to be a tall, strong, young black man who enjoys walking at night but innocently terrifies any lone woman. His solution to his night walking problems gives a nice twist to nonviolent resistance.

Brent Staples holds an MA and PhD in psychology from the University of Chicago. A former reporter for the Chicago Sun-Times, *Staples became the assistant metropolitan editor of the* New York Times, *then editor of the* New York Times Book Review, *and now writes on education, race, and culture for the* New York Times *editorial board. His memoir,* Parallel Time: Growing Up in Black and White, *was published by Pantheon Books in 1994 and has been hailed as one of the best coming-of-age books in recent years. The essay reprinted here was first published in* Harper's Magazine *in 1986. He's still whistling.*

What to Look For   Before you read the essay, look up the dash in a handbook of usage so you'll be on the lookout for Staples' use of it. He uses it in two different ways, but always appropriately.

1   My first victim was a woman—white, well-dressed, probably in her early twenties. I came upon her late one evening on a deserted street in Hyde Park, a relatively affluent neighborhood in an otherwise mean, impoverished section of Chicago. As I swung onto the avenue behind her, there seemed to be a discreet, uninflammatory distance between us. Not so. She cast back a worried glance. To her, the youngish black man—a broad 6 feet 2 inches with a beard and billowing hair, both hands shoved into the pockets of a bulky military jacket—seemed menacingly close. After a few more quick glimpses, she picked up her pace and was soon running in earnest. Within seconds she disappeared into a cross street.

2   That was more than a decade ago. I was 22 years old, a graduate student newly arrived at the University of Chicago. It was in the echo of that terrified woman's footfalls that I first began to know the unwieldy inheritance I'd come into—the ability to alter public space in ugly ways. It was clear that she thought herself the quarry of a mugger, a rapist, or worse. Suffering a bout of insomnia, however, I was stalking sleep, not defenseless wayfarers. As a softy who is scarcely able to take a knife to a raw chicken—let alone hold one to a person's throat—I was surprised, embarrassed, and dismayed all at once. Her flight made me feel like an accomplice in tyranny. It also made it clear that I was indistinguishable from the muggers who occasionally seeped into the area from the surrounding ghetto. That first encounter, and those that followed, signified that a vast, unnerving gulf lay between nighttime pedestrians—particularly women—and me. And I soon gathered that being perceived as dangerous is a hazard in itself. I only needed to turn a corner into a dicey situation, or crowd some frightened, armed person in a foyer somewhere, or make an errant move after being pulled over by a policeman. Where fear and weapons meet—and they often do in urban America—there is always the possibility of death.

3   In that first year, my first away from my hometown, I was to become thoroughly familiar with the language of fear. At dark, shadowy intersections, I could cross in front of a car stopped at a traffic light and elicit the *thunk, thunk, thunk, thunk* of the driver—black, white, male, or female—hammering down the door locks. On less traveled streets after dark, I grew accustomed to but never comfortable with people crossing to the other side of the street rather than pass me. Then there were the standard unpleasantries with policemen,

doormen, bouncers, cabdrivers, and others whose business it is to screen out troublesome individuals *before* there is any nastiness.

4   I moved to New York nearly two years ago and I have remained an avid night walker. In central Manhattan, the near-constant crowd cover minimizes tense one-on-one street encounters. Elsewhere—in SoHo, for example, where sidewalks are narrow and tightly spaced buildings shut out the sky—things can get very taut indeed.

5   After dark, on the warrenlike streets of Brooklyn where I live, I often see women who fear the worst from me. They seem to have set their faces on neutral, and with their purse straps strung across their chests bandolier-style, they forge ahead as though bracing themselves against being tackled. I understand, of course, that the danger they perceive is not a hallucination. Women are particularly vulnerable to street violence, and young black males are drastically overrepresented among the perpetrators of that violence. Yet these truths are no solace against the kind of alienation that comes of being ever the suspect, a fearsome entity with whom pedestrians avoid making eye contact.

6   It is not altogether clear to me how I reached the ripe old age of 22 without being conscious of the lethality nighttime pedestrians attributed to me. Perhaps it was because in Chester, Pennsylvania, the small, angry industrial town where I came of age in the 1960s, I was scarcely noticeable against a backdrop of gang warfare, street knifings, and murders. I grew up one of the good boys, had perhaps a half-dozen fistfights. In retrospect, my shyness of combat has clear sources.

7   As a boy, I saw countless tough guys locked away; I have since buried several, too. They were babies, really—a teenage cousin, a brother of 22, a childhood friend in his mid-twenties—all gone down in episodes of bravado played out in the streets. I came to doubt the virtues of intimidation early on. I chose, perhaps unconsciously, to remain a shadow—timid, but a survivor.

8   The fearsomeness mistakenly attributed to me in public places often has a perilous flavor. The most frightening of these confusions occurred in the late 1970s and early 1980s, when I worked as a journalist in Chicago. One day, rushing into the office of a magazine I was writing for with a deadline story in hand, I was mistaken for a burglar. The office manager called security and, with an ad hoc posse, pursued me through the labyrinthine halls, nearly to my editor's door. I had no way of proving who I was. I could only move briskly toward the company of someone who knew me.

9   Another time I was on assignment for a local paper and killing time before an interview. I entered a jewelry store on the city's affluent Near North Side. The proprietor excused herself and returned with an enormous red Doberman pinscher straining at the end of a leash. She stood, the dog extended toward me, silent to my questions, her eyes bulging nearly out of her head. I took a cursory look around, nodded, and bade her good night.

10   Relatively speaking, however, I never fared as badly as another black male journalist. He went to nearby Waukegan, Illinois, a couple of summers ago to work on a story about a murderer who was born there. Mistaking the reporter for the killer, police officers hauled him from his car at gunpoint and but for his press credentials would probably have tried to book him. Such episodes are not uncommon. Black men trade tales like this all the time.

11   Over the years, I learned to smother the rage I felt at so often being taken for a criminal. Not to do so would surely have led to madness. I now take precautions to make myself less threatening. I move about with care, particularly late in the evening. I give a wide berth to nervous people on subway platforms during the wee hours, particularly when I have exchanged business clothes for jeans. If I happen to be entering a building behind some people who appear skittish, I may walk by, letting them clear the lobby before I return, so as not to seem to be following them. I have been calm and extremely congenial on those rare occasions when I've been pulled over by the police.

12   And on late-evening constitutionals I employ what has proved to be an excellent tension-reducing measure: I whistle melodies from Beethoven and Vivaldi and the more popular classical composers. Even steely New Yorkers hunching toward nighttime destinations seem to relax, and occasionally they even join in the tune. Virtually everybody seems to sense that a mugger wouldn't be warbling bright, sunny selections from Vivaldi's *Four Seasons*. It is my equivalent of the cowbell that hikers wear when they know they are in bear country.

ORGANIZATION AND IDEAS

1. Reread paragraph 1. What expectations does it evoke in the reader? For paragraph 2, state in your own words what Staples means by "unwieldy inheritance." What effects does that inheritance have?

2. The body of the essay breaks into three paragraph blocks. In paragraphs 3–5, what effects does the author's walking at night have on others? On himself?

3. In paragraphs 6 and 7, Staples refers to his childhood. Why had he been unaware of his effect on others? What effect did the streets he grew up on have on him?

4. Summarize the causes and effects Staples brings out in paragraphs 11 and 12, and in one sentence, make a general statement about them. What does that statement imply about being a black male? About urban life? About American culture? Consider your answers to those questions, and in one sentence state the thesis of the essay.

5. Who are the "victims" in Staples' essay? What are they victims of?

TECHNIQUE AND STYLE

1. A large part of the essay's impact lies in the ironic contrast between appearance and reality. What details does Staples bring out about himself that contrast with the stereotype of the mugger?

2. In paragraph 1, Staples illustrates the two uses of the dash. What function do they perform? Rewrite either of the two sentences so that you avoid the dash. Which sentence is better and why?

3. Trace Staples' use of time. Why does he start where he does? Try placing the time period mentioned in paragraphs 6 and 7 elsewhere in the essay. What advantages does their present placement have? What is the effect of ending the essay in the present?

4. Examine Staples' choice of verbs in the second sentence of paragraph 5. Rewrite the sentence using as many forms of the verb *to be* as possible. What differences do you note?

5. Staples concludes the essay with an analogy. In what ways is it ironic? How does the irony tie into the essay's thesis?

SUGGESTIONS FOR WRITING

Journal

1. To what extent do you identify with the women in the essay? With Staples? With both? Explain.

2. Think about a time when, intentionally or unintentionally, you threatened or intimidated someone. Describe either the causes or effects.

Essay

1. You can develop either of the journal ideas above into a full-fledged essay. Or, if you prefer, think about a situation in which you have been

stereotyped and that stereotype determined your effect on others. Among the physical characteristics that can spawn a stereotype are

age
race
gender
physique
clothing

2. All of us have been in a situation in which we felt threatened. Select an incident that occurred to you and describe its effect on you.

Retreat into the iWorld

Andrew Sullivan

Andrew Sullivan was born in England, where he graduated from Oxford University and then won a fellowship to the John F. Kennedy School of Government at Harvard. There he received a master's degree in public administration and, later, a PhD in Political Science. His career in journalism, however, started by interning for The Daily Telegraph *and at the conservative Centre for Policy Studies, both in London, then in Washington, D.C., at the* New Republic *where at the age of 27 he rose to editor. A frequent guest on radio and TV news and talk shows, Sullivan has also written four books:* Virtually Normal *(1996),* Love Undetectable: Notes on Friendship, Sex, and Survival *(1999),* Same-Sex Marriage: Pro and Con *(2004), and* The Conservative Soul: How We Lost It, How to Get It Back *(2006). Though he is still a senior editor at the* New Republic, *he also writes for* Time *magazine, the* New York Times Book Review, *and the* Sunday Times *of London, where this essay appeared on February 20, 2005.*

What to Look For   If Sullivan is right, then most cities are full of iPod people, which means they are part of the audience for his essay. As you read it, keep track of how he tries not to alienate them.

1   I was visiting New York last week and noticed something I'd never thought I'd say about the city. Yes, nightlife, is pretty much dead (and I'm in no way the first to notice that). But daylife—that insane

mishmash of yells, chatter, clatter, hustle and chutzpah that makes New York the urban equivalent of methamphetamine—was also a little different. It was quieter.

2   Manhattan's downtown is now a Disney-like string of malls, riverside parks and pretty upper-middle-class villages. But there was something else. And as I looked across the throngs on the pavements, I began to see why.

3   There were little white wires hanging down from their ears, or tucked into pockets, purses or jackets. The eyes were a little vacant. Each was in his or her own musical world, walking to their soundtrack, stars in their own music video, almost oblivious to the world around them. These are the iPod people.

4   Even without the white wires you can tell who they are. They walk down the street in their own MP3 cocoon, bumping into others, deaf to small social cues, shutting out anyone not in their bubble.

5   Every now and again some start unconsciously emitting strange tuneless squawks, like a badly tuned radio, and their fingers snap or their arms twitch to some strange soundless rhythm. When others say "Excuse me" there's no response. "Hi", ditto. It's strange to be among so many people and hear so little. Except that each one is hearing so much.

6   Yes, I might as well own up. I'm one of them. I witnessed the glazed New York looks through my own glazed pupils, my white wires peeping out of my ears. I joined the cult a few years ago: the sect of the little white box worshippers.

7   Every now and again I go to church—those huge, luminous Apple stores, pews in the rear, the clerics in their monastic uniforms all bustling around or sitting behind the "Genius Bars", like priests waiting to hear confessions.

8   Others began, as I did, with a Walkman—and then a kind of clunkier MP3 player. But the sleekness of the iPod won me over. Unlike other models it gave me my entire music collection to rearrange as I saw fit—on the fly, in my pocket.

9   What was once an occasional musical diversion became a compulsive obsession. Now I have my iTunes in my iMac for my iPod in my iWorld. It's Narcissus heaven: we've finally put the "i" into Me.

10   And, like all addictive cults, it's spreading. There are now 22m iPod owners in the United States and Apple is becoming a mass-market company for the first time.

11   Walk through any airport in the United States these days and you will see person after person gliding through the social ether as if on autopilot. Get on a subway and you're surrounded by a bunch of Stepford commuters staring into mid-space as if anaesthetised by technology. Don't ask, don't tell, don't overhear, don't observe. Just tune in and tune out.

12   It wouldn't be so worrying if it weren't part of something even bigger. Americans are beginning to narrow their lives.

13   You get your news from your favourite blogs, the ones that won't challenge your view of the world. You tune into a satellite radio service that also aims directly at a small market—for new age fanatics, liberal talk or Christian rock. Television is all cable. Culture is all subculture. Your cell phones can receive e-main feeds of your favourite blogger's latest thoughts—seconds after he has posted them—get sports scores for your team or stock quotes of your portfolio.

14   Technology has given us a universe entirely for ourselves—where the serendipity of meeting a new stranger, hearing a piece of music we would never choose for ourselves or an opinion that might force us to change our mind about something are all effectively banished.

15   Atomisation by little white boxes and cell phones. Society without the social. Others who are chosen—not met at random. Human beings have never lived like this before. Yes, we have always had homes, retreats or places where we went to relax, unwind or shut out the world.

16   But we didn't walk around the world like hermit crabs with our isolation surgically attached.

17   Music was once the preserve of the living room or the concert hall. It was sometimes solitary but it was primarily a shared experience, something that brought people together, gave them the comfort of knowing that others too understood the pleasure of a Brahms symphony or that Beatles album.

18   But music is as atomised now as living is. And it's secret. That bloke next to you on the bus could be listening to heavy metal or a Gregorian chant. You'll never know. And so, bit by bit, you'll never really know him. And by his white wires, he is indicating he doesn't really want to know you.

19   What do we get from this? The awareness of more music, more often. The chance to slip away for a while from everydayness, to

give our lives its own soundtrack, to still the monotony of the commute, to listen more closely and carefully to music that can lift you up and keep you going.

20   We become masters of our own interests, more connected to people like us over the internet, more instantly in touch with anything we want, need or think we want and think we need. Ever tried a Stairmaster in silence? But what are we missing? That hilarious shard of an overheard conversation that stays with you all day; the child whose chatter on the pavement takes you back to your early memories; birdsong; weather; accents; the laughter of others. And those thoughts that come not by filling your head with selected diversion, but by allowing your mind to wander aimlessly through the regular background noise of human and mechanical life.

21   External stimulation can crowd out the interior mind. Even the boredom that we flee has its uses. We are forced to find our own means to overcome it.

22   And so we enrich our life from within, rather than from white wires. It's hard to give up, though, isn't it.

23   Not so long ago I was on a trip and realised I had left my iPod behind. Panic. But then something else. I noticed the rhythms of others again, the sound of the airplane, the opinions of the taxi driver, the small social cues that had been obscured before. I noticed how others related to each other. And I felt just a little bit connected again and a little more aware.

24   Try it. There's a world out there. And it has a soundtrack all its own.

ORGANIZATION AND IDEAS

1. Sullivan begins with a personal narrative. Where else in the essay does he return to that mode? What effects does it achieve?
2. Reread Sullivan's essay, marking each instance of cause and of effect. Which predominates?
3. In paragraphs 17 and 18, Sullivan uses comparison and contrast. In what ways does that mode contribute to the primary one of cause and effect?
4. Sullivan states a bare-bones thesis in paragraph 12. Given the essay as a whole, how can you flesh it out?
5. Test Sullivan's thesis against your own experience. How valid is it?

TECHNIQUE AND STYLE

1. Sullivan refers to "Narcissus heaven" (paragraph 9) and "Stepford commuters" (paragraph 11). What does he mean by these allusions?

2. Reread the essay looking for unusual or striking words. How would you characterize Sullivan's diction? What does he achieve by using it?

3. In paragraph 7, Sullivan sets out an analogy. What is being compared? How effective is the comparison?

4. Sullivan begins paragraph 15 with three incomplete sentences that amount to a short list. Rewrite them to make one or more complete sentences. What is gained? Lost?

5. Where in the essay does Sullivan use metaphor? Choose the one you like best and explain what it adds to the essay.

SUGGESTIONS FOR WRITING

Journal

1. If you have an iPod, how accurate do you find Sullivan's essay? If you don't have one, explain why you would or would not want one.

2. In paragraph 20, Sullivan argues for "allowing your mind to wander aimlessly through the regular background noise of human and mechanical life." Explain to what extent you agree or disagree with the value of letting your mind wander.

Essay

1. It's a rare invention or technical advance that doesn't have some drawbacks, major or minor. Think about the electronic or mechanical innovations that are now available, choose one, and analyze its effects, both positive and negative. Once you've weighed those effects, you can form your thesis for an essay. Suggestions:

camera phones
chat rooms
blogs
digital cameras
dvds
cell phone rings

2. Analyze Sullivan's essay to determine the extent to which he takes a stand. Is he arguing, explaining, speculating, musing, analyzing, what? Back up your interpretation with quotations and examples from the essay.

ADDITIONAL WRITING ASSIGNMENTS

Using Cause and Effect

1. Consider the causes of a problem that can arise in a familiar setting and its solution, a problem that might occur at work, school, home, a sports event, between friends, or within a marriage.
2. Analyze why you like what you like, your taste in hangouts, classes, teams, celebrities, food, or films.
3. Predict the future by analyzing why *x* is going to win a political race, crucial game, championship, stardom, prize, or contest.
4. Use your library or the Internet to research the causes of a particular disease, accident, chemical reaction, environmental problem, or safety measure.

Evaluating the Essays

1. Both Bjorn Skogquist and Brent Staples deal with how each affects others, depending on narration and example to support their theses. Of the two, which do you more closely identify with and why? The answer will be your thesis for an essay built around effect.
2. Oliver Sacks explains the healing power of music, while Andrew Sullivan examines the isolating effect of the iPod universe. Compare the two essays to determine which does a better job of explaining effects. Use evidence from both essays to make your point.
3. The idea of identification runs through the essays by George Felton and Brent Staples, though both writers treat it differently. Felton's interest is personal; pro wrestling provides a way for him "to take my id out for a walk" (p. 251). Staples' interest is both personal and general; he observes how people react to him as a black man. Felton's identification is harmless; the one Staples examines can be lethal. Which do you find the more interesting and why?
4. The essays in this chapter take up widely differing topics—the effects of music, teasing, the media, pro wrestling, of being young, black and strong—yet all depend on example, narration, and description to investigate and explain their subjects. Of the five, who faces the most difficult topic? How well does the writer deal with it? Use examples from the other essays for comparison.

On Using Argument

9

Up to Chapter 9, this book has focused on patterns of organization that can be used singly or in combination for various aims—to express how you feel, to explain, and, to a lesser extent, to argue. Those modes or patterns are the means to an end, ways to achieve your goal of self-expression, exposition, or argument. This chapter directly addresses the goal of argument, but because book after book has been written on the art of argument, think of what you have here as a basic introduction. In this chapter you will discover how to construct a short argumentative essay and how the various modes are used to support that aim. It's only appropriate, therefore, that the discussion start with a definition.

In everyday speech, ***argument*** is so closely associated with *quarrel* or *fight* that it has a negative connotation, but that connotation does not apply to essays. If you were to analyze an essay by examining its argument, you would be looking at the writer's major assertion and the weight of the evidence on which it rests. That evidence should be compelling, because you want the reader to respond in one of several ways:

- To adopt your view
- To rethink his or her previous position
- To take a particular action
- To keep reading

Though the last goal may seem a small one, many of the subjects of argumentative essays are ones your readers already have an opinion about, so if all you accomplish is having someone who disagrees with you keep on reading, you have constructed a successful argument.

Because an argumentative essay bases its thesis primarily on reason, the word *logic* may pop into your mind and raise images of mathematical models and seemingly tricky statements stringing together sentences beginning with *if*s and leading to one starting with *therefore*. Don't worry. The kind of argumentative essays you will be asked to write extends the kinds of essays you've written all along: your thesis is the heart of your argument, and examples, definitions, descriptions, and the like provide supporting evidence.

It's useful to distinguish between self-expression and argument. Open your local newspaper to the editorial pages, and you'll probably find examples of both. If you find a letter to the editor that rants about the financial "sins" of the Democratic Party and describes the "sinners" as "dishonest, lying cheats," it's unlikely a Democrat will finish it. The writer was letting off steam rather than trying to argue a point, steam based on emotion, not reason. But an editorial on the same page on the same general subject will use reason. Such an editorial may well state that although the media's focus highlights abuses within the Democratic Party, the Republicans are not altogether innocent. Both Democrats and Republicans are apt to read the editorial all the way through, and many from both parties may come to agree with the editor's thesis.

If you brainstorm the subject as a whole, not just your position on it, you can avoid relying on emotion instead of reason. Phrase the subject as a question, and then list the pros and cons.

If you are writing on gambling, for instance, you would ask, "Should gambling be legalized?" Then you would define your terms: Who would be legalizing it—the federal government, the state, the county, the city? What kind of gambling is involved—betting on horse races, on sports? Playing games such as bingo, video poker, slot machines, roulette? Buying tickets for a lottery? Answering those kinds of questions will help you to draw up your pros and cons more easily because your focus will be more specific. Once you've listed the arguments that can be used, you can then sort through them, noting evidence you can cite and where to find it. Having done all that, you then are in a position to choose which side you wish to take, and you know the arguments that can be used against you.

Reason is the backbone of argumentative writing, and to use it successfully, you will probably need to research your subject. Once your argument begins to take shape, however, you will find that dealing with one or two of the opposing views will not only strengthen your own case but will also earn you some points for fairness.

Argumentative writing ranges from the personal to the abstract and draws on the various patterns that can be used to structure an essay. For instance, waiting tables in a restaurant may have convinced you that tips should be automatically included in the bill. To make the case that the present system is unfair to those in a service trade, you might draw primarily on your own experience and that of others, though you need to make sure that your experience is representative. If you don't, your reader may discount your argument, thinking that one example isn't sufficient evidence. A quick check among others who are similarly employed or a look at government reports on employment statistics should show that your example is typical and, therefore, to be trusted.

The technical term for an entire argument based on only one example is **hasty generalization,** one of many logical fallacies that can occur in argumentative writing. **Logical fallacies** are holes or lapses in reasoning and, therefore, to be avoided. If you were to argue that the reader should consider only the present system of tipping or the one you propose, you will be guilty of **either–or reasoning,** which is false because it permits no middle ground such as requiring a minimum tip of 10 percent. Quote Michael Jordan on the subject and you will be citing **false authority;** he knows basketball but not the restaurant industry. And obviously, if you call a 10-percent tipper a cheap idiot, you will be accused quite rightly of name-calling, the **ad hominem** (to the person) fallacy.

Say you noticed one evening that as closing time loomed, your tips got smaller. Is that because people who dine late tip minimally or because your customers felt rushed or because someone miscalculated the tip or some unknown reason? If you conclude that people who dine late are poor tippers, you may well be mistaking a temporal relationship for a causal one. Two events may occur at times close to each other (small tip, late hour) without implying a valid cause-and-effect relationship. To confuse the two is called **post hoc reasoning.**

Often the best topic for an argumentative essay is the one you come up with on your own, but at times you may be assigned a topic. If so, your chances for success increase if you shape the topic so that you can connect to it. Because you already know something about the subject, you have done some thinking about it instead of starting from scratch or using secondhand opinions. Even abstract topics such as euthanasia can be made concrete and will probably be the better for it.

You may know little about mercy killing, but you may have had a member of your family who was terminally ill. Would euthanasia have been an appropriate alternative? Should it have been? In addition to using your own experience, consider using your local newspaper as a resource. Newspaper accounts and editorials can also help give form and focus to an abstract issue, as can book and periodical sources, and of course there's the Internet. The Web provides instant access to a huge and unfiltered amount of information, but always check out who or what is behind the information. Anyone can put anything on the Web. And does.

Audience and Purpose

Audience plays a greater role in argument than in any other type of writing, and therein lies a problem: you must adapt both form and content to fit your audience, while at the same time maintaining your integrity. If you shape your argumentative position according to its probable acceptance by your readers rather than your own belief, the result is propaganda or sensationalism, not argument. Knowingly playing false with an audience by omitting evidence or shaping facts to fit an assertion or by resorting to logical fallacies are all dishonest tricks.

Imagine, for example, that you are on the staff of your campus newspaper and have been given the assignment of investigating the rumors that the dean of the College of Business is going to resign. You know that the dean has been fighting with the president of your university, arguing that the College of Business is "grossly underfunded," a phrase you found in an earlier story on university finances. But you also read an interview with the dean and know that she has close ties to the local business community and may be offered a job heading a local company. Add to that your suspicion that not many colleges of business have deans who are women, a suspicion borne out by statistics you can quote, and you begin to scent a story. If you choose to write one that plays up the conflict with the president and implies sexism while ignoring the possibility of the dean being hired away from the university, you are not being true to your evidence and are, therefore, misleading your readers.

Within honest bounds, however, you have much to draw on, and a sense of what your audience may or may not know and of what the audience believes about a topic can guide you. Even if your topic is familiar, what you have to say about it will be new information. Censorship is a tired subject, but if you were to write on the banning of a particular book from a particular public school library, you would probably give the topic a new twist or two. A concrete example, often in the form of a short introductory narrative, makes an abstract issue more accessible and is apt to keep your reader reading.

If your subject is one many readers know little about, then you can begin by explaining the issue and its context. If your classmates are your readers, for example, they will know little about your personal life. And if you have an aunt whose health insurance was cancelled after her cancer returned, the action may compel you to research an insurance company's right to drop those it insures. Put your indignation together with what you discovered through your research and what your classmates don't know, and you have all the makings of a successful argumentative paper protesting what you see as an injustice.

Whether you start with what your audience does or does not know or with a narrative that illustrates the general situation and makes it concrete, your aim is to try to convince your readers to adopt your convictions, perhaps even to act on them.

Appealing to Reason, Emotion, and Persona

The appeal of **reason,** what the ancient Greeks called *logos,* is crucial. To present a logical pattern of thought, you will probably find yourself drawing on one or more modes, particularly definition, comparison, and cause and effect. If, for instance, you have a part-time job at a fast-food franchise, you may have noticed that most of the other employees are also part-time. The situation may strike you as exploitive, and you want to write about it.

You might start sketching out a first draft with the example of your job, then define what part-time means, using cause and effect to argue that franchise companies that depend primarily on part-time labor exploit their workers to create greater profits for the company. As you work, you will find that you are laying out a line of reasoning, the assertions—probably the topic sentences for paragraphs or paragraph clusters—that support your thesis. You will also have to do some research so that you place your example in a larger context, showing that it is clearly typical. Then, armed with some facts and figures, you can test your thesis and supporting sentences:

1. Am I making an assertion? Test the sentence by checking to see if it states an opinion.

   If yes, go to question 2.
   If no, review pp. 3–4 and revise the sentence.

2. Is the assertion supported by evidence? List the evidence and sources.

   If yes, go to question 3.
   If no, research the topic to gather more evidence.

3. Is the evidence sufficient? Check it to make sure it's directly related to the assertion.

If yes, the assertion checks out.

If no, gather more evidence.

If your thesis and supporting sentences check out, then you know your argument rests on reason.

Logical thinking must undergird all argumentative essays, even those that use an **emotional** appeal, or *pathos*, an appeal that often rests on example, description, and narration. In the example of the essay about health insurers, you would be using an emotional appeal if you began your essay with a brief narrative of your aunt's battle with cancer and the crisis caused by her loss of health insurance. And although the bulk of the essay would be taken up with the essay's appeal to reason, you might choose to close with an emotional appeal, perhaps reminding your readers of the number of people who cannot afford any kind of medical insurance and calling for a general reform of health care.

But the emotional appeal has its dangers, particularly when you are close to the subject. You would not want your description of your aunt's problems to slide into the melodramatic, nor would you want to create so powerful an impression that anything that comes after, which is the heart of your argument, is anticlimactic. Emotional appeals are often best left to snagging the reader's attention or calling for action—relatively small roles—than to serving a primary function in the essay. Emotion will have an impact; reason will carry the argument.

The ethical appeal, or *ethos,* rests on a credible **persona** and is more subtle than the others; the writer is not appealing directly to the reader's emotions or intellect but instead is using his or her persona to lend credence to the essay's major assertion. The point gets tricky. A fair and honest writer is one who is fair and honest with the reader. Such a writer takes on a persona, not like donning a mask to hide behind but like selecting a picture to show those elements in the personality that represent the writer at his or her best.

To understand how persona functions, think of the last time you took an essay test. What you were writing was a mini argument maintaining that your answer to the question is a correct one. Your persona, which you probably didn't even think about, was intended to create a sense of authority, the idea that you knew what you were writing about. You are so used to writing within an academic context that the elements of your persona come naturally. The tone you use for essay tests is more formal than informal, which means that your choice of words, your diction, is more elevated than conversational. And if a technical vocabulary is appropriate—the vocabulary of physics, sociology, the arts, and the like—you use it. Successful essay answers also use evidence and are tightly organized so that the line of thought is clear and compelling, all of which comes under the appeal of reason, but don't underestimate the appeal of persona. If two test answers contain the exact same information, the one that is written in the more sophisticated style that implies a more thoughtful response is apt to receive the higher grade.

Logical Fallacies

Logical fallacies abuse the various appeals. The introduction to this chapter has already pointed out the more obvious ones—hasty generalization, false authority, name–calling, post hoc and either–or reasoning—but there are many others as well. Advertising and political campaigns are often crammed with them.

If you receive a flyer asking you to vote for a candidate for the school board because he is a Vietnam veteran who has a successful law practice, the logic doesn't follow, a literal translation of the Latin term **non sequitur:** the claim leaves you wondering what being a veteran and an attorney have to do with the duties of a member of the school board. And if the flyer goes on to maintain that because the candidate has three children he can understand the problems of students in the public schools when you know that his three children go to private schools, then you've spotted a **false analogy,** a double one—public and private schools are quite different, and three children from the family of a professional are not representative of the public school student population.

Such a flyer is also guilty of **begging the question,** another fallacy. The main question for a school board election is "Can this person make a positive contribution?" Being a Vietnam veteran and the father of three children doesn't answer that question. A **shift in definition** is another form of begging the question. If this hypothetical candidate also claims to be a "good citizen" and then goes on to define that term by example, citing service to his country and fatherhood as proof, then as a voter, you're left with a very narrow definition. Good citizenship involves much more.

Often when you read or hear about the holes in an argument, you may also hear the term **straw man.** With this technique (yet another form of begging the question), your attention is drawn away from the main point, and instead the argument focuses on a minor point with the hope that by demolishing it, the main one will also suffer. Imagine that there's a move to increase local taxes, and you want to argue against it in a letter to the local paper. As you consider the points you can make, you come up with a short list: that the taxes are already high, that existing funds are not being spent wisely, and that schools, roads, government, and the like—all that the taxes support—while not outstanding are adequate. You start to gather information to use as evidence for each of these points (probably discovering several more) and run across a news story about a large amount of local taxpayers' money having been spent on rebuilding a bridge on a back road that averaged all of three cars a day. If you were to stop there and construct a thesis arguing taxes should not be raised because of waste in government, then making your case by basing it on the example of the building of the bridge, you would be constructing a straw man argument, one that avoids the major issues.

Organization and Ideas

The thesis of an argumentative essay should be readily identifiable: it is the conviction that you want an audience to adopt. Sometimes the thesis may be stated in the title, but more often you will state your position early on, then back it up with evidence in the body of your essay. If you organize your ideas by moving from the general (the thesis) to the particular (the evidence), you are using **deductive reasoning.** Most of the argumentative essays you run across will be using this kind of logical organization. As for the order in which you choose to present the evidence on which your thesis rests, you'll probably arrange it from the least important to the most important so that the essay has some dramatic tension. Putting the most important first doesn't leave you anywhere to go, rather like knowing from the start that the butler did it.

Although sometimes you may want to put your thesis as your first sentence, usually you will want to lead up to it, *introduce* it in the literal sense. Starting right off with the thesis will probably strike the reader as too abrupt, too sudden, a bit like being hit over the head. Often an argumentative essay will begin with a narrative or some explanation, ways of setting the scene so that when the thesis appears, it seems natural. As for the ending, you may want to return to the same narrative or information you started with or call for action or point out what may happen unless your view is adopted. Remember, by the time your reader finishes reading what you have to say, if all you have done is make the person reconsider ideas and rethink the argument, you will have succeeded. It's rare, though not impossible, for one essay to change a person's mind.

Now and then, you'll find yourself reading an argument that is organized by moving from the particular to the general, from evidence to thesis. What you have then is called **inductive reasoning,** and it's usually more difficult to write because it demands tight focus and control. Think of the essay's organization as a jigsaw puzzle. Your reader has to recognize each piece as a piece, and you have to build the evidence so that each piece falls into a predetermined place. The completed picture is the thesis.

If you want to construct an essay using inductive reasoning, you may find it easier to do if in your first draft you state your thesis at the beginning, baldly, just so you stay on track. Then, when you've shaped the rest of the paper, you simply move the thesis from the beginning to the last paragraph, perhaps even the last sentence.

You'll find that the essays in this section represent both kinds of organization, so you'll have a chance to see how others have developed their ideas to argue a particular point.

Useful Terms

Ad hominem argument Name-calling, smearing the person instead of attacking the argument. A type of logical fallacy. Smearing the group the person belongs to instead of attacking the argument is called an *ad populum* logical fallacy.

Appeal to emotion Playing or appealing to the reader's emotions.

Appeal to persona The appeal of the writer's moral character that creates the impression that the writer can be trusted and, therefore, believed.

Appeal to reason Presenting evidence that is logical, well thought out, so as to be believed.

Argument The writer's major assertion and the evidence on which it is based.

Begging the question Arguing off the point, changing direction. A type of logical fallacy.

Deductive reasoning Reasoning that moves from the general to the particular, from the thesis to the evidence.

Either–or reasoning Staking out two extremes as the only alternatives and, therefore, excluding anything in between. A type of logical fallacy.

False analogy An analogy that does not stand up to logic. A type of logical fallacy.

False authority Citing an expert on one subject as an expert on another. A type of logical fallacy.

Hasty generalization Reasoning based on insufficient evidence, usually too few examples. A type of logical fallacy.

Inductive reasoning Reasoning that moves from the particular to the general, from the evidence to the thesis.

Logical fallacy An error in reasoning, a logical flaw that invalidates the argument.

Non sequitur Literally, it does not follow. No apparent link between points. A type of logical fallacy.

Persona The character of the writer that comes through from the prose.

Post hoc reasoning Assuming a causal relationship where a temporal one exists. A type of logical fallacy.

Shifting definition Changing the definition of a key term, a form of begging the question. A type of logical fallacy.

Straw man Attacking and destroying an irrelevant point instead of the main subject.

POINTERS FOR USING ARGUMENT

Exploring the Topic

1. **What position do you want to take toward your subject?** Are you arguing to get your audience to adopt your thesis or to go further and take action? What is your thesis? What action is possible?

2. **How is your audience apt to respond to your assertion if you state it baldly?** How much background do you need to provide? Do you need to use definition? What arguments can the reader bring against your assertion?

3. **What examples can you think of to illustrate your topic?** Are all of them from your own experience? What other sources can you draw on?

4. **How can you appeal to your reader's emotions?** How can you use example, description, and narration to carry your emotional appeal?

5. **How can you appeal to your reader's reason?** How can you use example, cause and effect, process, comparison and contrast, analogy, or division and classification to strengthen your logic?

6. **What tone is most appropriate to the kind of appeal you want to emphasize?** Does your persona fit that tone? How can you use persona to support your argument?

Drafting the Paper

1. **Know your reader.** Estimate how familiar your reader is with your topic and how, if at all, the reader may react to it emotionally. Keeping those ideas in mind, review how the various patterns of development may help you contend with your audience's knowledge and attitudes, and decide whether your primary appeal should be to emotion or to reason.

   Description, narration, and example lend themselves particularly well to emotional appeal; process, cause and effect, comparison and contrast, analogy, example, and division and classification are useful for rational appeal. Use definition to set the boundaries of your argument and its terms as well as to clear up anything the reader may not know.

2. **Know your purpose.** Depending on the predominant appeal you find most appropriate, your essay will tend toward persuasion or argument; you are trying to get your reader not only to understand your major assertion but also to adopt it and perhaps even to act on it. Short of that, a successful writer of argument must settle for the reader's "Well, I hadn't thought of it that way" or "Maybe I should reconsider."

   The greatest danger in argumentative writing is to write to people like yourself, ones who already agree with you. You need not think of your audience as actively hostile, but to stay

(Continued)

POINTERS FOR USING ARGUMENT *(Continued)*

on the argumentative track, it helps to reread constantly as you write, playing the devil's advocate.

3. **Acknowledge the opposition.** Even though your reader may be the ideal—someone who holds no definite opposing view and indeed is favorably inclined toward yours but hasn't really thought the topic through—you should bring out one or two of the strongest arguments against your position and demolish them. If you don't, the reader may, and there goes your essay. The ideal reader is also the thinking reader who says, "Yes, but. . . . "

4. **Avoid logical pitfalls.** Logical fallacies can crop up in unexpected places; one useful way to test them is to check your patterns of development. If you have used examples, does your generalization or assertion follow? Sometimes the examples are too few to support the assertion, leading to a hasty generalization; sometimes the examples don't fit, leading to begging the question or arguing off the point or misusing authority; and sometimes the assertion is stated as an absolute, in which case the reader may think of an example that is the exception, destroying your point.

   If you have used analogy, double-check to see that the analogy can stand up to scrutiny by examining the pertinent aspects of the things compared. If you have used cause and effect, you need to be particularly careful. Check to see that the events you claim to have a causal relationship do not have a temporal one instead; otherwise, you fall into the post hoc fallacy. Also examine causal relationships to make sure that you have not merely assumed the cause in your statement of effect. If you claim "poor teaching is a major cause of the high dropout rate during the freshman year in college," you must prove that the teaching is poor; if you don't, you are arguing in a circle or begging the question.

   Non sequiturs can also obscure cause-and-effect relationships when an element in the relationship is missing or nonexistent. Definition also sets some traps. Make sure your definition is not only fully stated but also commonly shared and consistent throughout.

5. **Be aware of your persona.** The ethical appeal, the rational appeal, and the emotional appeal are fundamental concepts of

argument, and it is the persona, together with tone, that provides the ethical appeal. To put it simply, you need to be credible.

If you are writing on an issue you feel strongly about and, for example, are depending primarily on an appeal to reason, you don't want to let your dispassionate, logical persona slip and resort to name-calling (formally known as arguing ad hominem or ad populem). That's obvious.

Not so obvious, however, is some slip in diction or tone that reveals the hothead behind the cool pen. Your reader may feel manipulated or use the slip to discount your entire argument, all because you lost sight of the ethical appeal. Tone should vary, yes, but never to the point of discord.

6. **Place your point where it does the most good.** Put each of your paragraphs on a separate piece of paper so that you can rearrange their order as you would a hand of cards. Try out your major assertion in different slots. If you have it at the beginning, try it at the end and vice versa. Or extend the introduction so that the thesis comes closer to the middle of the paper. See which placement carries greater impact.

You may want to organize your material starting with examples that lead up to the position you wish to attack and to the conviction you are arguing for; in that case your thesis may occur somewhere in the middle third or at the end of the paper. On the other hand, you may want to use deduction—starting with the opposition, stating your position, and then spending 90 percent of the remaining essay supporting your case. Remember that you want to win your reader over, so put your thesis where it will do the greatest good.

Last Rites for Indian Dead

Suzan Shown Harjo

Suzan Shown Harjo is a columnist for Indian Country Today, *the foremost Native American newspaper, but, as her biography on the paper's Web site states, she is also "poet, writer, lecturer, curator and policy advocate." President and Executive Director of the Morning Star Institute, a national Indian organization dedicated to promoting their rights, cultures, traditions, and arts, Harjo was the first Native American to be honored by the Stanford University Haas Center for Public Policy. The essay that follows typifies her activism and her effectiveness. Writing as a Cheyenne, Suzan Shown Harjo points to a problem that affects Native Americans and, she argues, that raises an ethical issue for the rest of us. Her essay, which appeared on the editorial page of the* Los Angeles Times *in September 1989, is a good example of deductive reasoning. And her argument was effective: Congress passed the Native American Graves Protection and Repatriation Act in 1990.*

What to Look For   Conclusions are often difficult to write, but one way of ending an argumentative essay is to call for a specified action. That is what Harjo does for her essay, and it's a technique you can adapt for your own arguments.

1   What if museums, universities, and government agencies could put your dead relatives on display or keep them in boxes to be cut up and otherwise studied? What if you believed that the spirits of the dead could not rest until their human remains were placed in a sacred area?

2   The ordinary American would say there ought to be a law—and there is, for ordinary Americans. The problem for American Indians is that there are too many laws of the kind that make us the archaeological property of the United States and too few of the kind that protect us from such insults.

3   Some of my own Cheyenne relatives' skulls are in the Smithsonian Institution today, along with those of at least 4500 other Indian people

who were violated in the 1800s by the U.S. Army for an "Indian Cranial Study." It wasn't enough that these unarmed Cheyenne people were mowed down by the cavalry at the infamous Sand Creek massacre; many were decapitated and their heads shipped to Washington as freight. (The Army Medical Museum's collection is now in the Smithsonian.) Some had been exhumed only hours after being buried. Imagine their grieving families' reaction on finding their loved ones disinterred and headless.

4   Some targets of the Army's study were killed in noncombat situations and beheaded immediately. The officer's account of the decapitation of the Apache chief Mangas Coloradas in 1863 shows the pseudoscientific nature of the exercise. "I weighed the brain and measured the skull," the good doctor wrote, "and found that while the skull was smaller, the brain was larger than that of Daniel Webster."

5   These journal accounts exist in excruciating detail, yet missing are any records of overall comparisons, conclusions or final reports of the Army study. Since it is unlike the Army not to leave a paper trail, one must wonder about the motive for its collection.

6   The total Indian body count in the Smithsonian collection is more than 19,000, and it is not the largest in the country. It is not inconceivable that the 1.5 million of us living today are outnumbered by our dead stored in museums, educational institutions, federal agencies, state historical societies and private collections. The Indian people are further dehumanized by being exhibited alongside the mastodons and dinosaurs and other extinct creatures.

7   Where we have buried our dead in peace, more often than not the sites have been desecrated. For more than 200 years, relic hunting has been a popular pursuit. Lately, the market in Indian artifacts has brought this abhorrent activity to a fever pitch in some areas. And when scavengers come upon Indian burial sites, everything found becomes fair game, including sacred burial offerings, teeth and skeletal remains.

8   One unusually well-publicized example of Indian grave desecration occurred two years ago in a western Kentucky field known as Slack Farm, the site of an Indian village five centuries ago. Ten men—one with a business card stating "Have Shovel, Will Travel"—paid the landowner $10,000 to lease digging rights between planting seasons. They dug extensively on the 40-acre farm, rummaging through an estimated 650 graves, collecting burial goods, tools and ceremonial items. Skeletons were strewn about like litter.

9   What motivates people to do something like this? Financial gain is the first answer. Indian relic-collecting has become a multimillion-dollar industry. The price tag on a bead necklace can easily top $1000; rare pieces fetch tens of thousands.

10   And it is not just collectors of the macabre who pay for skeletal remains. Scientists say that these deceased Indians are needed for research that someday could benefit the health and welfare of living Indians. But just how many dead Indians must they examine? Nineteen thousand?

11   There is doubt as to whether permanent curation of our dead really benefits Indians. Dr. Emery A. Johnson, former assistant surgeon general, recently observed, "I am not aware of any current medical diagnostic or treatment procedure that has been derived from research on such skeletal remains. Nor am I aware of any during the 34 years that I have been involved in American Indian . . . health care."

12   Indian remains are still being collected for racial biological studies. While the intentions may be honorable, the ethics of using human remains this way without the full consent of relatives must be questioned.

13   Some relief for Indian people has come on the state level. Almost half of the states, including California, have passed laws protecting Indian burial sites and restricting the sale of Indian bones, burial offerings and other sacred items. Representative Charles E. Bennett (D-Fla.) and Sen. John McCain (R-Ariz.) have introduced bills that are a good start in invoking the federal government's protection. However, no legislation has attacked the problem head-on by imposing stiff penalties at the marketplace, or by changing laws that make dead Indians the nation's property.

14   Some universities—notably Stanford, Nebraska, Minnesota and Seattle—have returned, or agreed to return, Indian human remains; it is fitting that institutions of higher education should lead the way.

15   Congress is now deciding what to do with the government's extensive collection of Indian human remains and associated funerary objects. The secretary of the Smithsonian, Robert McC. Adams, has been valiantly attempting to apply modern ethics to yesterday's excesses. This week, he announced that the Smithsonian would conduct an inventory and return all Indian skeletal remains that could be identified with specific tribes or living kin.

16   But there remains a reluctance generally among collectors of Indian remains to take action of a scope that would have a quantitative

impact and a healing quality. If they will not act on their own—and it is highly unlikely that they will—then Congress must act.

17   The country must recognize that the bodies of dead American Indian people are not artifacts to be bought and sold as collectors' items. It is not appropriate to store tens of thousands of our ancestors for possible future research. They are our family. They deserve to be returned to their sacred burial grounds and given a chance to rest.

18   The plunder of our people's graves has gone on too long. Let us rebury our dead and remove this shameful past from America's future.

ORGANIZATION AND IDEAS

1. Paragraphs 1 and 2 introduce the essay by presenting a "what if" situation. Why might Harjo have chosen this kind of opening?
2. Paragraphs 9–12 explain why people dig up Indian burial sites. What reasons does Harjo give?
3. Harjo explains what is being done and what needs to be done about the situation in paragraphs 13–18. What solution does she call for?
4. Considering the situation Harjo describes, the steps that are being taken to address that situation, and what remains to be done, what is the thesis of the essay?
5. If you were in Harjo's position, what additional arguments might you add?

TECHNIQUE AND STYLE

1. Describe the audience the essay is aimed at as precisely as you can. What evidence do you base your description on?
2. How would you characterize the diction Harjo uses in connection with her examples? Choose one or two examples and substitute more or less loaded words. What is gained? Lost?
3. Based on the way the essay is written, what kind of person does Harjo appear to be? How would you describe her?
4. To what extent does the essay rest its appeal on Harjo's persona? On emotion? On logic? Which appeal predominates?
5. The essay concludes with a call for action. Evaluate its effectiveness.

SUGGESTIONS FOR WRITING

Journal

1. Imagine that you are on the board of a museum that owns Indian skeletons. Explain your response to Harjo's essay.
2. Harjo uses the term "shameful past" (paragraph 18). What other examples might Native Americans associate with that term?

Essay

1. Think of an action that was considered acceptable in the past but today is either questionable or unacceptable. Fifty years ago, for instance, no one thought much about the hazards of smoking, nor of cholesterol levels, nor of needing to inspect meat. Segregation was acceptable, as were other forms of racism. Choose a subject and think about the ethics involved and how present knowledge has changed how we live. Other suggestions:

   The sale of cigarettes
   The advertising of alcoholic beverages
   The popularity of natural foods
   The sale of diet products

2. Harjo states that "Indian relic-collecting has become a multi-million-dollar industry" (paragraph 9). Use your library or the Internet to research the degree to which relic-collecting is still a problem and what should be done about it.

Don't Impede Medical Progress

Virginia Postrel

Virginia Postrel began her writing career as a reporter for Inc. *and the* Wall Street Journal, *moving on first to become associate editor, then editor, and then editor-at-large of* Reason, *a monthly magazine of news, opinion, analysis, and reviews focusing on politics and culture. Her book* The Future and Its Enemies *(1999) examines the ways in which traditional political polarities, such as conservative and liberal, fail to deal with the major issues of our present time.* The Substance of Style: How the Rise of Aesthetic Value Is Remaking Commerce, Culture, and Consciousness *(2005), her new book, argues that the idea of aesthetics is increasingly important to society and to business. In addition to writing a regular column, "Commerce and Culture," for the* Atlantic, *where she is a contributing editor, she writes on economics for the* New York Times *and contributes to* Forbes *and the* Wall Street Journal, *where this article appeared on December 5, 2001.*

What to Look For   Just as comparison and contrast essays can be organized by block or point by point (p. 175), an argumentative essay can cite a position and then counter it or break the position into points, countering each one. As you read Postrel's essay, keep track of how she lays out her argument.

1   To many biologists, the recently announced creation of a cloned human embryo was no big deal. True, researchers at Advanced Cell Technology replaced the nucleus of a human egg with the genetic material of another person. And they got that cloned cell to start replicating. But their results were modest. It took 71 eggs to produce a single success, and in the best case, the embryo grew to only six cells before dying. That's not a revolution. It's an incremental step in understanding how early-stage cells develop.

2   And it's far from the 100 or so cells in a blastocyst, the hollow ball from which stem cells can be isolated. Scientists hope to coax embryonic stem cells into becoming specialized tissues such as nerve, muscle, or pancreatic islet cells. Therapeutic cloning, or nucleus transplantation, could make such treatments more effective.

3   In theory, it would work like this: Suppose I need new heart tissue or some insulin-secreting islet cells to counteract diabetes. You could take the nucleus from one of my cells, stick it in an egg cell from which the nucleus had been removed, let that develop into stem cells, and then trigger the stem cells to form the specific tissue needed. The new "cloned" tissue would be genetically mine and would not face rejection problems. It would function in my body as if it had grown there naturally, so I wouldn't face a lifetime of immunosuppressant drugs.

4   But all of that is a long way off. ACT and others in the field are still doing very basic research, not developing clinical therapies. Indeed, because of the difficulty of obtaining eggs, therapeutic cloning may ultimately prove impractical for clinical treatments. It could be more important as a technique for understanding cell development or studying the mutations that lead to cancer. We simply don't know right now. Science is about exploring the unknown and cannot offer guarantees.

5   Politics, however, feeds on fear, uncertainty, and doubt, and the word "cloning" arouses those emotions. While its scientific

importance remains to be seen, ACT's announcement has rekindled the campaign to criminalize nucleus transplantation and any therapies derived from that process. Under a bill passed by the House and endorsed by the President, scientists who transfer a human nucleus into an egg cell would be subject to 10-year federal prison sentences and $1 million fines. So would anyone who imports therapies developed through such research in countries where it is legal, such as Britain. The bill represents an unprecedented attempt to criminalize basic biomedical research.

6   The legislation's backers consider the fear of cloning their best hope for stopping medical research that might lead to gene-level therapies. Opponents make three basic arguments for banning therapeutic cloning.

7   The first is that a fertilized egg is a person, entitled to full human rights. Taking stem cells out of a blastocyst is, in this view, no different from cutting the heart out of a baby. Hence, we hear fears of "embryo farming" for "spare parts."

8   This view treats microscopic cells with no past or present consciousness, no organs or tissues, as people. A vocal minority of Americans, of course, do find compelling the argument that a fertilized egg is someone who deserves protection from harm. That view animates the anti-abortion movement and exercises considerable influence in Republican politics.

9   But most Americans don't believe we should sacrifice the lives and well being of actual people to save cells. Human identity must rest on something more compelling than the right string of proteins in a petri dish, detectable only with high-tech equipment. We will never get a moral consensus that a single cell, or a clump of 100 cells, is a human being. That definition defies moral sense, rational argument, and several major religious traditions.

10   So cloning opponents add a second argument. If we allow therapeutic cloning, they say, some unscrupulous person will pretend to be doing cellular research but instead implant a cloned embryo in a woman's womb and produce a baby. At the current stage of knowledge, using cloning to conceive a child would indeed be dangerous and unethical, with a high risk of serious birth defects. Anyone who cloned a baby today would rightly face, at the very least, the potential of an enormous malpractice judgment. There are good arguments for establishing a temporary moratorium on reproductive cloning.

11   But the small possibility of reproductive cloning does not justify making nucleus transfer a crime. Almost any science might conceivably

be turned to evil purposes. This particular misuse is neither especially likely—cell biology labs are not set up to deliver fertility treatments—nor, in the long run, especially threatening.

12   Contrary to a lot of scary rhetoric, a healthy cloned infant would not be a moral nightmare, merely the not-quite-identical twin of an older person. (The fetal environment and egg cytoplasm create some genetic variations.) Certainly, some parents might have such a baby for bad reasons, to gratify their egos or to "replace" a child who died. But parents have been having children for bad reasons since time immemorial.

13   Just as likely, cloned babies would be the cherished children of couples who could not have biological offspring any other way. These children might bear an uncanny resemblance to their biological parents, but that, too, is not unprecedented. Like the "test tube babies" born of in vitro fertilization, cloned children need not be identifiable, much less freaks or outcasts.

14   Why worry so much about a few babies? Because, say opponents, even a single cloned infant puts us on the road to genetic dystopia, a combination of Brave New World and Nazi Germany. A cloned child's genetic makeup is too well known, goes the argument, and therefore transforms random reproduction into "manufacturing" that robs the child of his autonomy. This is where the attack broadens from nucleus transfer to human genetic engineering more generally. An anti-therapeutic cloning petition, circulated by the unlikely duo of conservative publisher William Kristol and arch-technophobe Jeremy Rifkin, concludes, "We are mindful of the tragic history of social eugenics movements in the first half of the 20th century, and are united in our opposition to any use of biotechnology for a commercial eugenics movement in the 21st century."

15   But the "eugenics" they attack has nothing to do with state-sponsored mass murder or forced sterilization. To the contrary, they are the ones who want the state to dictate the most private aspects of family life. They are the ones who want central authorities, rather than the choices of families and individuals, to determine our genetic future. They are the ones who demand that the government control the means of reproduction. They are the ones who measure the worth of human beings by the circumstances of their conception and the purity of their genetic makeup. They are the ones who say "natural" genes are the mark of true humanity.

16   Winners in the genetic lottery themselves, blessed with good health and unusual intelligence, they seek to deny future parents the

chance to give their children an equally promising genetic start. In a despicable moral equivalency, they equate loving parents with Nazis.

17   Biomedicine does have the potential to alter the human experience. Indeed, it already has. Life expectancy has doubled worldwide in the past century. Childbirth is no longer a peril to mother and infant. Childhood is no longer a time for early death. The pervasive sense of mortality that down through the ages shaped art, religion, and culture has waned.

18   Our lives are different from our ancestors' in fundamental ways. We rarely remark on the change, however, because it occurred incrementally. That's how culture evolves and how science works. We should let the process continue.

ORGANIZATION AND IDEAS

1. Paragraphs 1–3 introduce the essay. What does the introduction accomplish?
2. What are the three main arguments in favor of outlawing nucleus transplants? How does Postrel counter them?
3. How fair is Postrel to the opposition?
4. To what extent does Postrel's argument appeal to reason? To emotion?
5. To what extent, if any, does Postrel persuade you to adopt her position?

TECHNIQUE AND STYLE

1. The procedures Postrel describes are complex. To what extent does she explain them clearly?
2. How would you describe Postrel's tone? What examples best support your view?
3. What reasons can you think of for the *Wall Street Journal* publishing the essay?
4. In paragraph 15, Postrel repeats the term "they are." Why might she have done so and what is the effect of the repetition?
5. To what extent, if any, can paragraph 16 be called an ad hominem attack?

SUGGESTIONS FOR WRITING

Journal

1. What effect would Postrel's essay have had if you knew she were a scientist? A politician?
2. What alternative titles can you think of for the essay? Which do you prefer and why?

Essay

1. Questions of ethics constantly arise in the field of medicine. Is it ethical to keep a dying patient alive? To sustain a two-pound "crack baby"? To give out clean needles at drug rehab centers? To sell organs for transplants? To use animals for research? Select one of these questions or another of your own choosing and research the topic, using your library or the Internet. Take a position and defend it in an essay.

2. Use your library or the Internet to bring Postrel's essay up to date. What is the current state of research in the United States? In England, Europe, and elsewhere? Should the laws in the United States be revised? Your answers to these questions and others that you uncover can evolve into an explanatory or argumentative essay.

Gay Marriages: Make Them Legal

Thomas B. Stoddard

What is traditional is not always what is right, or so Thomas B. Stoddard argues in the essay that follows. He calls for a redefinition of marriage that accommodates the legal status of matrimony to the present times. Stoddard was an attorney and executive director of the Lambda Legal Defense and Education Fund. He died in 1997, having spent most of his life fighting for equal rights for gays and lesbians and against AIDS-related discrimination. His essay was published as an opinion piece in the New York Times *in 1989. Since that time, a few states have legalized gay unions and Massachusetts recognizes gay marriage. The topic continues to be hotly debated.*

What to Look For Definition is a key element in argument. Note how careful Stoddard is to define marriage in paragraphs 4 and 5. When you write your own argumentative paper, you'll probably find it helpful first to identify the most important term and then to make sure early on in your paper that you define it carefully.

1   In sickness and in health, 'til death do us part." With those familiar words, millions of people each year are married, a public affirmation of a private bond that both society and the newlyweds hope will endure. Yet for nearly four years, Karen Thompson was denied the company of the one person to whom she had pledged lifelong devotion. Her partner is a woman, Sharon Kowalski, and their home state of Minnesota, like every other jurisdiction in the United States, refuses to permit two individuals of the same sex to marry.

2   Karen Thompson and Sharon Kowalski are spouses in every respect except the legal. They exchanged vows and rings; they lived together until November 13, 1983—when Ms. Kowalski was severely injured when her car was struck by a drunk driver. She lost the capacity to walk or to speak more than several words at a time, and needed constant care.

3   Ms. Thompson sought a court ruling granting her guardianship over her partner, but Ms. Kowalski's parents opposed the petition and obtained sole guardianship. They moved Ms. Kowalski to a nursing home 300 miles away from Ms. Thompson and forbade all visits between the two women. Last month, as part of a reevaluation of Ms. Kowalski's mental competency, Ms. Thompson was permitted to visit her partner again. But the prolonged injustice and anguish inflicted on both women hold a moral for everyone.

4   Marriage, the Supreme Court declared in 1967, is "one of the basic civil rights of man" (and, presumably, of woman as well). The freedom to marry, said the Court, is "essential to the orderly pursuit of happiness."

5   Marriage is not just a symbolic state. It can be the key to survival, emotional and financial. Marriage triggers a universe of rights, privileges and presumptions. A married person can share in a spouse's estate even when there is no will. She is typically entitled to the group insurance and pension programs offered by the spouse's employer, and she enjoys tax advantages. She cannot be compelled to testify against her spouse in legal proceedings.

6   The decision whether or not to marry belongs properly to individuals—not the government. Yet at present, all 50 states deny that choice to millions of gay and lesbian Americans. While marriage has historically required a male partner and a female partner, history alone cannot sanctify injustice. If tradition were the only

measure, most states would still limit matrimony to partners of the same race.

7   As recently as 1967, before the Supreme Court declared miscegenation statutes unconstitutional, 16 states still prohibited marriages between a white person and a black person. When all the excuses were stripped away, it was clear that the only purpose of those laws was, in the words of the Supreme Court, "to maintain white supremacy."

8   Those who argue against reforming the marriage statutes because they believe that same-sex marriage would be "antifamily" overlook the obvious: marriage creates families and promotes social stability. In an increasingly loveless world, those who wish to commit themselves to a relationship founded upon devotion should be encouraged, not scorned. Government has no legitimate interest in how that love is expressed.

9   And it can no longer be argued—if it ever could—that marriage is fundamentally a procreative unit. Otherwise, states would forbid marriage between those who, by reason of age or infertility, cannot have children, as well as those who elect not to.

10   As the case of Sharon Kowalski and Karen Thompson demonstrates, sanctimonious illusions lead directly to the suffering of others. Denied the right to marry, these two women are left subject to the whims and prejudices of others, and of the law.

11   Depriving millions of gay American adults the marriages of their choice, and the rights that flow from marriage, denies equal protection of the law. They, their families and friends, together with fair-minded people everywhere, should demand an end to this monstrous injustice.

ORGANIZATION AND IDEAS

1. Stoddard's paragraphs 1–3 present an example that holds a "moral for everyone." What is it?
2. Paragraphs 4 and 5 define marriage. What point does Stoddard make about it? To what extent is his definition complete?
3. Paragraphs 6–9 are aimed at countering arguments that can be used against Stoddard's view. Summarize them.
4. What is the effect of paragraph 10? What other paragraphs does it connect with?
5. The essay concludes with a statement of thesis and a call to action. Who should demand what, and how?

TECHNIQUE AND STYLE

1. What paragraph or paragraphs appeal to the reader's emotions? What examples can you find of loaded language?
2. What paragraph or paragraphs appeal to the reader's reason?
3. Where in the essay can you identify an ethical appeal, an appeal based on the author's persona?
4. Stoddard cites the arguments that can be used against his. Does he cite obvious ones? Is his treatment of them fair? How so?
5. How would you characterize Stoddard's audience? How well does his argument fit it?

SUGGESTIONS FOR WRITING

Journal

1. Reread paragraphs 4 and 5. To what extent do you agree with Stoddard's definition?
2. Select one of Stoddard's points and either support or refute it.

Essay

1. Think of an issue that ought to be covered by a law or one that is governed by law and should not be. The best place to start is probably with your own experience and what irks you, but after that you'll need to do some research so that you can present your position in a more objective and reasoned way. The use of outside sources will lend more weight to your ideas. Suggestions for laws that do exist but that some think should not:

   the given speed limit
   the legal drinking age
   particular zoning or IRS regulations
   banning of prayers in public schools

   Suggestions for laws that some think should exist but don't (varies by state):

   car insurance
   automobile safety seats for infants
   helmets for motorcycle riders
   neutering of pets

2. The word *marriage* combines religious connotations with civil rights. By legalizing civil unions, however, Vermont and Connecticut have split the civil contract away from the religious ceremony. Research the difference between civil union and marriage so that you can take a stand on what, if anything, should or should not be legal.

Dearly Beloved

Cal Thomas

Open the editorial page of almost any major newspaper in the United States, and you'll probably see a column by Cal Thomas. Over 600 newspapers carry his essays. Equally at home on the air, Thomas has worked for NBC, CNBC, PBS, and Fox as a political analyst. The quality of his commentary has won him a Peabody (for team reporting) as well as Associated Press and United Press International awards. His most recent books are The Wit and Wisdom of Cal Thomas *(2001), a collection of his writings, and* Blinded by Might: Can the Religious Right Save America? *(1999), a hard look at how the religious right tries to shape politics. Thomas's column that appears here was published in the New Orleans* Times-Picayune *on June 15, 2006.*

What to Look For   As you read Thomas's essay, keep track how he defines marriage: What role does religion play? What religion? What is and is not allowed, given his definition?

1   "Dearly beloved, we are gathered together in the sight of God and before these witnesses to join this man and this woman in holy matrimony."

2   So begins most "traditional" marriage ceremonies in Western culture for as long as anyone can remember. Now we are told such exclusivity of preserving marriage for men and women "discriminates" against people of the same sex who wish to "marry" each other. Some forms of discrimination are good, because they send a signal and provide an example that certain behavior is to be preferred over other behaviors for the betterment of society.

3   That a president of the United States would feel compelled, for whatever reason, to make a public statement that marriage should be reserved for men and women is a leading indicator of the moral state of the union. Imagine Calvin Coolidge saying such a thing, even in the "Roaring '20s." He might as well have stated the equally obvious that the sun rises in the east.

4   Today, right and wrong, an objective concept rooted in unchanging truth, has been dismissed in favor of the imposed rulings of federal judges guided by their own whims and opinion polls (various polls show the country equally split between those who oppose same-sex marriage and those who would allow it). We are now adrift to sort out our choices based on a weather vane principle: whichever way the wind blows is where we'll go.

5   When nothing is either true or false and all decisions about life and morals are based on personal choices and whatever new "trend" happens to capture our attention, we lose our moral sense, which, like an immune system, was established to protect us from cultural, as well as biological viruses.

6   The charge is made that President Bush is "again" using the issue of same-sex marriage to rally his base. But it is not the president who has made this a political issue. Those who would melt the glue of marriage, which has held societies together for millennia, are using the legal and political system for their own ends. In every state where same-sex marriage has been on the ballot, it has been decisively defeated. But like the war in Iraq, the "insurgents" in the culture wars believe all they must do is hang on long enough and the majority will surrender because protracted warfare interferes with our pursuit of pleasure and material consumption.

7   Some claim that heterosexuals ought to tend to their own marriages before they prohibit people of the same sex from marrying. While it is true that too many heterosexuals divorce (and too many others live together without becoming married), using this as a wedge to undermine a "norm," which, when practiced, serves children and society well, is not a sufficient reason for broadening—and therefore undermining—the traditional definition of what it means to be married.

8   Allowing same-sex marriage would be the ultimate in social engineering on a scale even grander than the judicial fiat that brought us abortion on demand. And it won't stop there. People whose beliefs about marriage are founded on religious doctrines can expect lawsuits accusing them of "discrimination" should they refuse to hire someone who is "married" to a person of the same sex. Some countries have enacted or are considering laws that prohibit anyone, including ministers, from publicly stating that homosexual practice is wrong, or a "sin." Remember sin? Sinful is what we were before we became "dysfunctional."

9   Religious groups who operate adoption agencies and schools under government contracts could face lawsuits for opposing same-sex marriages. Under Massachusetts' anti-discrimination law, for example, the state told Catholic Charities it must place foster children with same-sex couples, or lose its state license to operate its adoption agency. Faced with a choice between its beliefs and the heavy hand of government, Catholic Charities of Boston decided to get out of the adoption business.

10   We can expect more of this. A Utah polygamist has filed a federal lawsuit demanding that he not be discriminated against for wanting to marry more than one woman. His attorney cites last year's Supreme Court ruling that struck down a Texas sodomy law. Richard G. Wilkins, a law professor at Brigham Young University, notes, "If you can't require monogamy, how in the world can you deny the claims of the polygamists, particularly when it's buttressed by the claims of religion?"

11   Exactly. When there is no "no" to any behavior, then there must be "yes" to every behavior. If same-sex "marriage" is allowed, no one will ever be able to say "no" to anything again.

ORGANIZATION AND IDEAS

1. Like Stoddard, Thomas begins with a quotation from the traditional Christian marriage ceremony. In what ways is that quotation central to Thomas's argument?

2. How does Thomas define marriage? To what extent is that definition complete?

3. Thomas is concerned with the "moral state of the union" (paragraph 3). Where else in the essay does he allude to it? What is his overall view of the country's "moral state"?

4. Reread the essay noting all comparisons. Explain the degree to which they are fair.

5. Thomas concludes his essay with a claim and a prediction. What effect do they achieve?

TECHNIQUE AND STYLE

1. What paragraph or paragraphs appeal to the reader's emotions? What examples can you find of loaded language?

2. What paragraph or paragraphs appeal to the reader's reason?

3. Where in the essay do you find evidence of Thomas's persona? How would you characterize it?

4. What is the dominant appeal in Thomas's essay? What evidence supports your view?

5. Thomas is careful to cite the arguments that can be used against his positions. Does he cite obvious ones? Is his treatment of them fair? How so?

SUGGESTIONS FOR WRITING

Journal

1. To what extent do you agree with Thomas's definition of marriage?

2. Select one of Thomas's points and either support or refute it.

Essay

1. Like it or not, various courts and legislatures, as well as Congress, have made rulings or laws that affect people's marriages and intimate relationships. Select one of the topics below or come up with a similar one of your own choosing and research it, gathering enough information so that you can compose an informed argument on it.

   Vermont's laws on civil unions

   Massachusetts' laws on gay marriage

   The Supreme Court's decision on the Texas sodomy case

   Your state's laws on adoption by gay couples

   Congress's debate on the "marriage amendment"

2. In the course of constructing his argument, Thomas makes a number of arguable claims, some in the form of comparisons and some as statements, as in paragraph 4. Reread the essay, looking for examples, choose one, research it, and then write an essay supporting or refuting it.

Guest Workers and the U.S. Heritage

Jay Bookman

Jay Bookman holds degrees in history and journalism from Pennsylvania State University. After writing for newspapers in Washington, Nevada, and Massachusetts, he joined the staff of the Atlanta Journal-Constitution *and is now that paper's deputy editorial page writer. His columns appear on the editorial page twice weekly and are carried by other papers as well. His interests range from national and state politics to technology and the environment, the latter leading to his book* Caught in the Current: Searching for Simplicity in the Technological Age *(2004). Bookman's work has earned him recognition from various environmental groups such as the Wilderness Society and the National Wildlife Federation, and he has also received the Aldo Leopold Award, as well as the Scripps Howard and National Headliner awards. For his editorial work, he won a Eugene Pulliam Fellowship from the Society of Professional Journalists. The essay below appeared in the Austin* American-Statesman *on April 4, 2006.*

What to Look For   When you think about an issue that you want to take an argumentative stand on, you might try the approach that Bookman uses: analyzing the problem and the possible solutions. He discusses various solutions others have proposed, finds them unsatisfactory, and concludes with his own.

1   If the American people decide that 12 million illegal immigrants should be removed and sent back home, fine, we can try to do that.

2   The process would be hard and expensive and brutally inhumane at times, and it could never be entirely successful. But if we hardened our hearts and emptied our wallets, we could probably come somewhat close to achieving that goal.

3   Of course, banishing those millions from our borders would also mean that we would do without the labor they now provide in industries from construction to hotels and restaurants to agriculture to food processing. Some Americans—generally the most rabid and extremist among us—are ready to make that deal anyway, and there are politicians in Washington willing to pander to that crowd, at least in theory.

4   Others, however, are trying to find a way to retain the labor that illegal immigrants provide without offering them the right to live here permanently, let alone the right to pursue citizenship. It's an effort to solve a politically tough problem by cutting the baby in half, placating anti-immigrant fervor without denying American business the cheap, docile work force it relies upon.

5   That is in essence the proposal championed by President Bush, who advocates "legalizing" millions of immigrants now here illegally, but only on a temporary basis. After working several years, the temporary "guest workers" would be forced to return to their home countries to be replaced by new temporary workers.

6   That proposal has been condemned by extremists—most of them in Bush's own party—as offering "amnesty" to those who broke the law in coming here, as if punishment were more important than solving the problem. The more serious problem with that approach is practical; it assumes that workers will return home once their legal status has expired, and that's unlikely to happen.

7   It's also important to think about the guest worker approach in moral terms, in terms of the values that we claim to honor as Americans.

8   Under a guest worker policy, we will let the immigrants come here by the millions, but only temporarily. We will let them mangle their hands in our poultry plants and salt our farmlands with the sweat off their brows and break their backs at our construction sites and raise our children as nannies and clean our homes as maids, all at cut-rate wages.

9   But we will not allow them to dream—for themselves or their children—of sharing in the future they help to build here.

10 In other words, we are willing to let them serve us but not join us; they must by law be held apart and beneath us. We will import them to serve as a perpetually rotating servant class, and we will do so even while pretending to still honor that most American of principles, "that all men are created equal."

11 That system of second-class citizenship—far from slavery, but far from the full range of human rights as well—has precedent in American history. In colonial times, more than half of those who immigrated from Europe came here not as free people but as indentured servants.

12 In return for the cost of passage to the New World, they agreed to be legally bound to an employer for a number of years, unable to marry without permission and with no say over where they lived or how they worked. They could even be sold to another boss.

13 But even back then, when the period of bonded indenture ended—usually after seven years—the servant was freed and allowed to take his or her place as a full citizen.

14   In reality, there is nothing all that complicated about drafting a practical, humane policy on illegal immigration. It would have three basic components:

- Tighter border security, to cut off as much as possible the supply of illegal workers coming into this country;
- Much more effective enforcement against illegal employers, to reduce as much as possible the demand for illegal workers;
- A way to deal effectively and humanely with the illegal immigrants already here.

15   Any proposed solution that does not include all three components is neither workable nor serious. But in a consideration that is just as important, any proposal that condemns millions to a permanent menial class, even while profiting from their labor, is beneath us as a country and a betrayal of all we are supposed to represent.

ORGANIZATION AND IDEAS

1. What paragraph or paragraphs introduce the essay? How effective is that introduction?
2. Paragraphs 8–10 discuss the drawbacks of a guest worker program. What are they? How are they related to American "values"?
3. Bookman draws an analogy between a guest worker program and indentured servitude. Explain the degree to which the analogy is accurate.
4. State Bookman's thesis in your own words. What words or sentences did you draw on in Bookman's essay to form your statement?
5. In paragraph 14, Bookman spells out three "basic components" of a "practical, humane policy on illegal immigration." To what extent is his overall argument weakened by his not fleshing out the third component?

TECHNIQUE AND STYLE

1. Take a good look at the verbs in paragraph 8. What effects do you think Bookman wants to achieve by choosing those verbs?
2. Where in the essay do you find examples of loaded language? What effect does it have on you?
3. Read the last paragraph out loud with your ear tuned to the way it sounds. What alliteration do you find? What purpose does it serve?
4. How would you characterize Bookman's persona? Given what he says in the essay and how he says it, what sort of person does he appear to be?

5. Reread the essay, marking the various places where Bookman appeals to emotion, reason, and his own persona. Which appeal is dominant? What evidence supports your view?

SUGGESTIONS FOR WRITING

Journal

1. Choose a sentence from the essay that strikes you as particularly effective and explain why you find it so.
2. What other titles can you think of for the essay? Which do you prefer and why?

Essay

1. Immigration is such a hot topic that it has spun off any number of related issues. Listed below are some of the questions raised in the course of the debate:

   Should American citizens be required to have and carry identity cards?

   Should English be the official language of the United States?

   Should the official policy on asylum be modified?

   Should we build a wall on the U.S./Mexican border?

   Is deportation an effective solution for illegal immigration?

   Choose one of the topics or a similar one of your own, research it, and gather enough evidence so that you can make a your own argument.
2. In the heat of debate, *amnesty* can mean different things to different people. Use your library and other resources to discover how the word has been used in the past and how it is used in the current debate over immigration. Write an essay in which you argue for the "true" interpretation of the word.

We Don't Need 'Guest Workers'

Robert J. Samuelson

Any time you pick up Newsweek, *you will see Robert Samuelson's regular column on economics, but before joining the magazine in 1984, he was a reporter for the* Washington Post *and still contributes a column to that newspaper, one that also appears in the* Los Angeles Times *and the* Boston Globe. *There's hardly a journalism award that he hasn't won: the John Hancock Award for Best Business and Financial Columnist (1993), Gerald Loeb Award for Best Commentary (1993 and 1986), National Headliner Award for Feature Column on a Single Subject (1993 and 1992), as well as others. He is also the author of two books:* Untruth: Why the Conventional Wisdom is (Almost Always) Wrong *(2001) and* The Good Life and Its Discontents: The American Dream in the Age of Enlightenment *(1997). The essay below was published on March 22, 2006, in the* Washington Post.

> **What to Look For**   Like Samuelson, you will be doing a lot of research to back up your argument, but research, particularly if it involves statistics, needs to be made interesting. One way to do that is by varying your tone and diction. As you read Samuelson, look for the ways he uses informal language.

1   Economist Philip Martin of the University of California likes to tell a story about the state's tomato industry. In the early 1960s, growers relied on seasonal Mexican laborers, brought in under the government's "bracero" program. The Mexicans picked the tomatoes that were then processed into ketchup and other products. In 1964 Congress killed the program despite growers' warnings that its abolition would doom their industry. What happened? Well, plant scientists developed oblong tomatoes that could be harvested by machine. Since then, California's tomato output has risen fivefold.

2   It's a story worth remembering, because we're being warned again that we need huge numbers of "guest workers"—meaning

unskilled laborers from Mexico and Central America—to relieve U.S. "labor shortages." Indeed, the shortages will supposedly worsen as baby boomers retire. President Bush wants an open-ended program. Sens. Edward M. Kennedy (D-Mass.) and John McCain (R-Ariz.) advocate initially admitting 400,000 guest workers annually. The Senate is considering these and other plans.

3   Gosh, they're all bad ideas.

4   Guest workers would mainly legalize today's vast inflows of illegal immigrants, with the same consequence: We'd be importing poverty. This isn't because these immigrants aren't hardworking; many are. Nor is it because they don't assimilate; many do. But they generally don't go home, assimilation is slow and the ranks of the poor are constantly replenished. Since 1980 the number of Hispanics with incomes below the government's poverty line (about $19,300 in 2004 for a family of four) has risen 162 percent. Over the same period, the number of non-Hispanic whites in poverty rose 3 percent and the number of blacks, 9.5 percent. What we have now—and would with guest workers—is a conscious policy of creating poverty in the United States while relieving it in Mexico. By and large, this is a bad bargain for the United States. It stresses local schools, hospitals and housing; it feeds social tensions (witness the Minutemen). To be sure, some Americans get cheap housecleaning or landscaping services. But if more mowed their own lawns or did their own laundry, it wouldn't be a tragedy.

5   The most lunatic notion is that admitting more poor Latino workers would ease the labor market strains of retiring baby boomers. The two aren't close substitutes for each other. Among immigrant Mexican and Central American workers in 2004, only 7 percent had a college degree and nearly 60 percent lacked a high school diploma, according to the Congressional Budget Office. Among native-born U.S. workers, 32 percent had a college degree and only 6 percent did not have a high school diploma. Far from softening the social problems of an aging society, more poor immigrants might aggravate them by pitting older retirees against younger Hispanics for limited government benefits.

6   It's a myth that the U.S. economy "needs" more poor immigrants. The illegal immigrants already here represent only about 4.9 percent of the labor force, the Pew Hispanic Center reports. In no major occupation are they a majority. They're 36 percent of insulation

workers, 28 percent of drywall installers and 20 percent of cooks. They're drawn here by wage differences, not labor "shortages." In 2004, the median hourly wage in Mexico was $1.86, compared with $9 for Mexicans working in the United States, said Rakesh Kochhar of Pew. With high labor turnover in the jobs they take, most new illegal immigrants can get work by accepting wages slightly below prevailing levels.

7   Hardly anyone thinks that most illegal immigrants will leave. But what would happen if new illegal immigration stopped and wasn't replaced by guest workers? Well, some employers would raise wages to attract U.S. workers. Facing greater labor costs, some industries would—like the tomato growers in the 1960s—find ways to minimize those costs. As to the rest, what's wrong with higher wages for the poorest workers? From 1994 to 2004, the wages of high school dropouts rose only 2.3 percent (after inflation) compared with 11.9 percent for college graduates.

8   President Bush says his guest worker program would "match willing foreign workers with willing American employers, when no Americans can be found to fill the jobs." But at some higher wage, there would be willing Americans. The number of native high school dropouts with jobs declined by 1.3 million from 2000 to 2005, estimates Steven Camarota of the Center for Immigration Studies, which favors less immigration. Some lost jobs to immigrants. Unemployment remains high for some groups (9.3 percent for African Americans, 12.7 percent for white teenagers).

9   Business organizations understandably support guest worker programs. They like cheap labor and ignore the social consequences. What's more perplexing is why liberals, staunch opponents of poverty and inequality, support a program that worsens poverty and inequality. Poor immigrant workers hurt the wages of unskilled Americans. The only question is how much. Studies suggest a range "from negligible to an earnings reduction of almost 10 percent," according to the CBO.

10   It's said that having guest workers is better than having poor illegal immigrants. With legal status, they'd have rights and protections. They'd have more peace of mind and face less exploitation by employers. This would be convincing if its premise were incontestable: that we can't control our southern border. But that's unproved. We've never tried a policy of real barriers and strict enforcement against companies that hire illegal immigrants. Until that's shown to be

ineffective, we shouldn't adopt guest worker programs that don't solve serious social problems—but add to them.

ORGANIZATION AND IDEAS

1. Samuelson opens his essay with an example. How does it tie into the rest of the essay? How effective is it?
2. Reread paragraph 4, noting the causal relationships. What are the effects of poverty?
3. Where in the essay does Samuelson consider arguments that can be used against his points? How does he counter them?
4. Samuelson's argument rests on economic analysis. How effective is it?
5. Where in the essay is Samuelson's thesis? What effect does he achieve by that placement?

TECHNIQUE AND STYLE

1. How would you describe Samuelson's tone? What examples can you find to support your opinion?
2. Paragraph 3 consists of one sentence. What effect does it achieve?
3. The essay brims with facts and figures. How well does Samuelson judge his reader's tolerance for pure information? How clearly does he present it?
4. Reread the essay, marking examples of Samuelson's use of appeals. Which dominates? What evidence supports your opinion?
5. If Samuelson's essay were written for an academic audience instead of a popular one, all the information would be documented in notes. Opinion essays in newspapers, however, don't use notes but must present facts and figures credibly. How well does Samuelson do that?

SUGGESTIONS FOR WRITING

Journal

1. What fact or figure does Samuelson use that surprises you and why?
2. What do you associate with the word *immigrant*? After you've written a paragraph or two, reread what you've written and sum it up in one sentence. You then have a starting place for an essay.

Essay

1. Many arguments have been put forward as reasons to control illegal immigration:
   To protect national security
   To protect jobs and wages

To prevent increased pressure on health services and public schools

To prevent "back-door citizenship" (citizenship being granted automatically to children born in the US)

To preserve the English language

Choose one of these reasons and research it so that you can amass enough information to form an educated opinion you can then defend in an essay.

2. Samuelson's concluding paragraph suggests that illegal immigrants, lacking the "rights and protections" accorded to American citizens, are sometimes abused by their employers. Use research to explore the truth of that idea. You might start by picking a type of job that attracts illegal immigrants: house and garden work, restaurant jobs, construction, fruit and vegetable harvesting, and the like.

Direct, current, often abrasive, and savagely funny, political cartoons and comic strips are readily accessible forms of argument. The artists who draw them consider all subjects fair game, so it's not surprising that the debate over immigration appealed to a great many political satirists, Steve Kelley and Darrin Bell foremost among them.

All These Illegals

Darrin Bell

Darrin Bell is best known for Candorville, *an aptly named comic strip featuring a diverse inner-city cast. Writing as an African American, he depicts tough issues—race and poverty among them—in a way that is both honest and upbeat, and as a result the strip has a wide appeal. Now syndicated by the Washington Post Writers Group,* Candorville *is carried by newspapers such as the* Los Angeles Times, *the* Chicago Tribune, *and the* Detroit Free Press, *as well as* Al Dia, *a Spanish language paper published in Dallas. Bell grew up in Los Angeles, earned a degree in Political Science at the University of California, Berkeley, and now lives and works in Berkeley. His work has been published in two collections:* Another Stereotype Bites the Dust: A Candorville Collection *(2006) and* Candorville: Thank God for Culture Clash *(2005). Working with the writer Theorn Heir, Bell also draws the comic strip* Rudy Park. *The strip included here was published on April 10, 2006.*

Americans and Jobs

Steve Kelley

Steve Kelley's home base is the New Orleans Times-Picayune, *but his cartoons are syndicated and appear in many other papers, often showing up in the weekly collections gathered by the* New York Times, Newsweek, *and* The Week. *A graduate of Dartmouth College, Kelley's first job in journalism was at the* San Diego Union-Tribune. *While there, he helped start a program to raise money for the San Diego Child Abuse Prevention Fund. Since then, he has started "1,000 Laughs for 1,000 Smiles," to raise money for Mexican children in need of plastic surgery. Kelley has won numerous awards for his cartoons, including the Best of the West and National Headliner awards. The cartoon below was published on March 29, 2006.*

By permission of Steve Kelley and Creators Syndicate.

FOR DISCUSSION

1. To what extent are Kelley's characters "typical" Americans?
2. To what extent are Bell's characters typical? Stereotypical?
3. How does each drawing narrow the debate over immigration?
4. How does each drawing contribute a different perspective to the essays by Bookman and Samuelson?
5. Consider each cartoon as a political statement on the issue of immigration. What thesis would you give to each and why?

SUGGESTIONS FOR WRITING

Journal

Of the two, which do you prefer and why? Make specific reference to the drawings to support your point.

Essay

Perhaps a particular current issue interests you, or perhaps you're curious about how a certain political figure is portrayed, or maybe you want to know more about a political cartoonist. Can the cartoonist, for example, be labeled *liberal*? And if so, what sort of liberal and what positions does he or she take? Or think about how any prominent political figure is drawn by different artists. What is exaggerated? What is implied? Use a search engine to find cartoons or comic strips that deal with a current topic, political figure, or artist. More than likely, once you have brought up a site, you will be able to narrow a search so that you can explore the pertinent cartoons or comic strips. As you explore your topic, you will start to form a thesis that can be used for your essay, an essay that uses your description of the drawings and some examples of them to support your point.

ADDITIONAL WRITING ASSIGNMENTS

Using Argument

1. Choose a topic that has a direct impact on your life and take a stand: admission requirements for your institution, speed limits, collegiate athletics, bookstore policies, or parking on campus.
2. Choose a topic that relates to state politics and take a stand: campaign contributions, primaries, mail-in voting, limiting campaign time, or term limits.
3. Choose a topic that relates to national issues and take a stand: required ID cards, mandatory sentencing, universal health care, social security reform, or welfare.
4. Choose a topic that relates to international relations and take a stand: global warming, the International Monetary Fund, the United Nations, NATO peacekeeping, or free trade.

Evaluating the Essays

1. Suzan Shown Harjo argues against the mistreatment of dead relatives and their effects, and Virginia Postrel argues against the outlawing of research on nucleus transportation. Yet underlying both essays are the questions of what is moral and who should decide. Which writer answers those questions more thoroughly and effectively?
2. The subject of the essays by Thomas B. Stoddard and Cal Thomas is a sensitive one, and the views each writer expresses may not be shared by many readers. Reread the essays, looking for evidence that the writers are aware of their readers' potential sensitivity and that they may not agree with the writers' stands on the issue. Which writer does the better job of addressing his readers and how?
3. Both Jay Bookman and Robert Samuelson oppose a guest worker program for illegal immigrants. Bookman's argument rests on American values; Samuelson's rests on economic analysis. Which is the more effective and why?
4. The drawings by Steve Kelley and Darrin Bell add more arguments to those raised by Jay Bookman, and Robert Samuelson. Write an essay in which you stake out your own argument on immigration, taking into account the points made in the essays and drawings.

Multiple Modes, Varied Opinions

If you have ever been in a cast, you have some idea of the physical challenges that face the disabled. If you haven't been in that situation, next time you see someone in a wheelchair, look around at those nearby. You'll probably find that some look away, others duck their heads, several look through the wheelchair and the person in it, blanking them out, and few, if any, make eye contact. In the two essays that follow, Roger Rosenblatt and Bryan Tortolani take a close look at what it means to be disabled and some of the ways people react.

Roger Rosenblatt regularly appears on PBS's "The News Hour with Jim Lehrer," and his essays have been published in almost every major magazine. He won two George Polk Awards for his essays in *Time* and a Peabody and an Emmy award for his work on "The News Hour." He has taught writing and modern literature at Harvard, worked as a columnist and editor for *Life*, served as editor of *U.S. News & World Report*, been a columnist and member of the editorial board of the *Washington Post*, and editor-at-large at *Time*. Author of eleven books and best known for writing nonfiction, Rosenblatt has recently published a novel, *Lapham Rising* (2006). "Mind Over Matter" aired on "The News Hour" on May 3, 2004.

Bryan Tortolani wrote "Macho Man" when he was a student at San Joaquin Delta College in California. The essay then appeared in the 2005 issue of *Delta Winds*, a collection of student essays published annually by the English Department. His essay will tell you a lot about him but not that came to Delta, as the "About the authors" section states, a "happily married 36-year-old cancer survivor," armed with an eighth-grade education, a GED, and a "powerful motivation to succeed." Tortolani graduated from Delta and is now at Stanislaus State University, majoring in Sociology with a minor in English. He is a member of Phi Kappa Phi, a national academic honor society, and is on the editorial staff of *Penumbra*, the university's art and literary magazine.

Mind Over Matter

Roger Rosenblatt

1   Now there are more of them, men and women grievously wounded in Iraq, who have been blinded or consigned to wheel-chairs, or who walk very slowly, with a little help. They join a distinct population: The blind, the lame, and the halt.

2   They were once called that, in an age when those who wore their human injuries for all to see were set apart from the rest of us who were luckier. But now they move among us more readily, thanks to ramps in office buildings and special accommodations in theaters, stadiums, and other public places. Section 508 of the Rehabilitation Act did that. Because of Section 508 and a general advance in thinking about such things, the blind, the lame, and the halt find it easier to reenter the more mobile world.

3   And they improve it, for whenever we see them—usually fleetingly, out of the corner of an eye, with our heads turning away quickly, so as not to stare rudely—whenever we see them, the common thought is, "that could be me." And we know it could. Shrapnel from a hand grenade or a bomb; a terrible accident or disease; something acquired or inborn, and anyone would be among the bent, the slower.

4   The blind, the lame, and the halt serve others profoundly as exhibitions of Jefferson's creed: All people created equal, equally fragile, equally available to mishap, or equally strong, for that matter, since the disabled are able to do a lot.

5   Never mind the spectacular feats: The special Olympics; the wheelchair basketball games; runners racing with metal legs. The blind artists who sing seem to take their voices from heaven. These are the high-wire acts. Yet it is the so-called ordinary disabled who

take your breath away. Observe someone move from a wheelchair to a stationary boat or vice versa—the concentration on the act, the mastery of will.

6   For them, mind overcomes matter in two ways. The mind is who they are. It moves as fluidly as an all-American athlete. Television, in its good-hearted but absurd way, once tried to make a point about the disabled. For a while in the 1970s and '80s, TV created disabled heroes: Tate, a cowboy who had one arm, Raymond Burr as Ironside, the wheelchair-bound detective. James Franciscus played a blind detective who got into fistfights with criminals and won. I suppose the intention of these programs was to say, see, disabilities don't matter.

7   But, of course, they do matter. They encumber life with yet more difficulties. One would prefer to be rid of them, just as those differently disabled would prefer to be rid of neuroses, depression, guilt, corrosive malice, a tendency to lie and gossip, and other maladies less visible on the street. And that is why we are all served by being in one another's presence.

8   For the blind, the lame, and the halt observe the quicker population, too, and know, from hard experience, that everyone has a time of it. Everyone limps, rolls, needs a white cane. The disabled are people, not symbols. At the same time, they represent the entire race in all its weakness, power, and choice. That could be me. It is. I'm Roger Rosenblatt.

Macho Man—An In-depth Analysis of the Prejudices of Disability

Bryan Tortolani

1   Because I am large and healthy-looking, people think that I am weak, lazy or outright faking my disabilities. In reality, I am a strong, highly motivated man with many health conditions that are not always readily apparent to those around me. People do not see the scars of

the nearly twenty surgeries on my body, or the degenerative bone decay that is slowly eating away at my knees, hips, and shoulders, or the hepatitis that is turning my liver into a ball of scar tissue while spewing toxins throughout my system.

2   Most people have a preconceived notion of how a person with disabilities should look, and anyone who does not fit into that category often faces a wide range of prejudices throughout the day. For example, people are often outraged when they see me parking in a disabled parking spot or speeding past them in a four-wheeled electric cart because my appearance does not coincide with their perception of a disability. Similarly, when I use my Medicare at the doctor's office, cash my Social Security check at the bank, ride on the elevator, or simply pull my noisy backpack on wheels across campus, I am often perceived as a fat, lazy freeloader taking advantage of the services reserved for the "truly" disabled. This is because many people associate people with disabilities with outwardly noticeable disfigurements, with easily observable debilitating diseases, or with the elderly. Anyone who does not fit into their image of "disabled" is often perceived as perfectly healthy.

3   I have been living with such stereotypes since shortly after my nineteenth birthday, at which time I was diagnosed with late stage Hodgkin's disease. From the beginning, I did not fit the stereotype of a person with disabilities and therefore was often misjudged. Even after I lost my hair from chemotherapy treatments and a bone marrow transplant, I was still not perceived as "disabled" by many strangers who associated my baldness with the skinhead neo-Nazi gangs that were popular in the Seattle area during that time. I was often verbally assaulted with a barrage of accusations ranging from a deranged narrow-minded sociopath to a cowardly, parasitic racist bully. Although I can sympathize with the anger many people hold toward racist bigots, I strongly resent being associated with such evil merely on the basis of my appearance. More recently, I have experienced less dramatic prejudices; however, the end result is equally degrading and hurtful.

4   On a typical day I experience a dozen or more incidences of prejudice. For example, just last week I faced a crowd of extremely disturbed students after parking my car in the disabled parking spot at the community college I attend. Every day is the same in that many students race around and around the parking lot in the hopes of finding the perfect spot. Last week as

I defensively maneuvered my automobile, I noticed two anxious drivers who at the same time spotted a man backing out of his parking place. I sat back and watched this old Western-style showdown unfold. There was a brief pause as they made eye contact while revving up their engines. I could almost feel the intensity and determination from each driver's eyes as they locked for a moment in a penetrating stare. Their eyes darted back and forth between the newly available parking place and one another before the man in the large red truck made his move. The smaller sporty silver Honda quickly followed suit, and in a flash the two crazed drivers accelerated their two-ton automobiles in a mad dash for the spot. Once there, however, they soon realized that the space was reserved for the disabled.

5   As the two drivers grieved for a moment at their misfortune, I effortlessly guided my car into "their" parking place. I went about the task of retrieving my disabled placard from the glove box and hanging it from my rearview mirror, oblivious to the resentment that was building within my fellow students. It was not until I exited the car that I realized that the two drivers had not moved. As they sat in their automobiles, blocking traffic and wearing angry expressions on their young faces, a small crowd of students gathered on the sidewalk. I noticed some wore equally contemptuous expressions. I did my best to ignore them as I made my way toward my first class. Ignoring them became increasingly difficult as I drew closer. At first, the comments, although for my benefit, did not directly confront me.

6   "Can you believe the nerve of that guy, using handicapped parking when he's obviously not disabled?" shouted an indignant student from the crowd of student bystanders.

7   Then, the man from the red truck yelled, "Who do you think you're fooling—you ain't disabled. What kind of man takes his grandma's parking placard, anyway, just so he don't have to walk a few feet?"

8   The other students grew angry, watching what they perceived to be a perfectly healthy student take the best parking spot in the school.

9   Looking at the situation from their perspective, I could somewhat understand their confusion. I am six feet two inches tall, weigh over two hundred twenty-five pounds, look fairly young and healthy. Yet I was using disabled-parking placard. I did not even

have my cane with me because the rubber stoppers had been worn down. It was not because the cane did not work properly. Rather, I preferred the physical pain resonating from my knees to the psychological pain that accompanied the unwanted attention I received. This was because once the rubber stoppers wore down, the four metal prongs were exposed, making a loud "Ching, ching, ching" with every step. The sound would echo all across the campus as I hobbled through the crowded quad. It was then that I was subject to spiteful remarks and resentful looks from many of my fellow students.

10   This may seem like a trivial matter. But appearing different is difficult, especially when it is not consistent. My particular health condition fluctuates regularly; some days I look and feel a lot better than others. People are more comfortable with the familiar. It is easier to classify someone who is always a certain way because most people do not trust change and unpredictability. For example, if I were always seen riding in a wheelchair, people would eventually accept or reject me. Either way people would feel more comfortable with whatever label they had given me. But when dealing with inconsistencies, people's prejudices come into question.

11   An individual may classify people according to certain beliefs: "Men are strong, people with disabilities are always incapacitated, fat people are lazy, and skinny people are weak and nervous." When those perceptions are proven inaccurate, the individual tends to become uncomfortable. When facing the unfamiliar and uncomfortable, people often turn to further prejudicial classifications in order to maintain their familiar, safe, and structured worldview.

12   It takes great courage, intelligence, open-mindedness, and integrity to resist the temptations of prejudice, big and small. Although society has advanced in the fight against prejudice, it still has a very long way to go. Some prejudices are socially unacceptable, and others are not. Many people, while exhibiting guarded behavior in some circumstances, will openly participate in prejudicial behaviors toward those individuals who fall under the radar of political correctness. It is important for society to recognize this situation. Empathy for all groups of individuals who are different or unfamiliar should be the moral compass we follow.

ON MORALITY, VALUES, AND HIGHER EDUCATION

What is taught in colleges and universities is listed in their catalogues—various courses divided into various fields in support of various majors. But where do values fit in? Or should they? Do institutions of higher learning have an obligation to teach morality to their students? Alan Wolfe certainly thinks so. Stanley Fish disagrees.

Alan Wolfe teaches Political Science at Boston College, a private, coeducational Jesuit university, where he also directs the Boisi Center for Religion and American Public Life. The author of many articles in the *New Republic, Harper's,* the *Washington Post,* and the *New York Times,* among others, he has also written more than 10 books. His most recent ones are *Does American Democracy Still Work?* (2006), *Return to Greatness: How America Lost Its Sense of Purpose and What it Needs to Do to Recover It* (2005), *The Transformation of American Religion: How We actually Practice our Faith* (2003), and *An Intellectual in Public* (2003). The essay included here is one of a series published online in *Slate,* which asked well-known academics, "What should students be studying in college?" Wolfe's response appeared on November 15, 2005.

Stanley Fish teaches Law and Religion at Florida International University, an urban public research university, where he is the Davidson-Kahn Distinguished University Professor of Humanities and Law. Because many legal disputes hinge on language, it's only natural that Fish's initial concentration on English literature and language led to his current interest and position in law. His publications range from *How Milton Works* (2001) to *Professional Correctness: Literary Studies and Political Change* (1995). In addition, he has written over 200 books and articles, the latter appearing in leading law journals as well as the *New York Times* and *Harper's.* His essay "Aim Low" was published in the *Chronicle of Higher Education* on May 16, 2003. Its audience, as the name of the journal suggests, is composed of those who are involved in higher education—mainly teachers, administrators, and board members.

When Ideas Kill

Alan Wolfe

1   If consensus has disappeared over what, if anything, should be taught to all students who attend college, it has been lost most dramatically where morality is concerned. Colleges once required a senior capstone course, often taught by the college president, focusing on morality, usually from a Christian perspective. These days colleges are afraid of teaching any perspective at all for fear that someone will be excluded.

2   I would make morality central to any plan to revitalize general education. Students would be exposed to the great ethical thinkers who pondered the meaning of life and death, defined the differences between right and wrong, and tried to figure out what was good and what was evil. By its very nature, such a course would include religious figures, Christian ones along with others; Jesus, St. Paul, and Augustine come immediately to mind. But it would also include moral philosophers with hard-to-define religious views (Kant, Hume), as well as the resolutely secular (Bertrand Russell, Richard Dawkins).

3   It is easy to say that such a course could avoid the problem of taking sides by not taking them. But I wonder whether such resolute nonjudgmentalism would best serve the needs of contemporary students. Although I teach at a Catholic university, I find students reluctant to proclaim any one thing better than any other thing, including their own faith. Catholicism cannot, they believe, be the one true faith, which is another way of saying that any faith, even no faith, can be true. Their pluralism is admirable. Their inability to choose is lamentable.

4   Religion and morality are either serious subjects or they are not. If they are not, by all means let college reinforce the conviction of its students that there are no real convictions. But if they are serious subjects, part of teaching them involves preaching them. Let the best case be made for why Christianity offers a superior morality to Islam (or, for that matter, the other way around). And then let the students argue against whatever case is being made.

5   If religion should be taught with its sharp edges intact, so should the Enlightenment. My students are the products, if long removed, of

a revolution in thought that took place in the 18th century; had it not occurred, they would not be in college. They need to know why it was so important for modern science to break through the orthodoxies imposed by faith, one reason why they also need to know what those orthodoxies were in the first place.

6   We live at a time when ideas kill. Even in the United States, where killing over ideas is less likely to happen compared to the places we send our troops, people devote their lives, sacrifice potential income, and even break the law on behalf of conceptions of the world they hold to be true. For my students, by contrast, ideas are things found in books meant to be transcribed into blue books. My students are intelligent enough to know which ideas are important and which are not. But they lack the passion to choose between which ones are worth fighting for and which ones are not.

7   The "liberal" in liberal education is generally understood to mean openness of mind: a suspicion toward dogma and a willingness to allow truth to emerge from the clash of different viewpoints. Liberalism, however, also means the cultivation of dispassion, the capacity to evaluate ideas from behind what the American philosopher John Rawls called a "veil of ignorance." The most just social arrangements, Rawls famously insisted, are the ones we would choose if we were forbidden to know whether or not we would benefit from them. In a similar way, students must learn that an idea is not necessarily true because it just feels true or accords with a moral sensibility that, however strongly held, is not well grounded in reason.

8   In today's attack-and-defend style of politics, the very possibility of dispassion is denied; a typical cable television program features someone from the left and someone from the right, as if ideas were nothing more than the ideological categories imposed on them. Along similar lines, we are frequently told that each person's religious convictions are sacrosanct and that someone outside one tradition has no right telling another inside one what to believe. My aim for liberal education is to make students passionate about dispassion. I want them both to have strongly held views and to be able to stand outside their own views and judge them as if they were wrong or self-serving. Making morality central to the reform of general education is a way of recognizing that human minds have come up with radically different answers to the great questions of moral obligation, but that human practices have also found ways for people with different answers to live together short of war and chaos—at least most of the time.

Aim Low

Stanley Fish

1   On more than one occasion I have had an experience many of you will recognize. A student you haven't seen in years rushes up to you and says, "Oh, Professor, I think so often of that class in 1985 (or was it 1885) when you said X and I was led by what you said to see Y and began on that very day to travel the path that has now taken me to success in profession Z. I can't thank you enough!"

2   You, however, are appalled, because you can't imagine yourself ever saying X (in fact you remember spending the entire semester saying anti-X) and you would never want anyone to exit from your class having learned Y (a lesson you have been preaching against for 20 years) and you believe that everyone would be better off if profession Z disappeared from the face of the earth. What, you might ask, did I do wrong?

3   The correct answer is quite likely, "nothing." It is the question that is wrong because it assumes that we are responsible for the effects of our teaching whereas, in fact, we are responsible only for its appropriate performance. That is, we are responsible for the selection of texts, the preparation of a syllabus, the sequence of assignments and exams, the framing and grading of a term paper, and so on.

4   If by the end of a semester you have given your students an overview of the subject (as defined by the course's title and description in the catalog) and introduced them to the latest developments in the field and pointed them in the directions they might follow should they wish to inquire further, then you have done your job. What they subsequently do with what you have done is their business and not anything you should be either held to account for or praised for. (Charlton Heston once said to Lawrence Olivier, "I've finally learned to ignore the bad reviews." "Fine," Olivier replied, "now learn to ignore the good ones.")

5   The question of what you are responsible for is also the question of what you should aim for, and what you should aim for is what you *can* aim for—that is, what you can reasonably set out to do as opposed to what is simply not within your power to do.

6   You can reasonably set out to put your students in possession of a set of materials and equip them with a set of skills (interpretive, computational, laboratory, archival), and even perhaps (although this one is really iffy) instill in them the same love of the subject that inspires your pedagogical efforts. You won't always succeed in accomplishing these things—even with the best of intentions and lesson plans there will always be inattentive or distracted students, frequently absent students, unprepared students, and on-another-planet students—but at least you will have a fighting chance given the fact that you've got them locked in a room with you for a few hours every week for four months.

7   You have little chance however (and that entirely a matter of serendipity) of determining what they will make of what you have offered them once the room is unlocked for the last time and they escape first into the space of someone else's obsession and then into the space of the wide wide world.

8   And you have no chance at all (short of a discipleship that is itself suspect and dangerous) of determining what their behavior and values will be in those aspects of their lives that are not, in the strict sense of the word, academic. You might just make them into good researchers. You can't make them into good people, and you shouldn't try.

9   This is certainly not the view of the authors of a recent book, *Educating Citizens: Preparing America's Undergraduates For Lives Of Moral and Civic Responsibility* (Jossey-Bass, 2003). A product of the Carnegie Foundation for the Advancement of Teaching, the volume reports on a failure that I find heartening.

10   In 1987, Ernest Boyer in his report on undergraduate education in America, concluded that what our colleges do best is produce "competence—competence in meeting schedules, in gathering information, . . . in mastering the details of a special field." The authors of this new study reaffirm "that by and large undergraduate education is not meeting the challenge of going beyond competence to commitment."

11   Commitment to what? The answer has already been given in the subtitle: commitment to moral and civic responsibility. "If a college education is to support the kind of learning graduates need to be involved and responsible citizens, they must go beyond the development of intellectual and technical skills and . . . mastery of a scholarly domain. They should include the competence to act in the world and the judgement to do so wisely."

12   To this I would say, first, that whatever might be the meaning of "going beyond" the mastery of intellectual and scholarly skills, I would like to be confident (as the statement seems to be) that such a mastery is something our students routinely achieve and is therefore something we can now help them to go beyond.

13   Unfortunately, that is not the case, and one reason (although surely not the only one) that it is not is the success (even if limited) of the program this book urges on us, the program of promoting "moral and civic development" by inculcating in our students certain "capacities": "self-understanding or self knowledge; understanding of the relationship between the self and community; awareness of and willingness to take responsibility for the consequences of one's actions for others and society; informed and responsible involvement with relevant communities; pluralism; cultural awareness and respect; ability to understand the value of one's own and other cultures; appreciation of the global dimensions of many issues."

14   That last one is at least a possible academic topic; any number of disciplinary issues now look different in an era of globalization, and it is important to understand and analyze that difference. The rest, however, is a mish mash of self-help platitudes, vulgar multiculturalism (is there any other kind?) and a soft-core version of 60s radicalism complete with the injunction (although not in song) to "love one another right now."

15   It is at once too vague and too left-by-the-numbers and too ambitious, at least as a program for an institution with its own purposes and values. It is those purposes and values—as identified in this book: "intellectual integrity, concern for truth, and academic freedom—that are put on the back burner when, for example, respect for the other takes precedence over learning (via the disciplines of history, anthropology, biology, literature, and sociology) what, precisely, the other is.

16   Respect for the other may or may not be a moral imperative—you can get quite an argument going on that one—but it is certainly not an academic imperative and if it is made one, academic imperatives are likely to be slighted.

17   The authors complain that students' "impatience to complete their professional or vocational training . . . can make it difficult to interest them in broader goals of intellectual and personal development." Mine is the opposite fear, that the emphasis on broader goals and especially on the therapeutic goal of "personal

development" can make it difficult to interest students in the disciplinary training it is our job to provide. (This has spectacularly been the case in the teaching of writing where the twin emphasis on personal development and the appreciation of other cultures, especially those that have been marginalized and/or oppressed, has been an all-out disaster because very few students have actually been taught to write.)

18   But my main objection to moral and civic education in our colleges and universities is not that it is a bad idea (which it surely is), but that it's an unworkable idea.

19   There are just too many intervening variables, too many uncontrolled factors that mediate the relationship between what goes on in a classroom or even in a succession of classroom and the shape of what is finally a life. Evidence of a kind comes from the list of institutions offered by the authors of *Educating Citizens* as models of what they would propose for everyone. There are 12, of which four are religiously based, three identified strongly with a single ethnic group, one a branch of the military, one a pretigious private university, one a small liberal-arts college, and two state universities.

20   The thesis is that these instituitons "treat their students' moral and civic development as central to their mission" and thereby produce a culture in which a concern with community and social justice is widely shared. It is a thesis I would be inclined to credit in advance of any evidence with respect to eight of the 12 where a certain homogeneity of culture is the advertised point of the enterprise and the students who enter that culture can be said to have self-selected. This is not the life they are led to; it is the life they already lead and their college experience reinforces moral and civic choices they have made before matriculating.

21   The claim that good and moral citizens can be fashioned by a curriculum must stand and fall with the performances of those institutions that are not sectarian or ethnic-identified, or very very small.

22   I taught for almost 14 years at one of them—Duke University—and while Duke is a first-rate institution with many virtues, I saw no evidence whatsoever that its graduates emerged with a highly developed sense of civic responsibility as they rushed off to enter top 10 law schools, medical schools, and business schools.

23   And in the case of another of the hallowed 12, the claim to be able to induce moral behavior is given the lie by the mere mention

of the name—the United States Air Force Academy, touted in the book as an exemplary instance of the "virtues approach." Of course one scandal is hardly enough to discredit the grand and ambitious agenda put forward in *Educating Citizens*, and it must be said that some of our most prominent educators and educational philosophers are among those who support that agenda.

24   Even Derek Bok, former president of Harvard University, is on board and has written an essay with the predictable and melancholy title "Universities and the Decline of Civic Responsibility." I say "even" Derek Bok because his most recent publication, *Universities in the Marketplace: The Commercialization of Higher Education*, suggests that he should be on the other side, my side. In that book Bok explains that commercial values and academic values are not the same and that the confusion of the two "can easily damage the quality of education."

25   When I have been saying, and what Bok should see, is that democratic values and academic values are not the same and that the confusion of the two can easily damage the quality of education. The readers who applaud Bok's arguments will probably reject mine; for while academics are always happy to be warned against the incursions of capitalism, they are unlikely either to welcome or heed a warning against the incursions of virtue.

ON TORTURE

A suicide bomber pushes a button, a car packed with explosives roars into a crowded hotel lobby and blows up, a missile brings down an airliner, bombs go off in a subway—acts of terrorism fill the newspapers and television screens. Their potential targets feel anger, uncertainty, anxiety, and a general sense of helplessness. Who will strike what? Where? When? How? Surveillance satellites, listening devices, infiltrators, spies, informers all provide some information but it only goes so far. Perhaps torture could tell us more. Under the threat and horror of terrorism, nations that pride themselves on the rights of the individual and the rule of law are considering the idea. What follows are two opposing views on using torture; both writers maintain their views uphold "morality."

Hendrik Hertzberg is a senior editor and political writer for the *New Yorker*, where the essay included here appeared in the March 24, 2003, issue. After graduating from Harvard, Hertzberg covered San Francisco for *Newsweek*, then served a hitch in the Navy. After he was discharged, he went to work for the *New Yorker*, leaving to serve on the White House staff under Jimmy Carter, becoming President Carter's main speechwriter. When Carter was not reelected, Hertzberg joined the staff of the *New Republic*, serving off and on as editor and polishing his political interests as a fellow in two institutes at Harvard's John F. Kennedy School of Government. In 1992, Hertzberg rejoined the *New Yorker* where in 2006 his political analysis and commentary earned the magazine a National Magazine Award for Columns and Commentary. Many of his essays are collected in his book *Politics: Observations and Arguments, 1966–2004* (2004).

Mirko Bagaric is a professor of law and head of the Deakin Law School in Australia. His most recent books are *How to Live: Being Happy and Dealing with Moral Dilemmas* (2006) and *Torture: When the Unthinkable is Morally Permissible* (with Julie Clarke, 2006). The essay included here was published in the Australian newspaper *The Age* on May 17, 2005, and summarizes a longer article he wrote with Julie Clarke that appeared in the *University of San Francisco Law Review* in the spring 2005 issue. Douglas Wood, to whom Bagaric refers in paragraph 13, is an Australian citizen who had lived in the United States for some 40 years. In 2005, Wood was under contract to the U.S. military in Iraq when he was taken hostage by insurgents in May. Wood was later rescued in a raid by Iraqi and U.S. forces.

Terror and Torture

Hendrik Hertzberg

1   "**I** see that a man I know to be a ruffian is pursuing a young girl," Leo Tolstoy wrote in "The Kingdom of God Is Within You." "I have a gun in my hand—I kill the ruffian and save the girl. But the death or the wounding of the ruffian has positively taken place, while what would have happened if this had not been I cannot know. And what an immense mass of evil must result, and indeed does result, from allowing men to assume the right of anticipating what may happen. Ninety-nine per cent of the evil of the world is founded on this reasoning—from the Inquisition to dynamite bombs."

2   This is the traditional case for pacifism. It hangs on an insight about means and ends. "Thou shalt not kill": whether the commandment is seen as coming from God or simply from self-evident moral intuition, few dispute that to kill is to commit a wrong, and that to refrain from killing is to prevent a wrong. In war, killing is the means. The end—the "war aim," the putative goal of the killing—may be right, but it is speculative, possibly unachievable, off in a future that is more or less unknowable. By its example, and by its corrupting effect, killing begets killing, evil begets evil. To do evil today, in the expectation that in the future, at the end of a long chain of causation and chance, something good will emerge, is the wager that pacifists refuse to make.

3   Governments have little patience with this line of thought, whether or not they are willing to excuse its adherents from military service. (What if the ruffian had just been seen to murder the young girl's family? Tolstoy does not say.) Neither do the great majority of people, who, while seeing no virtue in killing, nevertheless believe that there are times when war is the preferred moral choice. But the logic of conscientious objection, which is also the logic of the Golden Rule, is powerful enough to make itself felt even at the level where states pursue their interests with all due lethality and hypocrisy. In the continuum of political violence—assassination, torture, terrorism, and war, reading from small-scale to large—international law deems war alone to be permissible, albeit only in extreme circumstances, and tries to tame it with rules and conventions. The rest are seen, theoretically at least, as outside the pale—as means that no end can be allowed to justify.

4   At the present dismal and disorienting moment, everything, as they say in Washington, is on the table. Before September 11, 2001, no one imagined that a time would come when the permissibility of torture would be an urgent topic of public discussion, let alone something like the official, though of course unacknowledged, policy of the United States. The arrest earlier this month, in Pakistan, of Khalid Shaikh Mohammed, an alleged senior lieutenant of Al Qaeda, touched off a round of speculation about how the government might try to separate him from his information. But for some time there have been reliable reports of American interrogators' subjecting terror suspects to what the C.I.A. calls "stress and duress" techniques. In a landmark *Washington Post* story last December 26th, Dana Priest and Barton Gellman listed some of those techniques: beating people; forcing them

to stand or kneel for hours, or holding them in awkward, painful positions; using bright lights or loud noises to deprive them systematically of sleep; if they are ill or have been wounded, withholding medical attention and painkillers; and turning them over to countries whose methods of inquiry are not so gentle.

5   It can be debated how many of these methods violate the United Nations Convention Against Torture, which defines torture as "any act by which severe pain or suffering, whether physical or mental, is intentionally inflicted." The last of them almost certainly violates the Convention's ban on sending anyone to a country "where there are substantial grounds for believing that he would be in danger of being subjected to torture." As the *Post* noted, suspects have been "rendered"—the verb is all too apt—to Egypt, Morocco, and Syria, all of which, according to the State Department's own human-rights reports, routinely use methods of pain infliction that are far more gruesome than lights and noise.

6   When the Senate ratified the Torture Convention, in 1990, it did so at the urging of the first President Bush, who, with war looming in the Persian Gulf, wanted to deny Saddam Hussein the slightest cover for mistreating any American soldiers his forces might capture. On the eve of a second Iraq war, a second President Bush lists ending torture as prominent among the war's aims. He mentioned it repeatedly during the news conference he held on March 6th. Earlier, in his State of the Union address, he catalogued "methods used in the torture chambers of Iraq: electric shock, burning with hot irons, dripping acid on the skin, mutilation with electric drills, cutting out tongues, and rape." And he said, "If this is not evil, then evil has no meaning."

7   There are obvious distinctions to be drawn between the C.I.A.'s "stress and duress" and the horrors of Saddam's dungeons—in their purposes (aborting terror attacks versus maintaining a tyranny) and, more important, in their degrees of cruelty. The distinctions are both real and slippery, like the distinction Palestinians make between suicide bombings in the occupied territories and in Israel proper. They get slipperier when prisoners are turned over to countries like Egypt, our fellow-signatory of the Torture Convention. And slipperiest of all is the slope from what has been called "torture lite" to torture dark. We simply do not know what goes on in the interrogation centers of Kabul and Guantánamo. We don't, most of us, want to know.

8   The argument is sometimes made that torture is useless—that it is a bad way to gather intelligence, because people under torture lie. Torture is "a wonderful way of getting false confessions out of innocent people," a human-rights activist said on television the other day, but "a terrible way of getting the truth out of guilty people." If matters were that simple, however, torture would be so rare that covenants abolishing it would be superfluous rather than ineffectual. All intelligence-gathering methods are imperfect; all produce "noise"; all are vulnerable to deceit and subject to verification. Torture, alas, is no worse than many. Over time, it probably ends up augmenting what it seeks to prevent, if what it seeks to prevent is terror. (A case in point is Ayman al-Zawahiri, whom Egyptian torturers made one of the deadliest terrorists on earth.) But, in the short run, torture, sometimes, "works."

9   War kills, maims, and otherwise destroys many more people than torture does, and most of them are innocent—not only civilians, who become "collateral damage," but also soldiers, many of whom are either unwilling conscripts or guilty simply of wishing to serve their country. Torture, per se, is not lethal, and its victims can be far from innocent, but the moral revulsion it provokes has a special sharpness, and in this lies the deepest reason to abjure it. In war, valor is possible; comradeship is possible; heroism is possible. Even terrorism and assassination can offer scope for an ugly kind of courage. But, just as the victims of torture are utterly helpless, the perpetrators of it are utterly debased. Like capital punishment, torture is abhorrent not only for what it does to the tortured but for what it makes of the torturer. It is the perfect opposite of what we like to think our country has stood for. It is surely not what we wish to become.

A Case for Torture

Mirko Bagaric

1   Our reflex rejection of torture needs to be replaced by recognition that it can be a moral means of saving lives.

2   Recent events stemming from the "war on terrorism" have highlighted the prevalence of torture. This is despite the fact that torture

is almost universally deplored. The formal prohibition against torture is absolute—there are no exceptions to it.

3   The belief that torture is always wrong is, however, misguided and symptomatic of the alarmist and reflexive responses typically emanating from social commentators. It is this type of absolutist and short-sighted rhetoric that lies at the core of many distorted moral judgements that we as a community continue to make, resulting in an enormous amount of injustice and suffering in our society and far beyond our borders.

4   Torture is permissible where the evidence suggests that this is the only means, due to the immediacy of the situation, to save the life of an innocent person. The reason that torture in such a case is defensible and necessary is because the justification manifests from the closest thing we have to an inviolable right: the right to self-defence, which of course extends to the defence of another. Given the choice between inflicting a relatively small level of harm on a wrongdoer and saving an innocent person, it is verging on moral indecency to prefer the interests of the wrongdoer.

5   The analogy with self-defence is sharpened by considering the hostage-taking scenario, where a wrongdoer takes a hostage and points a gun to the hostage's head, threatening to kill the hostage unless a certain (unreasonable) demand is met. In such a case it is not only permissible, but desirable for police to shoot (and kill) the wrongdoer if they get a "clear shot". This is especially true if it's known that the wrongdoer has a history of serious violence, and hence is more likely to carry out the threat.

6   There is no logical or moral difference between this scenario and one where there is overwhelming evidence that a wrongdoer has kidnapped an innocent person and informs police that the victim will be killed by a co-offender if certain demands are not met.

7   In the hostage scenario, it is universally accepted that it is permissible to violate the right to life of the aggressor to save an innocent person. How can it be wrong to violate an even less important right (the right to physical integrity) by torturing the aggressor in order to save a life in the second scenario?

8   There are three main counter-arguments to even the above limited approval of torture. The first is the slippery slope argument: if you start allowing torture in a limited context, the situations in which it will be used will increase.

9 This argument is not sound in the context of torture. First, the floodgates are already open—torture is used widely, despite the absolute legal prohibition against it. Amnesty International has recently reported that it had received, during 2003, reports of torture and ill-treatment from 132 countries, including the United States, Japan and France. It is, in fact, arguable that it is the existence of an unrealistic absolute ban that has driven torture beneath the radar of accountability, and that legalisation in very rare circumstances would in fact reduce instances of it.

10 The second main argument is that torture will dehumanise society. This is no more true in relation to torture than it is with self-defence, and in fact the contrary is true. A society that elects to favour the interests of wrongdoers over those of the innocent, when a choice must be made between the two, is in need of serious ethical rewiring.

11 A third counter-argument is that we can never be totally sure that torturing a person will in fact result in us saving an innocent life. This, however, is the same situation as in all cases of self-defence. To revisit the hostage example, the hostage-taker's gun might in fact be empty, yet it is still permissible to shoot. As with any decision, we must decide on the best evidence at the time.

12 Torture in order to save an innocent person is the only situation where it is clearly justifiable. This means that the recent high-profile incidents of torture, apparently undertaken as punitive measures or in a bid to acquire information where there was no evidence of an immediate risk to the life of an innocent person, were reprehensible.

13 Will a real-life situation actually occur where the only option is between torturing a wrongdoer or saving an innocent person? Perhaps not. However, a minor alteration to the Douglas Wood situation illustrates that the issue is far from moot. If Western forces in Iraq arrested one of Mr Wood's captors, it would be a perverse ethic that required us to respect the physical integrity of the captor, and not torture him to ascertain Mr Wood's whereabouts, in preference to taking all possible steps to save Mr Wood.

14 Even if a real-life situation where torture is justifiable does not eventuate, the above argument in favour of torture in limited circumstances needs to be made because it will encourage the community to think more carefully about moral judgements we collectively hold that are the cause of an enormous amount of suffering in the world.

15   First, no right or interest is absolute. Secondly, rights must always yield to consequences, which are the ultimate criteria upon which the soundness of a decision is gauged. Lost lives hurt a lot more than bent principles.

16   Thirdly, we must take responsibility not only for the things that we do, but also for the things that we can—but fail to—prevent. The retort that we are not responsible for the lives lost through a decision not to torture a wrongdoer because we did not create the situation is code for moral indifference.

17   Equally vacuous is the claim that we in the affluent West have no responsibility for more than 13,000 people dying daily due to starvation. Hopefully, the debate on torture will prompt us to correct some of these fundamental failings.

CREDITS

Page 22: "A Sandwich" by Nora Ephron. Reprinted by permission of International Creative Management, Inc. Copyright © 2002 by Nora Ephron. First appeared in the *New Yorker.*

Page 25: "The Bridge" by Jason Holland. Reprinted by permission of the author.

Page 29: "Countdown" by Johathan Franzen from the *New Yorker,* April 18, 2005. Copyright © 2005 by Jonathan Franzen. Reprinted by permission of the author.

Page 33: "El Hoyo" by Mario Suárez for *Arizona Quarterly,* Summer 1947, vol. III, no. 2. Copyright © by the Arizona Quarterly. Reprinted by permission.

Page 37: "Left Sink" by Ellery Akers from *Sierra,* 1990. Reprinted by permission of the author.

Page 57: "Designer of Audio CD Packaging Enters Hell" by Steve Martin from the *New Yorker,* April 19, 1999. Reprinted by permission of International Creative Management, Inc. Copyright © 1999 by Steve Martin. First appeared in the *New Yorker.*

Page 61: "Learning, then College" editorial by Meg Gifford, the *Baltimore Sun.* Reprinted with permission.

Page 64: "The Night of the Oranges" by Flavius Stan from the *New York Times,* December 24, 1995. Copyright © 1995 by the New York Times Co. Reprinted by permission.

Page 67: "Time to Look and Listen" by Magdoline Asfahani from *Newsweek,* December 2, 1996. Copyright © 1996 by Newsweek, Inc. Reprinted by permission of Newsweek, Inc.

Page 72: "Footprints on the Flag" by Anchee Min from the *New Yorker,* October 13, 2001. Copyright © 2001 by Anchee Min. Reprinted by permission of the author and the Sandra Dijkstra Literary Agency.

Page 84: "Chocolate Equals Love" by Diane Ackerman from *Parade,* February 9, 2003. Copyright © 2003 by Diane Ackerman. Reprinted by permission of William Morris Agency, LLC on behalf of the Author.

Page 88: "I Was a Member of the Kung Fu Crew" by Henry Han Xi Lau from the *New York Times,* October 19, 1997. Copyright © 1997 by The New York Times. Reprinted by permission of The New York Times.

Page 92: "The Handicap of Definition" from "Instilling Positive Images" by William Raspberry. Copyright © 1982 by the Washington Post Writers Group. Reprinted by permission.

Page 96: "Where Nothing Says Everything" by Suzanne Berne from the *New York Times,* April 21, 2002. Copyright © 2002 by the New York Times Co. Reprinted by permission.

Page 101: "Crippled by Their Culture" by Thomas Sowell from the *Wall Street Journal,* April 26, 2005. Copyright © 2005 by Thomas Sowell. Reprinted by permission of the author.

Page 117: "Sweatin' for Nothin'" by Michael Barlow. Reprinted by permission of the author.

Page 120: "Stop Ordering Me Around" by Stacey Wilkins from *Newsweek,* January 4, 1993. Copyright © 1993 by Newsweek, Inc. Reprinted by permission of Newsweek, Inc.

INDEX